Gabriel Garc

Titles in the series Critical Lives present the work of leading cultural figures of the modern period. Each book explores the life of the artist, writer, philosopher or architect in question and relates it to their major works.

Gabriel García Márquez

Stephen M. Hart

REAKTION BOOKS

To Danyl, for putting up with me

Published by Reaktion Books Ltd
33 Great Sutton Street
London EC1V 0DX, UK

www.reaktionbooks.co.uk

First published 2010

Printed and bound in Great Britain
by CPI Antony Rowe, Chippenham, Wiltshire

British Library Cataloguing in Publication Data
Hart, Stephen M.
     Gabriel García Márquez. – (Critical lives)
     1. García Márquez, Gabriel , 1928–
     2. Authors, Colombian – 20th century – Biography.
     I. Title II. Series
     863.6'4-DC22

ISBN: 978 1 86189 763 3

Contents

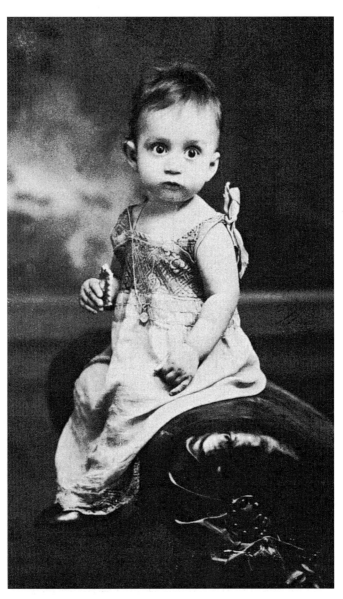

Gabito on his first birthday.

1

'He won't be playing chess any more'[1]

Gabriel José García Márquez was born at nine in the morning[2]
during a storm on 6 March 1927,[3] to Gabriel Eligio García and Luisa
Santiaga Márquez Iguarán in a town in Colombia called Aracataca
– a word based on the conjunction of two Amerindian words, *ara*
(river) and *cataca* (chief). His parents had married a year earlier
(on 11 June 1926),[4] against the wishes of Luisa's parents. He was
born with the umbilical cord around his neck which was said to
have led to his suffering from claustrophobia in later life,[5] weighing
nine pounds and five ounces. He was rubbed with rum and blessed
with baptismal water in case of further mishap. When Gabito – as
García Márquez was affectionately known in his youth – was still
a baby he was packed off to live with his maternal grandparents,
Colonel Nicolás Márquez Mejía and Tranquilina Iguarán Cotes,
while his parents, who were suffering from money troubles, went
off to live in the coastal town of Riohacha. Gabriel Eligio and Luisa
Santiaga went on to have ten more children together,[6] but they left
Gabito living in his grandparents' house where he seemed most
comfortable; Gabito was joined by the third child, Margarita
(better known by her nickname Margot) who came to live with
him in their grandparents' house when García Márquez was three
and a half years old.[7] Gabriel García Márquez was baptized on
27 July 1930 in the local church by the priest of Aracataca, Father
Angarita,[8] who had become famous the previous year for being
the author of a letter read out in the House of Representatives

Luisa Santiaga Márquez Iguarán (1905–2002), García Márquez's mother, before her marriage.

denouncing the army's actions in Aracataca during the banana massacre of December 1928.[9]

The house in which García Márquez lived with his grandparents, with its ghosts and stories, had a decisive impact on the young child. He clarified this in an interview with Plinio Apuleyo:

My most constant and vivid memory is not so much of the people but of the actual house in Aracataca where I lived with my grandparents. It's a recurring dream which persists even now. What's more, every single day of my life I wake up with the feeling, real or imaginary, that I've dreamt I'm in that huge old house. Not that I've gone back there, but that I am there, at no particular age, for no particular reason – as if I'd never left it.[10]

His grandparents' house would be a recurrent theme in García Márquez's work – indeed his first idea for a novel was called *La casa* (*The House*), and the first draft of this was the seed for the novel which made him famous when he was in his early forties, *One*

The marriage of Gabriel Eligio and Luisa Santiaga, Gabo's parents, in Santa Marta, 11 June 1926.

Hundred Years of Solitude (1967). Gabo slept in the house in a hammock and all night long the candles were lit next to the family saints which were as big as real people; they used to scare Gabo because he thought they were looking at him.[11] To make matters worse, his grandmother, Tranquilina, said that the house was haunted by her sister's ghost, Aunt Petra Cotes, who had died in one of the bedrooms of the house many years before. Tranquilina, with Aunt Francisca (Nicolás' cousin), and her sister-in-law, Wenefrida (Nicolás' sister) would sit in the corridor of begonias and talk about witches and ghosts and *la llorona* (the weeping woman) and Gabo, playing in the corridor with his toy cars, used to listen to them and ended up 'hearing' the ghosts in the house. Francisca used to say to Gabito that if he was naughty she would take him to the Dead Man's House.[12] This was the house in which a Venezuelan called Antonio Mora hanged himself; his ghost could be heard coughing in the house for years afterwards. García Márquez recalls that he went into the house once as a young child

Servants' abode in the grandparents' house in Aracataca.

in search of a rabbit (the same rabbit, one might presume, that is depicted in one of his early drawings),[13] and went into the toilet, and it was there that he saw the ghost, who was sitting on the toilet; he knew it was the ghost because of his 'beautiful black man's teeth'.[14] García Márquez to this day suffers from nightmares, and he has said that they go back to the childhood he spent in his grandparents' house in Aracataca; to this day he sleeps with the light on.[15]

At the back of the grandparents'property there was a huge chestnut tree which would have an important role as a prop in *One Hundred Years of Solitude*; this was the tree to which the character José Arcadio Buendía is tied. There were also guava trees: Tranquilina picked the fruit and made sweets of it, and sold it to the neighbourhood; this was the smell that García Márquez associated with his childhood and with the Caribbean – that's why his best friend, Plinio Apuleyo, called his collection of interviews with García Márquez *El olor de la guayaba* (The Fragrance of Guava, 1982). When the Colombian critic J. G. Cobo Borda visited the Aracataca house in 1987 all that was left was a pile of tin lying on the floor, with an old abandoned shoe, a trunk and solitary chair in the middle for good measure. María Mejía Brochero, the local curator, told him at the time that there were plans to turn the house into a museum 'soon' but, as Cobo Borda knew only too well, 'soon' in the Caribbean is a rather elastic term which could mean a 'year' or even a 'century'.[16] I visited the house in Aracataca in February 2009 and it has now been completely rebuilt based on the original plans.

García Márquez's official biographer, Gerald Martin, gives a vivid image of what Tranquilina was like:

Dressed always in mourning or semi-mourning, and always on the verge of hysteria, Tranquilina floated through the house from dawn to dusk, singing, always trying to exude a calm and unflustered air, yet always mindful of the need to protect her charges from the ever-present dangers: souls in torment ('hurry, put the children to bed'), black butterflies ('hide the children, someone is going to die'), funerals ('get the children up, or they'll die too').[17]

The house in Aracataca had a patio garden where Tranquilina used to grow roses so she could make rose water to give to the children to keep them healthy.[18] Margot remembers that Tranquilina was very superstitious:

> In the house there was an immense garden with a small fountain where the frogs would congregate. . . . At night, when we heard a frog croaking, my grandmother would say: 'That must be a witch; that's Nicolasito who's got a woman and she's sent me a witch.' Our grandfather would go down to the workshop, heat up the pincers until they were red hot and he would catch the poor frog with them to kill it.[19]

The curious part of this anecdote is that it demonstrates that Tranquilina's superstitions were anything but innocent, for they were based on the knowledge that her husband was carrying on with other women (of which more later): in this case her use of superstition was an indirect way of castigating her husband for his waywardness. Likewise indicative of how this critique had hit home is the fact that the grandfather would kill the offending 'witch', in effect paying penance for his adultery. It was a ritual played out within the displaced language of superstition.

Martin gives the following description of García Márquez's grandfather: 'He was sixty-three when Gabito was born, quite European-looking, like his wife, stocky, of average height with a broad forehead, balding and with a thick moustache. He wore gold-rimmed glasses and by that time was blind in the right eye because of glaucoma. On most days he would wear a spotless white tropical suit, a panama hat and brightly coloured braces.'[20] Gabo was adored by his grandfather, and spoiled. Anything that he wanted to have, his grandfather would give it to him; they just walked together to the store over the road from the house in Aracataca, and his grandfather would buy it for him; he was like the 'prince of the house'.[21]

One can speculate that it was during this time that the young Gabito first became aware of the existence of illegitimate children within his grandfather's extended family. It is clear that a number of episodes such as the touching of ice in the United Fruit Company Shop across the road, the stories his grandfather used to tell about the War of a Thousand Days, and his grandmother's supernatural tales were the soil in which his magical-realist style would later flourish – but there was, I will be arguing, one further element which would become the matrix of his early and later fiction. This was the discovery of the double life of Colonel Márquez. A colonel who had seen distinguished service in the War of a Thousand Days, he was the mayor and treasurer of Aracataca, an upright and wealthy member of the Aracataca elite; yet he still managed to father between nine and nineteen (probably twelve) illegitimate children,[22] and it is this conflicting picture of his grandfather which would be crucial to García Márquez's work. Indeed, the illegitimate family, metaphorically speaking, is the double of the legitimate family (rather like a mirror image, both families have an oldest child and a youngest child) and deconstructs the legitimacy of the legitimate family. Its naturalness (in Colombia an illegitimate child is called *un hijo / una hija natural*) undermines the cultural constructedness of the legitimate family. It is clear also that one of the overriding tropes of the illegitimate family is its mystery; *hijos naturales* by definition escape the rational and empiric parameters of identity as understood within a modern society – *hijos naturales* are often not baptized and sometimes do not have their father's surname; they operate thus within a socially undefined limbo zone, produced by nature rather than a father. It comes as no surprise, for example, that at least three of Nicolás' illegitimate children, though known to exist by the García Márquez family, have not been identified; they were outside society's hermeneutic net, functioning in effect like ghosts within the sphere of the legitimate family home in Aracataca.[23] García Márquez told Dasso Saldíva, his Colombian biographer, that when his grandfather's illegitimate children turned up in Aracataca, which they normally did at Christmas time, they would be taken into the family home by Tranquilina.[24]

Given the significance that the theme of illegitimacy would take in García Márquez's later fiction (particularly *One Hundred Years of Solitude*), it is important to evaluate the social context of this phenomenon in Latin American society. Concubinage and illegitimacy were much more common in Latin America during the colonial period than they were during the same period in Europe,[25] to such an extent that they have been called 'endemic' by one critic.[26] *Barraganía*, the custom whereby an unmarried couple lived together freely, was common during the colonial period in Bogotá;[27] children born from such a union were able to retain their father's name, were capable of being declared legitimate and also able to inherit.[28] Colonel Nicolás Márquez and Tranquilina Iguarán got married in Riohacha in 1885, and while there are no relevant figures for Riohacha at that time, there are some for a nearby city, Barranquilla, for 1892. Parish records show that of the children baptized in that year, 80.6 per cent were *hijos naturales* and 18.6 per cent were legitimate.[29] Parish records also demonstrate that, in the same year, it was more common than not for couples to come to the altar having already had an *hijo natural*.[30] It could be argued then, that it would not have been anomalous for Nicolás Márquez to have had *hijos naturales* before his marriage; indeed, this was the case: he had already sired two children with Altagracia Valdeblánquez before appearing at the altar to marry Tranquilina.[31]

It was also common for members of the elite of Barranquilla to have a second family created by what was termed *queridazgo* (a second family with the *querida*, or lover).[32]

Colonel Nicolás Márquez lived for a period of his life in Barranquilla and he had three legitimate children with Tranquilina (one of whom was García Márquez's mother, Luisa Santiaga, the other two being Juan de Dios Márquez Iguarán and Margarita Miniata Márquez Iguarán) as well as twelve or so *hijos naturales*, some of whom took his name.[33] It is important to bear in mind these contextual cultural factors because they show the parameters of permissibility in the society of the time. While *queridazgo* were commonly accepted, it is clear that Colonel Nicolás Márquez went beyond even these bounds in that he had not one but multiple *queridas* with whom he had children at different times of his life. The fact that his *hijos naturales* outnumbered his legitimate children by four to one (three legitimate compared to twelve *hijos naturales*) shows the unusual level of his interest in siring children with a variety of women – one could almost call it a Genghis Khan syndrome. The young Gabito played an interesting role in his grandfather's affairs, as the autobiography makes clear:

I know now that it had been my grandmother who insisted that her husband take me with him on his twilight excursions, for she was certain they were pretexts for visiting his real or hypothetical lovers. It is possible that at times I served as his alibi, but the truth is that he never took me anywhere that was not on the anticipated itinerary. I have a clear image, however, of a night when I was holding somebody's hand and happened to pass a strange house and saw my grandfather sitting like the lord and master in the living room. I could never understand why I was shaken by the intuition that I should not tell this to anyone.[34]

Aracataca was, indeed, something of a Wild West town in the 1920s and '30s when the Márquez family lived there. When the United Fruit Company closed down in the late 1920s, and people had no work, this had a direct impact on the prostitutes who used to ply their trade in the main street of Aracataca; they began to fight over any client, punching and scratching each other.[35] So the mayor of Aracataca decided to slap a fine on any women caught fighting in the main street, and as a result raised enough money to build the park which is in the main square of Aracataca opposite the church.[36]

Quite apart from the 'witches' that Tranquilina imagined near the back garden pool, there was, of course, one other ghost in the house in Aracataca, the man that García Márquez's grandfather had killed in a duel on 19 October 1908 in Barrancas, Medardo Pacheco Romero,[37] and which filled Nicolás Márquez Mejía's latter years with sorrow.[38] Saldívar gives the details of how the duel came about,[39] and some of these details would find their way into *One Hundred Years of Solitude*. When, for example, Colonel Nicolás Márquez was asked if he had killed Medardo Pacheco Romero he replied: 'I killed Medardo Romero and if he comes back to life, I'll kill him again', and in *One Hundred Years of Solitude* José Arcadio Buendía says something very similar to Prudencio Aguilar when his ghost appears in the house in Macondo.[40] This incident would weigh heavy on the colonel's conscience, and would also be transmitted to Gabito, who was told when he was about six or seven years old by his grandfather: 'You don't know how heavy a dead man is!'[41] Intriguingly, many years later in December 1952, when García Márquez was having a beer in the small town of La Paz, he met a strapping tall man who asked him if he was anything to do with Colonel Nicolás Márquez. When García Márquez said he was the latter's grandson, the man replied: 'So your grandfather killed my grandfather.'[42] At the most unexpected times, the ghost of the past could return. The man's name was Lisandro Pacheco and

García Márquez and he put their differences behind them and drank to the memory of their dead grandfathers.[43]

The young Gabo was fascinated by his grandfather's stories of the War of a Thousand Days in which he had fought as a young man, and he was amazed when he once caught sight of the bullet wound close to his grandfather's groin, as he remembers in his memoirs.[44] One day Gabo, who was five years old at the time, told his grandfather that he had seen some fish which were like stones in the United Fruit Company shop, and his grandfather explained that the fish were frozen because they had been laid in ice. So he took his grandson to the UFC shop and had the fridge opened to show his grandson what ice was like,[45] an event which would become famous once transmuted poetically in *One Hundred Years of Solitude*. His grandfather often used him to take him for a walk around Aracataca. As Martin suggests: 'One of their favourite walks was on a Thursday to the post office to see if there was any news about the Colonel's pension from the war twenty-five years earlier. There never was, a fact which made a big impression on the child.'[46] This detail would find its way into *No One Writes to the Colonel*. Living with his grandparents turned the young Gabito into a mature child. Margot remembers that he was unlike his brother, Luis Enrique, who was mischievous and unruly; Gabo never used to play football and get up to mischief like the other boys.[47] As Luisa, his mother, once said: 'Gabito was always old; when he was a child he knew so much he seemed like a little old man. That's what we called him, the little old man.'[48] One possibly decisive difference between Gabo's life and that of his brothers and sisters is that he was frequently able to listen to his grandfather's friends telling stories of the war:

Gabito lived glued to his grandfather, listening to all the stories. Once a friend from Ciénaga came to visit; he was one of the old men who had fought in the War of a Thousand

Days with granddad. Gabo, who was always all ears, stood next to the gentleman and it turns out that the leg of the chair that they drew up for him to sit down on got stuck on Gabito's shoe. He put up with it without making a sound until the visit was over, because he thought: 'If I say something, they'll surely realise I'm here and throw me out.'[49]

Such was his determination to listen that the future novelist would put up with severe discomfort in order to experience the immense pleasure of listening to stories. The important point to underline here is that García Márquez was exposed from an early age to two types of story – the mad stories about ghosts from his grandmother and the serious stories about war from his grandfather and friends, and that his later fiction was to produce a magical balance between the two genres. As Saldívar put it: 'His grandmother used to tell him stories about dead people who carried on living, and his grandfather told him stories about people who really did die. His grandmother spoke of a world that was intimate, domestic, ghostly, and his grandfather spoke of a world that was epic, historic and external.'[50]

One of Gabito's most vivid memories as a child was of Don Emilio, a Belgian, who arrived in Aracataca after the First World War, on crutches with a bullet in his leg. A talented jeweller and cabinet maker, Don Emilio would play chess or cards with the colonel of an evening until the day he went to see *All Quiet on the Western Front* and went home and killed himself with a slug of cyanide.[51] It is important, indeed, to point out that García Márquez has said that his childhood was the most important archive for the stories he would one day write, to such an extent that he once dramatically said in an interview that nothing of importance happened to him after his grandfather died (when he was nine years old). We might legitimately question this – would this mean, for example, that García Márquez's readings in literature counted for nothing? But there is a kernel of truth in this in that the magical side of his writing echoes the narrative style of the ghost stories that his grandmother told him. The formula was enhanced and improved by his reading of Kafka, but the mixture of the real and the magical was one which would recur at crucial times in his later fiction, as we shall see. As a result of the rather more retiring life that he experienced living with his grandparents, Gabo became more reclusive and pensive, and his conversations with the grown-ups led him to compete at an early age with their stories. He developed his skill at the *mot juste*. Thus his only comment when discovering that Don Emilio had committed suicide was: 'Ya no jugará al ajedrez . . .' ('He won't be playing chess any more').[52] The fact that, as he recalls in his memoirs, he was feted by his grandfather for his wit is an indication of the motivation he had to impress others with stories, witty comments, artful language:

> It was a simple idea, but my grandfather told it to the family as if it were a brilliant witticism. The women repeated it with so much enthusiasm that for some time I ran from visitors for fear that would say it in front of me or oblige me to repeat it. This also revealed to me a characteristic of adults that would be very useful to me as a writer: each of them told the story with new details that they added on their own, until the various versions became different from the original.[53]

As a young boy Gabo initially found it quite difficult to read, but when suddenly the secret of language was opened to him, he became fascinated by reading, writing, and telling stories.[54]

García Márquez's autobiography, *Vivir para contarla* (*Living to Tell the Tale*), builds up a picture of a young boy with an extraordinarily vivid imagination; he remembers the shock he experienced when an enormous petroleum tanker arrived in Barranquilla on 28 May 1935, the amazement he experienced when he saw a plane crash-land, as well as the surprise which gripped everyone when the radio hit town.[55] On one occasion he happened to see the Indian woman who used to serve the drinks in the house taking her dress off; he had never seen a naked woman before and was surprised to see that she was hairy down below. It was an image that stuck in his mind and which he used in order to create Remedios la Bella in *One Hundred Years of Solitude*, the woman who transfixes men and is not quite of this world.[56] Indeed, the same wide-eyed wonder can be found in the extraordinarily poised and literary descriptions of the advances of the technological world taking an 'undeveloped world' by storm, which feature so heavily in chapter one of *One Hundred Years of Solitude*. In particular García Márquez's memoirs describe the irruption of modernity into the town of Barranquilla, and he picks on details with the eye of a novelist:

> The city also had its first radio station, a modern aqueduct that became a tourist and pedagogical attraction for displaying the new process of water purification, and a fire department whose sirens and bells were a fiesta for children and adults from the moment they were heard. At about the same time the first convertible automobiles came in, racing along the streets at lunatic velocities and smashing into smithereens on the new paved highways. The undertaking establishment La Equitativa, inspired by the humour of death, set up an enormous sign at the exit from the city: 'Take your time, we're waiting for you.'[57]

The acute sense of the disjunction between the old and the new which underlines this paragraph is an insight which can be found at the heart of *One Hundred Years of Solitude*.

Some of García Márquez's most powerful childhood memories are associated with his grandfather. It is from his grandfather, for example, that he derived his fascination with Simón Bolívar. In his memoirs he recalls the day his grandfather hung a picture of Bolívar on the wall, and read aloud a poem:

Then, in a tremulous voice that did not seem his, he read me a long poem that hung next to the picture, of which I remembered only and forever the final verses: 'Thou, Santa Marta, wert charitable, and in thy lap thou gavest him that piece of the ocean's strand to die.' From then on, and for many years afterward, I had the idea that Bolívar had been found dead on the beach. It was my grandfather who taught me and asked me never to forget that he was the greatest man ever born in the history of the world.[58]

Margot remembers the day their grandfather attempted to capture the parrot which had escaped from his cage and was sitting on one of the water cisterns high up near the tree in the garden. He was seventy-two years old at the time and went up a ladder to capture the bird, but his foot slipped and he fell down on to his back, harming some internal organs; this was the inspiration for García Márquez's portrayal of Juvenal Urbino's death in *Love in the Time of Cholera*.[59] Colonel Márquez died three years later, on 4 March 1937, when Gabo was just two days away from his tenth birthday. As a result Gabo and Margot moved to their parents' house in Sucre and they both found it difficult to adjust. Whereas before, it seemed, they could have anything they wanted, in their parents' house they found that they could have either lunch or dinner but not both.[60] That the magic of his childhood was finally gone was brought home to Gabo when he went back to the house in Aracataca and witnessed his grandfather's belongings, his white suits, his hats, being burned; for Gabito it was as if they were burning everything that was dear to him in the world.[61]

Life in Sucre was a world apart from the paradise of Aracataca. Now ten years old, Gabo had to attend the Colegio San José de la Compañía de Jesús in Barranquilla,[62] and, more importantly, he had to reinvent himself as the son of his parents. This was easy when it came to his mother, Luisa Santiaga, to whom García Márquez had always been very close. García Márquez mentioned to Plinio Apuleyo that 'it's probably the most serious relationship I've ever had. I believe there's nothing she and I can't tell each other and no subject we can't talk about',[63] and it is not by chance that the first defining moment in his autobiography focuses on a meeting and subsequent mission with his mother.[64] This closeness probably explains why Luisa was always such a sharp reader of her son's fictions over the years (indeed, right up until her death in 2002). As García Márquez puts it: 'When she reads my books she instinctively eliminates all the bits that are added on and identifies the main vertebra, the core around which I construct the character. Sometimes when she's reading, you can hear her say, "Oh, my poor *compadre*, he's been turned into a real pansy here."'[65] García Márquez's relationship with his father, Gabriel Eligio, the telegrapher of Aracataca, though, proved to be more troublesome. Saldívar suggests that Gabriel Eligio considered his first-born son as not only the very spoilt grandson of his grandfather, but also a *mentiroso* (liar).[66] Margot stated the following: 'Gabito was also very afraid of dad. The truth is that he was a strange person, we saw him more as an uncle, a distant person. He loved us, that much I know, but I didn't feel he was my dad and that made me suffer a great deal.'[67] Aída, his young sister, offers a similar take on the situation: 'When he [Gabo] came to live with us and he realised that dad wasn't as loving and free-and-easy [*consentidor*] as granddad, he began to miss the atmosphere of the grandparents' house; dad gave orders where granddad was pure affection.'[68] García Márquez confirms this impression in an interview: 'Not long ago he told a friend that I thought I was one of the chickens born without any help from the cockerel. He said it good-naturedly, with his fine sense of humour, as a sort of mild reproach because I always talk about my relationship with my mother and rarely about him.'[69]

There were, though, some similarities between García Márquez's grandfather and his father which have not, perhaps, been sufficiently

Gabo with siblings; left to right, Aída, Luis Enrique, Gabito, cousin Eduardo García Caballero, Margot and Ligia as a baby, in Aracataca, 1939. The photograph was taken by the García Márquez children's father, Gabriel Eligio.

underscored. One was the predilection both had for siring children outside the family unit.[70] Thus when Gabriel Eligio and Luisa Santiaga got married in Santa Marta in 1926, Gabriel Eligio – following in Colonel's Márquez's footsteps, it would seem – had already had two *hijos naturales*; again, this would not have been unusual for the time. Although we do not have figures for Santa Marta, only for Barranquilla, it is likely the lay of the land would have been similar. Parish baptism records for Barranquilla in that year (1926) – no doubt as a result of a pro-marriage campaign by the Catholic Church in the first few decades of the twentieth century – indicate that legitimate children brought to baptism only just outnumbered *hijos naturales*.[71] Very much confirming the prevalence of *hijos naturales* in his memoirs, García Márquez alludes to the 'atavistic prejudice' which 'has turned us into a vast community of unmarried women and men with their flies unzipped and numerous children born out of wedlock'.[72] When García Márquez won the Nobel Prize he went to see his former teacher in Aracataca, Rosa Elena Fergusson (of English extraction) and she said to him: 'Gabo, I could have been your mother.' And he replied: 'Yes, you used to take me to school when my grandmother couldn't.' 'No,' she replied, 'for a while I was your father's girlfriend.'[73] There was sexual scandal in the Gabriel Eligio–Luisa Santiaga household. As Martin suggests: 'A woman in a nearby settlement hired a lawyer who accused Gabriel Eligio of raping her while under anaesthetic and although he denied the more serious charge of rape he admitted he was indeed the father of her child.'[74] This was, furthermore, not an isolated event; another woman later came along and said the same thing. Luisa Santiaga, after an angry show-down with her husband, decided to take the child in. Gabo's brother, Jaime, recalls that the illegitimate children were accepted into the household by Luisa as if they were her own.[75] Gabo himself heard his mother once say: 'I don't want the family blood going wandering around the world.'[76]

It is clear from comments like this just how much of the fantastic world of Macondo grew out of the vivid metaphors and narratives García Márquez heard from his mother's and grandmother's mouths; there is a famous scene in *One Hundred Years of Solitude* in which the blood of the Buendía family weaves its way through the streets of Macondo on its way back to the family home. Though Gabriel Eligio did practise *queridazgo* – he went on to have a total of four llegitimate children (Abelardo García Ujueta, Carmen Rosa García Hermosillo, Germaine (Emy) García Mendoza, and Antonio (Toño) García Navarro) – he favoured his legitimate family, having eleven children with Luisa Santiaga (Gabriel José (Gabo), Luis Enrique, Margarita (Margot), Aída, Ligia, Gustavo, Rita del Carmen, Jaime, Hernando (Nanchi), Alfredo Ricardo (Cuqui), and Eligio Gabriel (Yiyo), who all of course took his name), and in this he differed from Colonel Márquez (who had three legitimate children versus twelve to nineteen illegitimate children).

Though a proclivity for sexual experimentation was clearly in his blood García Márquez chose not to follow in his father's footsteps. In the telegraph office where he worked Gabriel Eligio 'had a bachelor's cot with well-oiled springs for whatever the night might offer him. At one time I was somewhat tempted by his furtive hunter's ways, but life taught me it is the most arid form of solitude.'[77] It is important to recall, though, that García Márquez was certainly no angel during his adolescence, as his brother pointedly observes in an interview with Silvia Galvis titled 'I am not a devil nor is Gabo a saint'.[78] During the holidays in Sucre García Márquez as a young man would help his father out, running errands for him, and collecting debts owed to his father's pharmacy. While out collecting some unpaid invoices, when he was twelve years old, García Márquez lost his virginity to a prostitute. He was calling to collect a debt at a brothel called La Hora, and what happened next is described with literary flair in his autobiography:

I went up to the half-closed door of a room that opened onto the street, and I saw one of the women from the house, barefoot and wearing a slip that did not cover her thighs, taking a nap on an air mattress. Before I could speak to her she sat up on the mattress, looked at me half asleep, and asked me what I wanted. I told her I had a message from the father for Don Eligio Molina, the proprietor. But instead of giving me directions she told me to come and bar the door, and with an index finger that said everything she signaled to me:
'Come here.'
I went there, and as I approached, her heavy breathing filled the room like a river in flood, until she grasped my arm with her right hand and slipped her left inside my fly. I felt a delicious tremor.
'So you're the son of the doctor with the little drops,' she said as she handled me inside my trousers with five agile fingers that felt like ten. She took off my trousers and did not stop whispering

warm words in my ear as she pulled her slip over her head and lay face-up on the bed wearing only her red flowered panties. 'This is something you have to take off,' she told me. 'It's your duty as a man.'

I pulled down the zipper but in my haste I could not remove her panties, and she had to help me by extending her legs and making a swimmer's rapid movement. Then she lifted me by the armpits and put me on top of her in the academic missionary position. The rest she did on her own, until I died alone on top of her, splashing in the onion soup of her filly's thighs.[79]

His childhood was over.

García Márquez's first love affair occurred in Barranquilla in 1942 with a woman called Martina Fonseca, whom he describes as 'a white cast in the mold of an intelligent, autonomous mulatta'.[80] She invited him around to her house after mass on Ash Wednesday; her husband, who worked on a boat which sailed along the Magdalena River, was away for twelve days, and, despite the Ash Wednesday cross on their foreheads, they made love. As García Márquez recalls: 'What was strange about his wife inviting me on a casual Saturday for hot chocolate and cruellers? Except that the ritual was repeated for the rest of the year when her husband was away on his ship, and always from four to seven.'[81]

In 1940 he won a scholarship to the Liceo Nacional de Zipiquirá, a boarding school near Bogotá, as a result of a good stroke of luck; by chance he had struck up a friendship on his way to Bogotá with a stranger who turned out to be the national director of scholarships for the Ministry of Education, Adolfo Gómez Tamara, and this friendship turned out to be a very productive one since he got the scholarship.[82] While at boarding school, García Márquez developed his interest in the fairer sex. García Márquez has admitted that he feels more comfortable with women than with men: 'my intimacy with the maids could be the origin of a thread of secret communication that I believe I have with women and that throughout my life has allowed me to feel more comfortable and sure with them than with men. It may also be the source of my conviction that they are the ones who maintain the world while we men throw it into disarray with our historic brutality.'[83] García Márquez soon discovered he had a way with women; indeed, he often got himself into scrapes as a young man because of his amorous activities. While at school in Zipiquirá, he had an affair with a woman whom he chooses to give the pseudonym of Nigromanta, or Necromancer: 'She would turn twenty at Christmas, and she had an Abyssinian profile and cocoa skin. Her bed was joyful and her orgasms rocky and agonized, and she had an instinct for love that seemed to belong more to a turbulent river than to a human being.'[84] Her husband, a police-man, had the body of a giant and the voice of a little girl. They lived opposite a graveyard and her neighbours used to complain about the noises she made during love-making which they said were enough to wake up the dead.[85] García Márquez would visit when her husband was out working. On one occasion he had to leave in a hurry at four o'clock in the morning because they mis-calculated the time of the husband's return, and he got out just in time. He crossed paths with the policeman in the street, who happened to ask him for a cigarette, and he said: 'Shit, Gabito, you've just come from La Hora [a local brothel] and you stink so much of whores that a goat wouldn't jump over you.'[86] The following Wednesday he was caught in bed with Nigromanta by her husband and forced to play a game of Russian roulette. The policeman put the gun to his own head, pulled the trigger, it clicked, and then he handed it to García Márquez for his turn. He couldn't do it, and expected to be killed. But he was lucky this time. The wronged husband eventually let him go because García Márquez's father had some years before cured him of a particularly nasty dose of gonorrhoea.[87]

Even though his amorous exploits were increasing in number García Márquez was falling deeper in love with a young girl, Mercedes Barcha, the granddaughter of an Egyptian immigrant and the woman whom he would one day marry.[88] As García Márquez told Plinio Apuleyo:

> I met Mercedes in Sucre, a town just inland from the Caribbean coast, where both our families lived for several years and where she and I spent our holidays. Her father and mine had been friends since they were boys. One day, at a students' dance, when she was only thirteen I asked her to marry me. Looking back I think the proposal was a metaphorical way of getting around all the fuss and bother you had to go through in those days to get a girlfriend. She must have understood it this way because we saw each other very sporadically, and always very casually, but I think neither of us had any doubt that sooner or later the metaphor would become fact. It actually became fact some ten years after the fiction, without our ever really having been engaged. We were just two people waiting, unhurriedly and imperturbably, for the inevitable.[89]

A poem appeared under the pseudonym Javier Garcés, published on 31 December 1944 in *El Tiempo*, when García Márquez was seventeen years old, entitled 'Canto' ('Song'); the last stanza runs as follows: 'I think – the rain falls – / Of your tender gaze. / Girl like fresh fruit, / Joyful as a fiesta, / Today your name is twilighting / Here in my poem'.[90] It is the love-sick song of an adolescent, pure Verlaine, for Mercedes. It is, indeed, possible to interpret García Márquez's adolescent years as caught between the pure love which must be deferred (for one thing, because of Mercedes Barcha's very young age at the time) and the sexual excesses of relationships with the likes of Nigromanta. If anything these episodes provide an indication of the extraordinarily deft way in which García Márquez has been able to transpose an experience of his own life into his fiction, allowing it to appear lived, although, as we soon learn, he was able to fuse a number of layers into his fiction. There is a part of Florentino who is based on García Márquez's adolescent years, and yet the trick is to see how the reality has been turned into art, and how, in a sense, García Márquez was able to use his own life as a tapestry in which he weaves and binds the longings and ironies of human life.

2

'10 per cent inspiration, 90 per cent perspiration'[1]

While García Márquez was studying in the capital (he had enrolled on a law course at the Universidad Nacional de Colombia in February 1947), Jorge Eliécer Gaitán, the Liberal candidate, was gunned down at 1.10 p.m. on 9 April 1948, on 14–55 of carrera 7 between Jiménez de Quesada and calle 14,[2] an event which changed García Márquez's life irrevocably. When the murder took place García Márquez was eating lunch with his brother, Luis Enrique, and some friends in a *pensión* where they were living in the Calle Florián only a couple of streets away.[3] They rushed out to see what had happened. The mayhem – looting and burning – was about to begin. The urban disturbance caused by Gaitán's murder was so radical that it led to the creation of a new word in the Spanish language, the *bogotazo*.[4] Luis Villar Borda remembers meeting a very distressed-looking García Márquez later on that day, just a few steps from where Gaitán had been shot, and the writer told him: 'They've burned down my pension and I've lost all my stories.'[5] The account given in García Márquez's autobiography is rather more varnished, but it is clear that he was as concerned about his career as a writer and, indeed, a journalist, as much as about Gaitán's death. Although they did not meet on that occasion García Márquez and Fidel Castro were both in Bogotá at that time (at any one time probably no more than a couple of streets away from each other) – Castro had met Gaitán on 7 April and they had agreed to meet again at 2.00 p.m. on 9 April: the meeting was doomed. The *bogotazo* would simmer in García Márquez's soul and stoke the flames of a political urgency which would develop in his life years later. Later on, of course, García Márquez would throw in his lot with the Cuban Revolution and, even when his friends such as Vargas Llosa turned away from the Revolution, he would remain a staunch friend of Fidel Castro. If nothing else, the *bogotazo* allowed García Márquez to see naked injustice at first hand and also witness the unstoppable anger of the 'pueblo' when roused.

Just as important, though, as his first-hand experience of political violence in Bogotá, was the manner in which these events were transformed in the sieve of García Márquez's vivid imagination. As we read in the autobiography:

Bands of bootblacks armed with their wooden boxes tried to knock down the metal gates of the Granada drug stores, where the few police on duty had locked away the attacker to protect him from the angry mob. A tall man, very much in control of himself and wearing an irreproachable gray suit as if he were going to a wedding, urged them on with well-calculated shouts that were so effective the owner of the pharmacy had raised the metal gates for fear they would burn his stores. The attacker, clutching a police officer, succumbed to panic at the sight of the maddened crowds rushing toward him.

'Officer,' he pleaded, almost without a voice, 'don't let them kill me.'

I will never be able to forget him. He had disheveled hair, a two-day beard, a dead man's gray color, and eyes that bulged with terror. He had a very worn brown suit with vertical stripes, its lapels ripped by the first tugs of the mob. It was an instant-aneous and eternal apparition, because the bootblacks tore him away from the police with blows of their boxes and then kicked him to death. The first time he went down he had lost a shoe.

'To the Palacio!' shouted the man in gray, who has never been identifed. 'To the Palacio!'[6]

Given that no other account of the *bogotazo* – and there are many accounts – mentions a man in gray who, in García Márquez's words, 'has never been identified', there is the distinct possibility that this is an example of a 'false memory', created as a result of the various vivid stories told to García Márquez soon after the event, and then woven together over time in the crucible of his mind.[7] Indeed, according to a number of other testimonies, García Márquez did not witness either Eliécer Gaitan's murder or the murder of his attacker,[8] and this lends further credence to the possibility of a false memory. As he suggests later on in the account: 'I remained at the scene of the crime for ten more minutes, surprised by the speed with which the accounts of witnesses were changing in form and substance until they lost all resemblance to reality.'[9] He concludes with a revealing point:

> Fifty years later, my memory is still fixed on the image of the man who seemed to incite the crowd outside the pharmacy, and I have not found him in any of the countless testimonies I have read to this day. I had seen him up close, with his expensive suit, his alabaster skin, and a milimetric control of his actions. He attracted my attention so much that I kept an eye on him until he was picked up by too new a car as soon as the assassin's corpse was dragged away, and from then on he seemed to be erased from historical memory. From mine, until many years later, in my days as a reporter, when it occurred to me that the man had managed to have a false assassin killed in order to protect the identity of the real one.[10]

How believable is this man? The description of his 'expensive suit' and 'alabaster skin' begins to ring a few of those 'verisimilitude' alarm bells, especially given – according to the majority of other accounts – the pandemonium which was taking place around Eliécer Gaitán's dead body. That he should have 'milimetric control' over his actions, and, furthermore, that he would be secretly picked up by 'too new a car' begins to beggar belief. Rather than it being the case, as García Márquez suggests, that this man was 'erased from historical memory', is it surely not more reasonable to assume that he has been added to the historical memory as a result of the Colombian writer's vivid imagination?

It is instructive to compare García Márquez's account with contemporary newspaper reports. *El Tiempo* on the front page of its 12 April 1948 edition, for example, gave a full account of the events. Gaitán was leaving his office in the Agustín Nieto building at about 1.10 p.m. on Friday 9 April 1948, accompanied by a number of colleagues including Jorge Padilla, Plinio Mendoza Neira, Alejandro Vallejo and Francisco Gaitán Pardo, when he was approached by a slight, short man dressed in gray, whom no one had noticed until that point, who pulled out his gun unexpectedly and then shot Gaitán four times. A police officer who happened to be nearby, Ciro Efraín Silván, apprehended the assassin. He and another officer attempted to protect the assassin from the gathering crowd but the mob eventually was able to prise the man from the policemen's grasp and began to beat him to death.[11] In this version there is no mention of a man directing the operation from the sidelines as in García Márquez's account. In the account provided by Jaime Quijano Caballero of the event which he witnessed at first-hand, he mentions that there was a shout of 'A palacio' ('To the palace') but – unlike García Márquez's account which states that this was shouted by a man who was masterminding the operation from the sidelines – he remembers it as one of various shouts emanating from the crowd, which included 'Muera el asesino!' ('Kill the assassin!'), and 'A palacio! A palacio! A que expliquen!' ('To the palace! To the palace! Let them explain!').[12]

The above is not to deny that García Márquez's is an accurate description but it is strange that none of the extant accounts appear to concur with it. What we have is an example of the false memory which nevertheless captures the most extraordinary part of the assassination. To this day, Juan Roa Sierra's motives have never been satisfactorily explained – since he does not appear to have had any clear political affiliation which might explain such a radical act – and García Márquez is able to express this by introducing an element of mystery into the event itself (even though other accounts suggest that the individual concerned only really existed in the Colombian writer's imagination). Indeed, the compelling detail in García Márquez's autobiography is the role that memory clearly played in this event, for it is only years later, as he suggests in his account, that it occurred to him that the man 'had managed to have a false assassin killed in order to protect the identity of the real one'. One possibility here is that García Márquez has used the narrative of the 1962 assassination of John F. Kennedy, which spawned an extraordinary number of conspiracy theories, in order to re-invoke the memory of the event and then re-present the event as an amalgamation of different 'real' events. This creation over time of a verisimilar but not empiric false memory offers a key to the way in which García Márquez creates his mesmerizing fiction. However one interprets this event – and it could be argued that its emotional importance to him can be measured by the intensity with which he recreated the event in his imagination, shaping it, personalizing it, giving it an intrinsic weight – the *bogotazo* proved too much for Gabo.

In early 1948, he and his brother, Luis Enrique, travelled back to the north to escape the violence and get some Caribbean peace and quiet. García Márquez left for Cartagena on 20 April 1948,[13] and, soon after his arrival, happened to bump into an old friend, Manuel Zapata Olivella (later the author of an extraordinary Afro-Caribbean novel, *Changó, el gran putas*, 1983),[14] who provided him with the shoo-in to a job as a journalist for the local newspaper, *El Universal*. It was a stroke of luck because it allowed García Márquez to pursue a career from which he later said he learned the stock in trade for his fiction.[15] He would never resume his university studies.

García Márquez's first article, 'Punto y aparte' ('New Paragraph') came out in *El Universal* on 21 May 1948.[16] The editor of *El Universal*, Clemente Manuel Zabala, was a bespectacled, discreet gay man with slicked-back hair and very vocal liberal views.[17] He was famous for berating the Conservatives not only for their erroneous political principles but also because of their bad grammar.[18] García Márquez later went on to write a series of 'New Paragraph' articles, edited closely by Zabala's legendary red pen, which already have a recognizable style – they are short (about a paragraph long), witty, pick on details which illustrate the moral of the tale in an entertaining way, and often have a political bite.[19] Typically they pick up on an everyday scene or event – perhaps the bell sounding the curfew, a scarecrow, a boat ride, a Thursday or a literary writer such as George Bernard Shaw or Arthur Conan Doyle – which then leads into a reflection on weightier matters (the historical significance of events, the fact that ghosts are no longer in fashion, and so on).[20] At times they are very imaginative and show the novelist polishing his writing style, such as the article on the special resonance that days of the week have (a Monday is like a ring on the finger, Tuesday is a day to get married or go on a long voyage, Wednesday is indecisive, Thursday is a hybrid day, while Friday is an elegant day to die).[21] García Márquez revealed his linguistic talent in these early articles; according to Colombia's most famous contemporary poet, Álvaro Mutis, García Márquez of all the writers of the Spanish-speaking world is the one with the deepest understanding of the Castilian language.[22] That García Márquez's experience of the *bogotazo* was already paying literary dividends is clear if we compare his articles with the literary short stories he had been writing around this time, all of which are intriguing but, ultimately, rather whimsical.[23] His journalism taught him to give his work a social edge. Once he put the two skills together – being able to write like a Colombian Faulkner, let's say, as well as writing edgy journalism – there was no stopping

García Márquez, second on the right, working at his desk as a journalist in Barranquilla, 1950.

him.[24] Indeed, it is possible that the investigative journalism García Márquez carried out in the late 1940s for *El Universal* of Cartagena provided inspiration for his most Cartagena-focused novel, *Of Love and Other Demons* (the prologue, after all, makes it quite clear where the novel is set). The 25 October 1949 edition of *El Universal*, for example, published a story about a dog called Calavera (Skull) which had unearthed the dead body of a baby – the story had been written by none other than García Márquez[25] – and it may well have inspired some details in *Of Love and Other Demons*.[26]

García Márquez began to make quite a name for himself with his journalism, and he was soon offered a job by Alfonso Fuenmayor, the editor of *El Heraldo*, a newspaper based in Barranquilla. In the Christmas of 1949 he moved to Barranquilla, and on 5 January 1950 he began work for *El Heraldo*, publishing on that day his first 'Jirafa' ('Giraffe') columns.[27] Ligia, Gabo's sister, has suggested that Gabo left *El Universal* to go to work in Barranquilla so he could be near Mercedes; indeed, the name of his column was inspired by Mercedes's long, elegant neck.[28] García Márquez soon became part of the Barranquilla literary group, consisting of two veterans, José

Mercedes Barcha in Barranquilla before her marriage to García Márquez.

Félix Fuenmayor and Ramón Vinyes, along with Obregón, Cepeda Samudio, Fuenmayor, and Vargas.[29] The main inspiration for García Márquez was Vinyes, 'the man who had read all the books', as Gabo would call him,[30] a man who would one day be given a role in García Márquez's fiction as himself (this was one of his tricks: he often put his friends in his fiction as themselves) in *One Hundred Years of Solitude*.[31] Soon after he started working for *El Heraldo* – where he regularly used to smoke two packets of cigarettes a day – García Márquez took up residence in a four-storey building in Barranquilla which was called the skyscraper because there were not many buildings of that height in the coastal city at that time. The building was on the Calle Real (now called Paseo Bolívar) near the Plaza Colón (now called Plaza San Nicolás), over the street from the offices of *El Heraldo* in a run-down district. On the ground floor there was a notary's office and other businesses, and the upper floors were a brothel; García Márquez lived on the top floor, and the rent was 1 *peso* 50 *centavos* per night. He became good friends with many of the prostitutes who plied their trade there; he would write letters on their behalf and they would wash and iron his clothes. When he did not have the rent he would leave the manuscript he was working on at the time as a surety with the porter. The contrast with García Márquez's present home in Colombia, a large three-storey house in Cartagena, designed by the Colombian architect Rogelio Salmona,[32] on the corner of the Paseo de la Muralla and the Calle del Curato,[33] with superb views of the Caribbean sea, could not be more striking.

The 'Giraffes' García Márquez wrote for *El Heraldo*, beginning in January 1950 and running until December 1952, are witty and break the mould of conventional journalism. One called 'In Defence of Coffins' (March 1950) begins with the rather startling opening sentence: 'The most optimistic of mortals might ask, on an afternoon like this one, where in the world is the tree that will be used to make his coffin.'[34] Another, 'Tarzan's Orphanhood' (March 1950), begins: 'As occurred with Popeye the Sailor Man, Tarzan will survive many years longer than his creator, Edgar Rice Burroughs, who died yesterday at his Californian ranch.'[35] Apart from writing for other newspapers, he also tried his hand at setting up his own newspaper and he and some friends founded a literary and cultural magazine, *Crónica*, the first number of which came out on 29 April 1950.[36] It was while working at *El Heraldo* that he developed his penchant for hard work. According to his brother Luis Enrique, his secret is that he writes consistently, every day.[37] The secret to his success, as García Márquez once said, is 10 per cent inspiration, 90 per cent perspiration.

Then disaster struck. One of his best friends, Cayetano Gentile, was hacked to death in Sucre on 22 January 1951, accused of taking the virginity of a local girl, Margarita Chica, and dishonouring her family. Margarita's brothers killed Gentile. Soon after the murder Gabriel Eligio, Gabo's father, decided to uproot the family and move to Cartagena, where García Márquez was then installed, working as a journalist for *El Universal*. The reason for this move has never been satisfactorily explained. It was clearly not for political reasons,[38] since Gabriel Eligio was a conservative and Sucre was, like the land-locked lake on whose banks it lay, a small, conservative, politically 'stagnant' town. The murder of Cayetano Gentile, though ostensibly provoked by the need to wash away Margarita Chica's sexual sin, had been committed by her brothers, Manuel and Víctor, who were (rather appropriately) butchers by trade. Since the victim was from the land-owning aristocracy, it was a clear sign that the *ancien régime* of sexual exploitation of lower-class women by upper-class men – including such customs as *queridazgo* and *ius primis noctis* – would no longer hold sway. Gabriel Eligio had always played by the rules of the old order – he had sired four *hijos naturales* – and it is quite possible that his awareness of a sea change in Sucre, coupled with the fact that Gentile was a relative of his wife – led him to make the decision to move the family to Cartagena. García Márquez meanwhile had decided that he wanted to write a novel about his friend's murder, but he was persuaded to hold off at least until Gentile's mother passed away. *Chronicle of a Death Foretold*, which is based on the murder, was published thirty years later.

García Márquez set up his own newspaper in September 1951, calling it *Comprimido* (*Compressed*); it aspired to be 'the smallest newspaper in the world', and was a reaction to the 'scarcity of paper, advertising and readers' as announced in the editorial of the first edition which was published in Cartagena on 18 September 1951. It was 24 inches long in its entirety,[39] and therefore eminently transportable. Financed by Guillermo Dávila and written almost entirely by García Márquez, it had a print-run of 500 copies – and folded after six days.[40] It had a section called 'Love Hospital', in which readers' heartaches would be solved. One went as follows:

> Q: I also want to say a lot of things to a man I like a lot, but when I'm near him my temperature drops and I get a cold sweat all over my body and I start to shiver. What can I do?
> A: Go and see a doctor. You might be suffering from malaria rather than love.[41]

Comprimido, which ran from 18 until 23 September 1951, is valuable in that it provides insight into García Márquez's rather quirky humour. It is in works such as these that the Caribbean strain within García Márquez's work is evident, which favours humour, spontaneity, the oral and the popular.[42] It was the only newspaper edited solely by the Colombian author.

Meanwhile García Márquez was writing his first novel. As early as March 1952 he wrote to Gonzalo González who was working at the time for *El Espectador* that he was working on a 600-page novel called *La casa* (*The House*).[43] Jacques Gilard has argued that in García Márquez's journalism of the late 1940s and early '50s there could be detected the spirit of the novel which would revolutionize the novelistic tradition, *One Hundred Years of Solitude*, and his statement led to a famous debate between himself and Ángel Rama, who argued that the journalism and the fragments of *La casa* were still a long way off from the artistry of *One Hundred Years of Solitude*.[44] García Márquez's father, meanwhile, was not happy with his eldest son's new-found career; when Gabo told his father he wanted to be a writer, his father said bluntly: 'You will eat paper.'[45]

His awareness of his grandfather's double life was one of the reasons why in 1952–3 García Márquez decided to go on a journey in the Magdalena region in search of his roots. The opportunity came to him serependitously in the form of an offer from Julio César Villegas, a Peruvian entrepreneur in exile who had just set up a business in Barranquilla selling books by instalments, and who asked García Márquez to be his agent. This was in December 1952, and García Márquez accepted the offer since it allowed him to make some money as well as research his roots. He went off to Santa Marta where he met his brother Luis Enrique, and from there they went together through various towns looking for customers for Villegas's books, to Ciénaga, Valledupar, La Paz and Manaure, with stop-offs in Guacamayal, Sevilla, Aracataca, Fundación and El Copey.[46] When Enrique returned to Ciénaga, García Márquez carried on his journey with Rafael Escalona and, later on, met Lisandro Pacheco, the grandson of Medardo whom his grand-father, Colonel Márquez, had killed in 1908. But they put their past behind them and went on the journey together around the region of La Guajira. They travelled to Riohacha, passing through Urumita, Villanueva, El Molino, San Juan del César, Fonseca, Bar-rancas (where the duel between Gabo's grandfather and Lisandro Pacheco's grandfather had taken place in the main square) and Tomarrazón.[47] García Márquez met a number of the colonel's *hijos naturales* on his travels, nineteen of them as he later told Dasso Saldívar. By the time he had returned to Barranquilla (May–June 1953) he had confirmed the 'other' image of his grandfather, which he had glimpsed years before as a child when he had seen his grandfather sitting in the living room of another house with a woman next to him, as naturally as if he had been at home with Tranquilina. Gabo's visit to La Guajira proved his grandfather had led a double life.

He managed to read some novels during this trip when he was not selling Villegas's books. He reread Virginia Woolf's *Mrs*

'La tercera resignación' ('The Third Resignation') published in *El Espectador*, 13 September 1947.

Dalloway and read Hemingway's *The Old Man and the Sea* for the first time, which impressed him deeply.[48] Perhaps most important, he discovered how the novelistic chassis of these novels could be remoulded in order to tell the story of his family with his grandfather as the patriarch. A novel he had read some years before, Fyodor Dostoevsky's *The Double*, probably in the Spanish translation by Alfonso Nadal,[49] may have helped in the artistic formulation of his novelistic vision.[50] Dostoevsky's story is about a man, Jakov Petrovitch Golyadkin, who is tortured by the existence of his double,[51] whom he meets at the climax of the novel, at which point he accepts his 'destiny' and is led off, either to a sanatorium or to his death, the novel does not make clear. García Márquez's early fiction is valuable not only because it allows us access to his obsessions (particularly, the doubleness of his family) but also because it allows us to track the emergence of a new literary style, one in which five techniques are gradually perfected, namely, magical realism, the portrayal of time as a truncated, dislocated reality, the lapidary one-liner, black humour, and political allegory.[52]

García Márquez's first published short story was 'La tercera resignación' ('The Third Resignation'); it appeared in *El Espectador* on 13 September 1947 and he did not even have enough money to buy a copy (it cost five *centavos*). García Márquez asked a passer-by if he could have his copy. As a result of a gift from a random individual García Márquez saw his first story in print.[53] 'The Third Resignation' does not contain a social or political critique since it is a psychological short story.[54] Above all, it is a story about living death, and particularly the thoughts running through the mind of someone who is alive but about to be buried: 'He was in the coffin, ready to be buried, and yet he knew that he wasn't dead' (p. 69).[55] It does not supersede the portrayal of consciousness beyond the grave familiar in much nineteenth-century fiction, and the dialogue is rather wooden if not downright unverisimilar: '"Madam, your child has a grave illness: he is dead. Nevertheless," he went on, "we shall do everything possible to keep him alive beyond death"' (p. 69).

His second story, 'Eva dentro de su gato' ('Eva is Inside her Cat'), published in *El Espectador* on 25 October 1947, confirms García Márquez's early fiction as fixated on death but shows hints of ori–ginality in its depiction of the uncanny. 'Eva is Inside her Cat'[56] reveals García Márquez experimenting – like an impromptu jazz musician – with his repertoire of techniques. A rewriting of Kafka's 'Metamorphosis',[57] it explores like a number of the early short stories the realm of non-rational consciousness (before expressed as the unconscious or dream or life after death) but now does so in terms of the consciousness of a cat. Like the other stories, techniques such as expression of the uncanny or the absurd are present; they are inchoate, unarticulated, but it is important to note that this story shows the emergence of one new technique within his *oeuvre*, that is, the lapidary one-liner, which would come to dominate his

'Tubal-Caín forja una estrella' ('Tubal-Cain Forges a Star') published in *El Espectador* on 17 January 1948.

best fiction in later years, and it occurs at the end of the story: 'Only then did she understand that three thousand years had passed since the day she had had a desire to eat the first orange' (p. 91).

García Márquez's third story, 'Tubal-Caín forja una estrella' ('Tubal-Cain Forges a Star') was published in *El Espectador* on 17 January 1948,[58] with a striking illustration by Enrique Grau.[59] García Márquez's story is an extraordinary piece of writing; though described by Vargas Llosa as 'diffuse to the point of incoherence',[60] it can be interpreted as an allegory of the subconscious fear of the others (the illegitimate children) who threaten the author's sense of identity. It begins with the description of a scene which could be a dream as much as the realistic description of someone walking down a street in Bogotá. The protagonist (a thinly veiled projection of García Márquez himself) feels he is being followed, and the short story begins: 'He stopped. The "other" stopped as well'.[61] This is then followed by a list of anxious thoughts caused by the 'other'. Facing the other means returning to the past: 'The man who was living inside his body trembled.' The experience forces the protagonist to feel an overwhelming sense of vertigo, which somehow leads to a memory of his father who is now dead, particularly of the time when 'he came to sit on the side of the bed'.[62] The story suddenly takes a magical turn as it describes the way in which the dead father descends and begins to multiply before his eyes:

He could already see him descending. Soon he would turn into a small minimal being, who would split into a double of himself [se desdoblaría] and he would multiply himself in all the corners of the room, into a handful of equal figures, which were identical and moved quickly [movedizos], who would run around in a disorganised manner, like ants dispersed by fire. He liked to witness this atrocious feast; he felt positive pleasure, which was irrational, when he saw his father multiplied. He felt satisfaction as he pursued that army of Lilliputians who congregated fearfully in the corners, looking at him with their sharp, malicious little eyes, bumping into each other, multiplying themselves more and more until they completely filled the room up.

The protagonist then goes on to describe his pleasure in capturing ten or fifteen of these Lilliputian beings: 'They were all the same, exactly the same.' Then he would kill them: 'With what satisfaction he saw them tremble when he began to clench his fingers, closing his fist so as to squeeze them, and destroy them inside his fist.' As the story goes on: 'Now he understood perfectly. The return of "the other" implied the return of all those of those morbid sensations.' The story then returns to the present – the man who is walking along the street and who feels fear when he hears the sound of the other's footsteps. The story expresses vividly a young man's anguish as caused by the Lilliputian ghosts created by his father, which I interpret here as a projection of García Márquez's existential unease once he discovered his grandfather's double life. Though it has not received the attention it deserves, this short story offers insight into the dilemma which had been torturing García Márquez since his childhood. 'Tubal-Cain Forges a Star' shows García Márquez confronting his family's ghosts.

'La otra costilla de la muerte' ('The Other Rib of Death', 1948) can also be read as a meditation on the rivalry between the legitimate child and the *hijo natural*, who takes the form of the dead twin/other in this story. The story does not have any plot to speak of but is rather the description of a sequence of thoughts which go through the protagonist's mind, as inspired by an initial nightmare about the death of someone called his brother. Any idea that the figure of the brother ('his brother, the other, his twin')[63] might be a projection of one of the author's real brothers, such as Luis Enrique, is soon dispelled by the fact that the protagonist and the twin/other both form part of 'another body which came from further back than his own body, which had been lying with him through the branches of an ancient genealogy; who was with him in the blood of his four pairs of great-grandfathers' (p. 29). The reference to how the two twins – the narrator and the other – were as one in the blood of their great-grandparents makes it possible to interpret the other projected in the story as an *hijo natural* sired by García Márquez's grandfather, Colonel Nicolás Márquez, and who now (i.e. in 1948) is living (García Márquez creatively imagines) a parallel life. The narrator of 'La otra costilla' imagines the 'other brother' as 'leaping from generation to generation, night to night, from kiss to kiss, from love to love, descending through arteries and testicles until he arrived as if in a nocturnal journey, at the matrix of his recent mother' (p. 29).

It is at this point in the story that the moment of artistic epiphany appears, in which the truth of the connection between the two twins is revealed: 'The mysterious ancestral journey now appeared to him as powerful and true, now that the balance had been broken and the equation definitively solved. He knew that there was something missing from his personal harmony, his formal, everyday integrity: Jacob had been irrevocably freed from his ankles!' (pp. 29–30). The biblical allusion (Gen 25:50) to Jacob and his twin brother, Esau, is a double-edged sword since while on the one hand, it resolves the mystery of the protagonist's identity (the equation is solved in the sense that the two twins are half each of one whole), it also leads to a sense of (existential) unease since this awareness leads to a sense of incompleteness. The other unnerving part of the existence of the other is that it is projected as already-dead though intimately part of his being: 'that dead body was not something alien to him, rather it was made of the same earthly substance he was, it was a repetition of him . . .' (p. 30). As the narrator subsequently exclaims; 'It was the consciousness of doubling! His double was a dead body!' (p. 30). García Márquez has clearly taken the horror of meeting one's double from Dostoevsky's *The Double* and turned it into an allegory of the bipolar identity within the Colombian family, the struggle between legitimate son and *hijo natural*. Though one is dead (which might be interpreted as social death in the sense of the lack of social acceptance) and one alive, they are 'two identical brothers, worryingly repeated' (*inquietamente repetidos*; p. 31). Perhaps the most intriguing feature of this short story is the dream described in the second paragraph:

Behind a tree there was his brother, the other, the twin, the one who had been buried that afternoon, gesticulating – this has happened to me on one occasion in real life – in order to stop the train. Convinced that his message was useless, he began to run after the train carriage until he collapsed, breathless, to the floor, his mouth full of foam. (p. 24)

As the narrator of 'La otra costilla' recognizes, the dream in itself does not appear to justify the horror it inspires: 'It was certainly an absurd, irrational dream but not one which justified at all that fitful awakening' (*despertar desasosegado*; p. 24), and this lack of an objective correlative would appear to vindicate an interpretation of the dream as more sinister than it first seems. The dream also has another curious detail in that it describes the other as 'attempting to extract his left eye with some scissors' (p. 24; my translation), which might well be an allusion to the famous opening of Buñuel's *Un Chien andalou*.[64] It is possible to read this story as a rewriting of the Oedipus myth (Oedipus of course blinded himself once he realized who he really was), which would become the mythical bedrock of the anagnorisis scene in *One Hundred Years of Solitude* nineteen years later. But, given its temporal proximity to 'Tubal-Cain Forges a Star', it is legitimate to interpret 'The Other Rib of Death' as an expression of the quasi-biblical struggle between legitimate son and the *hijo natural* within his own family. Intriguingly the *hijo natural* is always already-dead and therefore is seen as destabilizing the primacy of the legitimate self.

'The Other Side of Death' (1948) returns to the theme of the supernatural but does so in a traditional, unimaginative way; there is no dialogue but there are the stirrings of a new awareness of the timelessness of time, as we read in the final paragraph of the story. The narrator is looking at a drop which is forming in the middle of the ceiling above him and he muses: 'Maybe that room would fill the room in the space of an hour or in a thousand years and would dissolve that mortal armour, that vain substance, which perhaps – why not? – between brief instants would be nothing but a sticky mixture of albumen and whey' (p. 82).[65] There is a hint of the use of absurd humour in the sense of an awareness of the absurd though not the expression of that awareness via humour: 'Resigned, he listened to the drop, thick, heavy, exact, as it dripped in the other world, in the mistaken and absurd world of rational creatures' (p. 82).

'Dialogue with the Mirror' (1949) shows a more concrete sense of the passing of time than previous stories ('eight-twelve', p. 92; 'eight-seventeen', p. 94; 'eight-eighteen', p. 95).[66] There is an improvement in the expression of dialogue in 'Bitterness for Three Sleepwalkers' (1949), but it was only in a story published a year later, 'Eyes of a Blue Dog' (1950) that we find punchy dialogue along with lapidary one-liners.[67] The story opens with what looks like an ordinary enough domestic setting which is gradually subverted by a set of more and more intriguing one-liners as the story develops: '"I think I'm going to catch cold," she said. "This must be a city of ice"' (p. 103). This is continued throughout the story until we reach the final section, which is lapidary but also has a twist: '"You're the only man who doesn't remember anything he's dreamed after he wakes up"' (p. 107; translation revised by author). It throws the reader's expectations into disarray since the site of consciousness, the perceptor of the narrative, has been told that he is actually the site of non-knowledge, thereby reversing the dichotomy knowledge/ignorance established up until that point in the short story. But it was 'The Woman Who Came at Six O'clock' (1950)[68] which excelled in the use of punchy, semantically resonant dialogue:

José went over to where she was. He put his great puffy face up to the woman while he tugged one of his eyelids with his index finger.

'Blow on me here,' he said.

The woman threw her head back. She was serious, annoyed, softened, beautified by a cloud of sadness and fatigue.

'Stop your foolishness, José. You know I haven't had a drink for six months.' (p. 109)

It is in 'Nabo: The Black Man who Made the Angels Wait . . .' (1951) that we find the first glimpse of that most elusive of García Márquez's techniques, magical realism, for Nabo is dead although he does not know it, and we as readers only find out gradually. Nabo was killed by being struck by a horse's hoof in a stable, and some angels are attempting to persuade him to come to heaven and sing in their choir. This supernatural sequence of events is presented in realistic terms, as if Nabo were alive, sleeping in a stable, and a man outside was asking him to wake up. 'Come on, Nabo. You've slept enough already' (p. 137), is the angel's first remonstrance. But Nabo is more interested in recollecting the details of his life, and also wants to know where the horses are, the horses that he used to sing his beautiful songs to. It is possible to read the story to mean that Nabo was kicked by a horse, survived the experience but lost his mind, and was locked up in the stable, and began to hear voices, that is, angels' voices, or that he is already dead, but unaware of this fact, and it is difficult to be definite one way or the other since there is no independent source of evidence with which to measure these hypotheses. Indeed, the story is deliberately kept ambiguous.

García Márquez perfected the technique of magical realism two years later by, in 'Someone Has Been Disarranging These Roses' (1952),[69] letting us hear a ghost speak to us in a dead-pan, natural way. The ghost, as he explains, is attempting to take some roses to his child's grave, and the roses he tries to take are those the woman he visits every Sunday puts on her altar. The story is obscure – deliberately so – but it appears that the ghost is that of a young boy who died when the stairs in the stable collapsed underneath him (p. 120), and who was like a brother to her (p. 119). This supposition, however, does not square with the other possibility, i.e. that the ghost is that of an older individual (for how else could he have had a child at whose grave he wants to lay flowers, as indicated at the beginning of the story? – p. 118).

Clearly the story is built around an aporia, since the different components cannot all add up:

> That's the way she's been for twenty years, in the rocker, darning her things, looking at the chair as if now she weren't taking care of the boy with whom she had shared her childhood afternoons but the invalid grandson who has been sitting here in the corner ever since the time his grandmother was five years old. (p. 120)

If we presume the invalid grandson to be the child whose body now 'rests, mingled now, dispersed among snails and roots' (p. 118) then we are clearly faced with a *non sequitur*, not only because it is difficult to know how the individual referred to as 'Boy! Boy!' (p. 120) could have had a child, and also because it is difficult to imagine how a grandson can have been sitting in a corner ever since 'his grandmother was five years old'. García Márquez has clearly telescoped individuals from different generations into a single person, undoing the Gordian knot of sequentiality, cause and effect. 'Someone Has Been Disarranging These Roses' is an extraordinary piece of fiction and, in retrospect, can be seen as the point in his career when García Márquez perfected the technique of magical realism, giving a tantalizing hint of what was to come.

3

'Same difference'[1]

Although much has been made of García Márquez's apparent dis-
taste for Bogotá – one critic has argued that the capital of Colombia
inspired in the Nobel laureate an 'anthropological allergy'[2] – it is
clear that he needed the discipline of the Andean city in order to
forge his career both as a journalist and a novelist. When García
Márquez was invited to stay with Álvaro Mutis in Bogotá in January
1954 (Mutis was working at the time as a publicist for Esso), *El
Espectador* offered him 900 *pesos* a month to work as a member of
staff, which was considerably better than the pay in Barranquilla
(which worked out at 3 *pesos* per *jirafa*).[3] He accepted the offer
not only because he could live comfortably on that salary but also
because it would enable him to help out with the family finances,[4]
and it would allow him to attend the best literary tertulias in
Colombia at the time, which met in El Molino and El Asturias
on Carrera 7.[5]

García Márquez learned new skills in Bogotá; thus he took over
as film critic at *El Espectador* on 22 February 1954,[6] establishing
himself as one of the pioneers of film criticism in Colombia.[7] The
film which most impressed García Márquez during this period
was Vittorio De Sica's *Bicycle Thieves* because of its humanity and
closeness to life.[8] García Márquez's film criticism at the time was
quite uncompromising and did not mince its words. As a result
there were complaints from the film distributors in Bogotá, and
some distributors even pulled their advertising from *El Espectador*.[9]

It is clear that García Márquez was using his film criticism as a means of distilling his own thoughts about literature. For example, in his review of De Sica's *Miracle of Milan*, which was published in *El Espectador* on 24 April 1954, he suggests that the film manages to 'humanize fantasy' by fusing together 'fable' with 'crude Italian realism'; he furthermore suggests that this aspect of the film reminds him of *Bicycle Thieves* in which a 'fantastic episode was fused in such a clever way with elements drawn from reality that its supernatural essence went unnoticed',[10] a comment which might be applied word for word to his later novel, *One Hundred Years of Solitude*. He also decided to put his film knowledge in the abstract to concrete use by getting involved in the filming of *La langosta azul* (*The Blue Lobster*), which was shot in Barranquilla in 1954–5, and directed by Álvaro Cepeda Samudio.[11]

One gets a good sense of García Márquez's development as a journalist from the selection of articles put together by him in *Crónicas y reportajes* (*Chonicles and Reports*, 1976), based on the articles he wrote for *El Espectador* from March 1954 until September 1955. The first three articles, published in March 1954, focus on the magic, superstitions and folklore found in the Colombian coastal region of La Sierpe, a place governed by a Spanish woman called *La Marquesita* (on whom the Big Mama of 'Big Mama's Funeral' would be based), who can order snakes to seek out and bite her enemies ('La Marquesita de la Sierpe', p. 15), be in more than one place at the same time, and even walk on water (p. 15). In La Sierpe Good Friday is not a moveable feast but happens on the last Friday of March (p. 13), and its inhabitants believe in curses such as that a man can have a *mico* (a monkey) magically inserted into his stomach.[12] La Sierpe, as García Márquez's articles suggest, is a place where the veneration of local shrines has reached extra-ordinary proportions, such that the villagers can do nothing for a whole year when their local wooden statue of Christ, *Jesusito*, goes missing ('La extraña idolatría de la Sierpe', pp. 27–41), and where the dead are thought to be happy if their bodies can be heard banging against the inside of the coffin when they are carried along bumpy roads.[13]

A decisive formative influence on García Márquez during this period was Álvaro Cepeda Samudio, not only in terms of his fiction (he had published *La casa grande*) and his interest in film-directing, but also his knowledge of the new genre of news reporting emanating from the United States. Cepeda Samudio had spent some time in the States where he had learned about New Journalism, and it is clear that this had an impact on García Márquez.[14] Tomás Eloy Martínez has epitomized neatly the difference between the two journalistic styles:

> The old style of journalism used to say: 'In the tsunami which took place yesterday in South East Asia X people died; a large wave advanced kilometres and reached towns and cities . . .', while New Journalism would begin a news item like that as follows: 'Tapa Raspatundra was on the shore of her village in Java when an enormous rain cloud on the horizon gave a presentiment of the catastrophe which was about to begin . . .' You tell the reader about the horror of the wave and you make the reader identify with a character who is living at the heart of the tragedy. The story takes the reader to the heart of the story.[15]

The publication of 'Relato de un náufrago' ('The Story of a Shipwrecked Sailor') in 1955 confirmed García Márquez's success as a journalist in the new style. On 28 February 1955 Luis Alejandro Velasco, a twenty-year-old sailor travelling on the destroyer Caldas of the Colombian Navy, had been shipwrecked along with seven other crew members in a journey from Mobile, Alabama, to Cartagena. His friends all perished, but Velasco managed to survive for ten days on a raft, eating a seagull and a fish, fighting with sharks, and finally running aground in Uraba, south Colombia, to the consternation of his family and indeed the whole country, since he had already been declared dead. García Márquez interviewed Velasco in 'three exhausting weeks',[16] and the interview was published as a first-person account on fourteen consecutive days in *El Espectador*, with the first instalment appearing on 5 April 1955.[17] It was a story that gripped the nation, and, as a result, *El Espectador*'s circulation doubled;[18] more intriguingly, it also had a political sting in its tail, since Velasco stated that the reason the destroyer capsized was that it was overloaded with illegal merchandise, such as fridges, TVs and washing machines. The Colombian authorities officially denied the story, but this was revealed to be a cover-up when *El Espectador* published photographs of the trip in a special supplement edition, which infuriated the government and eventually led to the newspaper being closed down.[19]

The story is a gripping one which already shows some of García Márquez's artistry at work. He ratchets up the suspense, describing Velasco's nervousness about his future voyage as a result of seeing a film about a shipwreck the night before he sets sail ('Relato de un náufrago', p. 11); mentioning that one of the crew members will be dead at the bottom of the sea within seventy-two hours (p. 14); and emphasizing certain details – the sharks which always return at five o'clock in the afternoon, the pain of Velasco's leg wound, the arrival of seagulls with its biblical resonances (calling to mind the dove that arrives at Noah's Ark with an olive leaf in its beak, indicating that land is near). All this provides the reader with an aesthetically contoured sense of being present in the story. Also already evident here is a rough cut of what would become a distinctive feature of García Márquez's style, namely the matter-of-fact description of a ghostly apparition, as when Velasco 'sees' one of his drowned friends, Jaime Manjarrés, sitting on the raft:

I felt so tired that I leaned my head on the oar, and prepared myself for death. It was then that I saw him sitting on the deck of the destroyer, Jaime Manjarrés the sailor; he was pointing towards the port with his index finger. . . . I know that I was completely awake, completely lucid, and I could hear the wind whistling and the sound of the sea above my head. I felt hungry and thirsty. I had not the slightest doubt that Jaime Manjarrés was travelling with me in the raft.

   – Why didn't you bring enough water in the ship? he asked me.
   – Because we were getting close to Cartagena – I replied.[20]

The fourteen episodes were immediately reissued in book format, which did extremely well. The story's political bite soon became clear; it revealed the deep level of corruption in the Colombian Navy. It profoundly embarrassed the Colombian government and it was clear that García Márquez would need to leave the county for a while until the storm died down.

García Márquez was hastily offered the post of European correspondent by *El Espectador* and he left for Geneva. García Márquez, indeed, dramatizes the importance of this moment in his life by having his autobiography, *Living to Tell the Tale*, stop precisely at the point when he embarks on his European venture. Given that García Márquez had not exactly planned to go to Europe in 1955, it is understandable that he was at something of a loose end when he first arrived in the Old World. He reached Paris and then made his way to Geneva, arriving there on 17 July 1955, where he was to cover the Geneva Meeting of the Big Four nations – the Soviet Union, the United Kingdom, the United States and France.[21] From there he went to Venice to cover the Venice Film Festival, and by October he was in Rome where he enrolled on a course on Directing at the famous Centro Sperimentale di Cinematografia in Rome, helped out by the Argentine documentarist, Fernando Birri.[22] He found the course too academic but he stuck it out for two months,[23] and it was an experience which would inspire him to set up a similar film school in Cuba in the mid-1980s, and also gave rise to one of the most charming of the short stories in *Strange Pilgrims: Twelve Stories* (1992). But the most memorable thing that happened in 1955 for García Márquez was that he published his first novel, *La hojarasca* (*Leaf Storm*), described as 'Colombia's first modern novel' by Raymond Williams.[24]

Leaf Storm is an extraordinarily dense piece of fiction which focuses on the creation of an atmosphere, the overwhelming and stifling atmosphere surrounding a doctor hated by everyone in the town of Macondo because he once refused to tend to the injured – and who has just committed suicide by hanging himself. There is little action in the story, the narrative mainly comprising the reactions of the characters to the doctor's dead body lying in a coffin in the living room of the house of the most powerful man in town, the colonel. This is interrupted at certain junctures by the recollection of past events, such as the time when the doctor arrived in the town, called on the colonel, and then lived in a back room in the house for years, and his gradual displacement by other doctors arriving to look after the workers on the banana plantation. The story takes place on 12 September 1928 from 2.30 p.m. – when a young boy, the colonel's son, arrives at the house – until 3 p.m., when the coffin is about to be taken out into the street and led to the plot just outside the graveyard where the doctor will be buried. The townspeople's hatred of the doctor is such that they would prefer the doctor be refused a Christian burial; this is a reworking of Sophocles' *Antigone,* in which King Creon denies Polynices a proper burial. The connection between the two texts is further emphasized by *Leaf Storm*'s epigraph, which quotes *Antigone*.[25]

Gerald Martin has argued that *Leaf Storm* is the most autobio-graphical of García Márquez's fictions: that the 'central characters are a holy trinity forming a three-way family romance based on Gabito, Luisa and Nicolás' which allowed García Márquez 'to fantasize while he wrote that his mother never really loved Gabriel

Eligio, and that it was Gabriel Eligio, the father, who became separated from her, not himself, Gabito, the son'.[26] Just as interesting as the Oedipal anxiety in *Leaf Storm*, though, is the artistry with which its story is enunciated. A striking characteristic of the novel is its skilful creation of consciousness about the doctor's death from three different points of view, beginning with the child (p. 3), passing to his mother, Isabel (p. 7), and then to Isabel's father, the colonel (p. 14), and finally criss-crossing between these perspectives in such a way as to transform the narrative 'I' into an amalgamation of three consciousnesses composed of the three generations of one family. This mosaic of perspectives gives a sense of plot and narrativity as enclosed within memory, somehow making time timeless. A point made about Meme,[27] the house servant who had been the doctor's concubine, might be applied to all of the characters of the novel:

> It was obvious that Meme felt like recalling things that night. And while she was doing it, one had the impression that over the past years she'd held herself back in some unique and timeless static age and that as she recalled things that night she was putting her personal time into motion again and beginning to go through her long-postponed ageing process.[28]

For García Márquez the fact that we can remember past time means that time is reversible: 'Then everything began to go backward, she said' (*Leaf Storm*, p. 25). As Ángel Rama suggests, García Márquez's fiction often portrays time as an 'oscillating movement which carries us forward and backwards, and which constantly returns us to the present'.[29] Pointing in a similar direction, J. G. Cobo Borda has highlighted the use of an 'unreal preterite, that legendary preterite in which each accident becomes necessary, which encapsulates García Márquez's novelistic artistry'.[30]

Leaf Storm also trips over a number of mysteries as it goes along, such as why the doctor committed suicide, what really happened to

Meme (p. 9), and why the town is so opposed to the doctor (for it could be argued that the objective correlative – being reluctant to tend to some patients on one occasion – is not enough to explain the depth of the town's hatred towards him). Perhaps most striking about the story is that the leaf storm, though providing the novel's title, is surprisingly absent from the narrative per se – other than in a few almost off-hand references such as when Isabel's parents oppose her going to the cinema because 'they're amusements from out of the leaf storm' (p. 51). Its meaning is explained in the rather poetic prologue to the novel, where the leaf storm is shown to be a metaphor of the havoc created by the arrival of the banana company.

> Suddenly, as if a whirlwind had set down roots in the center of the town, the banana company arrived, pursued by the leaf storm. A whirling leaf storm had been stirred up, formed out of the human and material dregs of other towns, the chaff of a civil war that seemed ever more remote and unlikely. The whirlwind was implacable. It contaminated everything with its swirling crowd smell, the smell of skin secretion and hidden death. In less than a year it sowed over the two the rubble of many catastrophes that had come before it, scattering its mixed cargo of rubbish in the streets. (p. 1)

It is true that the banana company does bring disaster in particular to one individual in the novel: the doctor. It deprives him of his livelihood by offering medical treatment to its workers, thus causing him to lose all his patients, then deprives him of his dignity by implicitly questioning whether he is really qualified to be a doctor as a result of new legislation requiring all professionals to register their degrees (p. 49), and it is possible that this is the reason why he committed suicide. But the novel does not focus on the 'many catastrophes' brought about by the banana company's arrival, and at most focuses on one – the doctor's demise. Given the novel's title and its powerful opening prologue the reader is encouraged to presume that the leaf storm will be the novel's overriding focus, but its apparent absence from the text in fact suggests that García Márquez is using the iceberg strategy in this novel[31] – that the main tragedy of Macondo is happening offstage in a place to which the reader is not privy but whose effects he can see, as it were, onstage. *Leaf Storm* therefore raises the possibility that what is not seen is more important than what is seen. Indeed, the novel is haunted by mysteries: as suggested above, they include the question of what happened to Meme, and why the doctor committed suicide; but these and others are subsumed within the greater mystery: Where is the leaf storm?[32]

Other stories written during the mid-1950s show García Márquez experimenting with the short story form, polishing its edges and individualizing it. 'Monologue of Isabel Watching it Rain in Macondo' (1955) recreates the thoughts going through the mind of a pregnant woman called Isabel, who is terrified by the rain. It expresses that Caribbean sense of the devastating and all-powerful reality of nature, providing an extraordinarily viscous sense of rain in the Caribbean: 'Then it rained. And the sky was a gray, jellyish substance that flapped its wings a hand away from our heads' (p. 129). The rain is so persistent that it begins to penetrate their senses: 'we hadn't eaten since sunset on Monday and I think that from then on we stopped thinking. We were paralyzed, drugged by the rain, given over to the collapse of nature with a peaceful and resigned attitude' (p. 132).

Despite the defiantly Caribbean mindset reflected by his mid-1950s fiction, it was written at a time when García Márquez was busy Europeanizing himself. He travelled from Rome to Paris in December 1955, moving into the Hôtel de Flandres at 16 Rue Cujas.[33] But then disaster struck. The Colombian government decided to close down *El Espectador*, in effect making García Márquez penniless overnight. This had been his only form of income. Despite having no money, he decided to stay in Europe. Luckily, Plinio Apuleyo, who was at the time living in Venezuela, offered him some freelance journalism. The problem was that Plinio Apuleyo's money orders did not always arrive promptly – an experience García Márquez (rather felicitously) transposed in his portrayal of the colonel waiting for his letter in *No One Writes to the Colonel*.[34] In late 1956 García Márquez moved into a *chambre de bonne* with Tachia Quintana, a Basque actress, in the Rue d'Assas; it was a brief but intense love affair.[35] But the love of his life was clearly still the girl he had first met when she was just nine years old, Mercedes Barcha, who was waiting for him back in Colombia. Gabo and Mercedes began writing to each other two to three times a week.[36] It was in their letter writing that they both developed an awareness of how much they loved each other. One could even argue that this was the juncture in their lives when they truly fell in love.

With hindsight, it is clear that the journalism that García Márquez began to write in Europe had an incisive wit, a cosmo-politanism and a sense of historic irony that were not there before; the essays are now collected in *Cuando era feliz e indocumentado* (*When I was Happy and Undocumented*, 1973). The article 'El año más famoso del mundo' ('The Most Famous Year in the World'), for example, begins with a visual image – García Márquez's trademark for his fiction – Sir Anthony Eden waves goodbye at 10 Downing Street, and then 'broke with party members, visited Queen Elizabeth for the last time, presented his resignation, packed his bags, left the house and retired from political life', all in two hours.[37] Various events from 1957 are brought together, and often it is the strange detail which is highlighted – Humphrey Bogart dies with the comment 'The only thing going well is my bank account' (p. 12), Andrei Gromyko rises (to power in the Soviet Union) while Brigitte Bardot's décolletage falls (pp. 13–14). While working as a journalist in Europe García Márquez had perfected his skill at drawing the reader into the heart of the story he is narrating, by creating a communality of sympathy viewed from the perspective of a shared quotidianity. One of his articles about a murder in Italy shows his craftmanship:

> Vicente Hernández Marval ate dinner with his wife, rested for an hour smoking cigarettes on the terrace and at ten o'clock at night he left the house. This was the last time he did so. He was a stocky, 34-year-old taxi-driver, a good conversationalist, a passionate fan of Copei's political programme and a practising Catholic. On that day, the 24th of March 1952, when he left his home for the last time he was not doing anything out of the ordinary. He had worked in his black Mercury since six in the evening, he had returned for his evening meal at 8.30 and he had promised his wife that he would back as usual at two in the morning. But he did not return until the next day, on the last page of the newspaper, which reported how Vicente Hernández Marval had been shot dead, along with his friend, inside his own car.[38]

In 1957 García Márquez visited the Eastern Bloc countries with Plinio Apuleyo, the latter's sister, Soledad, and Luis Villa Borda; Apuleyo had bought a Renault and offered to go on the trip with García Márquez.[39] They travelled to East Germany, West Germany, Czechoslovakia, Poland, Russia, and Hungary. In the articles García Márquez subsequently wrote on his journeys, now collected as *De viaje por países socialistas* (*A Journey Through the Socialist Bloc*), it is clear that his political acumen was being sharpened. In some ways the Colombian writer's journalism is similar to César Vallejo's reportage on the Soviet Union of some fifty years before in that García Márquez, like Vallejo, draws conclusions about life in a communist country based on his impressions of places and people, and his conversations. The impression derived from García Márquez's journalism, unlike Vallejo's, however, was overwhelmingly negative; in the Socialist Bloc countries García Márquez thought they could not get anything right, even prostitution![40] According to Plinio Apuleyo, who accompanied García Márquez on this trip, García Márquez's subsequent interest in communism and socialism derived from his natural sympathy with Cuba, rather than his affiliation with the Soviet Union and its satellite nations.[41]

After his trip to the Eastern Bloc, García Márquez went to London for six or seven weeks, ostensibly to learn English but in fact to polish his short stories for publication.[42] He was then offered work as a journalist for *Momento* in Caracas, through the intercession of Plinio Apuleyo, and he arrived in Venezuela on 24 December 1957.[43] Thus it was that he was present in Caracas in January 1958 when dictator Marcos Pérez Jiménez was ousted from power, and shared in the popular and public jubilation that accompanied this event. García Márquez once more brought his magic touch to the publication he worked for; the issue of *Momento* he and Plinio Apuleyo put together, published a day after Pérez Jiménez's flight from Venezuela on 23 January 1958, in which they celebrated the return of democracy, had a print run of 100,000 copies and sold out within hours.[44] Despite their initial success, however, Plinio Apuleyo and García Márquez were later sacked from *Momento* by the editor Carlos Ramírez MacGregor for political differences over Richard Nixon's visit to Venezuela in May 1959.[45]

It was while he was living in Caracas that García Márquez decided to follow through on an offer and a promise that he had made many years ago. In the spring of 1958 he was drinking with Plinio Apuleyo and some friends in Caracas's Gran Café when 'he looked at his watch and said, 'Fuck it, I'm going to miss my plane.' Plinio asked him where he was going and García Márquez said, 'To get married.'[46] He had taken some time off work from *Momento*, and he flew down to Barranquilla where Mercedes Barcha was waiting for him. They got married on 21 March 1958 in the Perpetuo Soccoro church on the Avenida 20 de Julio.[47] One of Garcia Marquez's brothers, Yiyo, thought Mercedes looked stunning, like Sophia Loren.[48] García Márquez took his newly wed wife back to Venezuela with him to begin their life together.[49] It was to be a very happy marriage. Gabo and Mercedes were very well suited. As a friend has pointed out, Mercedes is 'the practical one, the one who looks after their properties, the lioness who looks after him. He would be totally lost without her.'[50] On 24 August 1959 their first child, Rodrigo, was born, and their second, Gonzalo, on 16 April 1962.

Meanwhile the political map of Latin American was become more explosive by the day. Fidel Castro ousted Fulgencio Batista from Cuba in a revolutionary coup on 1 January 1959. García Márquez and Plinio Apuleyo were invited to Cuba to participate as journalists in Fidel Castro's 'Operation Truth'; they arrived in Havana on 19 January 1959, and it was during this visit that García Márquez met Castro for the first time.[51] García Márquez commented: 'For those of us who had lived in Caracas throughout the previous year, the feverish atmosphere and the creative disorder of Havana at the beginning of 1959 were no surprise.'[52] It was the beginning of García Márquez's conversion to Caribbean-style communism.[53] García Márquez was invited to open the Bogotá office of the recently founded Cuban press agency, Prensa Latina, and, then in January 1961, he was invited to work in Prensa Latina's New York office. Mercedes and his two-year-old son, Gonzalo, went with him, but they had a hard time of it. The workers in the Prensa Latina were routinely subjected to abusive phone calls from anti-Castro refugees living in New York. Even Mercedes got a threatening phone call from someone saying he knew where they lived and where they took their child for a walk (in Central Park).[54]

Then, in June 1961, on the spur of the moment, García Márquez decided to leave New York, and he, Mercedes and little Rodrigo travelled on a Greyhound bus down to Mexico. It was intended as

García Márquez working for Prensa Latina, Bogotá, 1959.

a pilgrimage through Faulkner's Deep South, but in Atlanta they came face to face with the harsh racism of the southern states. They were not allowed into hotels because they were thought to be Mexican,[55] and were greeted with signs that said 'No dogs or Mexicans allowed'. In New Orleans they picked up a cheque for $120, sent by Plinio Apuleyo from Bogotá, which was waiting for

them at the Colombian consulate.[56] On their way to Mexico García
Márquez saw with his own eyes Faulkner's vision of the terrible
life of Yoknapatawpha County.[57] The hot, dust-filled town and the
hopeless people reminded him of the world of Aracataca which
he had evoked in his earlier fiction.[58] Gabo, Mercedes and Rodrigo
arrived in Mexico City on 26 June 1961.[59] García Márquez struggled
to find work, and eventually – in September of that year – agreed
to work as the editor of Gustavo Alatriste's two popular magazines,
The Family and *Stories for Everyone*.[60] He also turned to writing film
scripts, which, in retrospect, was a distraction.

The year 1962 was significant for García Márquez, being the
annus mirabilis of his fiction: the year when he published three
major works: *La mala hora* (*In Evil Hour*), *El coronel no tiene quien le
escribe* (*No One Writes to the Colonel*) and *Los funerales de la Mama
Grande* (*Big Mama's Funeral*). There are clear connections between
the three texts.[61] *In Evil Hour* has some of the same characters as in
the other two – such as Big Mama herself, Don Sabas, the Widow
Montiel, and Isabel – and some of the scenes replay episodes from
the other stories; thus the description of how the mayor has his
tooth pulled out by the dentist is a longer version of the action
depicted in the short story 'One of These Days', from the collection
Big Mama's Funeral. As in *No One Writes to the Colonel*, the local
cinema owner in *In Evil Hour* has to check with the local priest to
see if he can show a particular film.[62] The world depicted in *In Evil
Hour* is a desperate one: a world in which the mayor is corrupt,
violent and all-powerful; in which the population live in constant
fear of the 'pasquines' posted early in the morning in prominent
places informing all and sundry of the vices committed by members
of the community; a world bounded at one end by the revenge of a
cuckolded husband (César Montero shoots Pastor dead for carrying
on with his wife) and at the other by the cruel killing of a jailed man
by the mayor's henchmen. There are phrases in here which will
appear in the later fiction, such as mayor's statement 'This town is

García Márquez in 1962.

a happy one' (*La mala hora*, p. 85), which will be repeated in *One Hundred Years of Solitude*. Rather than being a novel in the traditional sense of the word, in which plot is central, *In Evil Hour* offers a visceral impression of a town caught in a timeless hell of stagnation, corruption and aimless violence. It is almost as though giving the novel a plot would have been to impose a spurious sense of direction on a world which does not have any such thing.

Filmic and objectivist, *No One Writes to the Colonel* manages within a hundred pages or so to conjure up the political atmosphere of Colombia in the 1950s. The plot is so simple as to be almost non-existent. A man, the colonel, has been waiting for fifteen years for a letter which he believes to be imminent and in which he will receive news of his military pension. Much of the novel is taken up with the description of the various things he and his wife – referred to simply as 'the wife' – do in order to survive, while retaining their dignity. It takes place in a short period of time from October to December in an unspecified year in the 1950s (although it is probably 1956 since this was the year of the Suez crisis, which is mentioned twice in the narrative; *El coronel*, p. 25, p. 41).[63] No details are provided by an omniscient third-person narrator; instead the reader is seduced into constructing the outline of the characters' lives based on a number of asides which we, as readers, overhear. As we soon find out, the colonel and his wife are severely affected by the loss of their son, Agustín, who, as it gradually emerges, was involved in anti-government activities, for which he paid with his life. The most elusive part of this novella concerns not the letter which appears in the title, but the cockerel which the colonel refuses to sell, even though he and his wife are practically starving to death. It comes to have a symbolic value, being associated with leftist ideology, with the couple's dead son (it once belonged to Agustín), with the people's hope for a brighter future (the 'illusion' mentioned towards the end of the novella; *El coronel*, p. 70), as well as (rather ominously) with death (*El coronel*, p. 71). Thus, the cock comes to stand for the people's determination to survive even in the face of the most abject political oppression. The main theme of *No One Writes to the Colonel*, as Rubén Celayo suggests, is the corruption of the powerful in Colombia.[64]

García Márquez had been writing *No One Writes to the Colonel* since his days spent in Paris and, as Gerald Martin has suggested,

there is a level at which this story is a recreation in fictional terms
of the everyday reality of the affair that he was pursuing at that
time with the Spanish actress Tachia.[65] Just as important is the
powerful sense of waiting conveyed in the novel; in effect García
Márquez creates a compelling vision of a Colombian Godot:
'While he was waiting for the tea to boil, sitting next to the fired
clay stove . . . the colonel felt as if poisonous mushrooms and lilies
were growing in his intestines. It was October' (pp. 5–6). The
grotesqueness of the image of mushrooms and lilies growing
within his body – recalling, of course, the fixation with death in
García Márquez's early fictions – is set against a very personal
reference. Whereas for T. S. Eliot it is April that is the 'cruellest
month', in García Márquez's own personal repertoire of symbols,
it is always October which is associated with death, bad luck,
pava.[66] Thus there is clearly a sense in which the colonel is a projection of the author (both are waiting for a cheque which never
arrives; both feel as if they are already dead; both hate October).
What this story indicates to us is how layered the fiction is; as
García Márquez has pointed out, the 'point of departure for *No
One Writes to the Colonel* was the image of a man waiting for a
launch in the market-place in Barranquilla. He was waiting with
a kind of silent anxiety. Years later in Paris I found myself waiting
for a letter – a money order probably – with the same anxiety and
I identified with the memory of that man.'[67] Then there is the
childhood memory: in this case it is the memory of his grandfather
who had been waiting for years for his pension as a result of his
service to the country in the War of a Thousand Days, fought
between 1899 and 1902 (see above, p. 17). Thirdly there is the
allegorical political level since the novel is also as much about
the political tensions in Colombia, particularly the horrors of
La Violencia, which surfaces in one-liners such as the colonel's
comment, 'This funeral is an event . . . It's the first person to die
of natural causes for years' (p. 11), and in the never quite explained

death of their son, Agustín. Fourthly, the novel was based on De Sica's *Umberto D.*;[68] García Márquez, like García Espinosa and Titón, was very much influenced by Italian neo-Realism in terms of the style of the fiction he wrote at this time. Last but not least, there is the personal, autobiographical, happening-now type of influence as evident in the details which are drawn from his relationship with Tachia and transposed into the novel.

This is the beauty of García Márquez's fiction; there are at least five levels in terms of its sources, including (i) a striking visual image; (ii) a memory of childhood; (iii) details drawn from his life at the time of writing; (iv) a literary technique used to structure the story, namely, to transpose it into art (in the case of *No One Writes to the Colonel* this technique was inspired by De Sica, and in the early 1950s it was Kafka); and (v) the political allegory (aided in its gestation by the literary metaphor) which often surfaces in apparently throwaway lines which are in fact the tip of an iceberg. The weaving together of these five levels, such that they can only be picked at with a very delicate knife – *ars celare artem* – so that, for example, the abortion that Tachia had[69] is mysteriously associated with the loss of the liberal cause (both of which ideas are encapsulated in the now dead son, Agustín) is part of the reason why García Márquez's fiction has a ring of truth, for it is four-fifths real and one-fifth fiction. The only problem is that it is never just one reality; it is the product of the amalgamation of four real situations that have been aestheticized with just one layer of art. It is real but it never happened. *No One Writes to the Colonel* is a tour de force which manages to combine the allegorical portrayal of the destiny of a nation within the apparently over-small frame of the everyday life of an ageing couple. García Márquez's fiction of this period (the mid- to late 1950s) is, indeed, often characterized by the portrayal of a latent political anger within a country which, in Ángel Rama's words, 'lives in a permanent state of violence, which is either open, or underground and threatening' (my translation).[70]

It was in the short story 'Los funerales de la Mamá Grande' ('Big Mama's Funeral') that García Márquez inaugurated the political allegory in Latin American literature, when he uses the funeral of a woman conveniently named Big Mama to allegorize the grotesque nature of postcolonial political reality in Latin America. 'Big Mama's Funeral' was written between May and June 1959,[71] which means that the short story can almost be seen as a direct response to the ideology underlying the Cuban Revolution. At first flush, there is nothing in this story which specifically defines it as a political allegory, but the list of powers over which Big Mama specifically has control are such as to persuade the reader that this tale is an allegory of the folly and misuse of power initiated by the Spanish conquistadors, which continued to the present day – and the re-action to the story when it came to greater public attention in the 1960s can only have been a revolutionary one. All of the details – particularly with regard to the various material and abstract entities to which Big Mama lays claim – gradually turn the 'récit' into a *reductio ad absurdum*. How can Big Mama, for example, really be the owner of

the richness of the subsoil, territorial waters, the colours of the national flag, national sovereignty, traditional parties, the rights of man, citizens' rights, citizens' freedoms, the first magistrate, the second official request, the third debate, letters of recommendation, historical proof, free elections, beauty queens, traditional speeches, grandiose demonstrations, distinguished young ladies, upright gentlemen, military honour, his illustrious lordship, the supreme court of justice, import-banned articles, liberal ladies, the problem of the flesh, linguistic purity, examples for the world, legal order, a free but responsible press, the Athens of South America, public opinion, democratic elections, Christian morals, lack of hard currency, the right to asylum, the communist threat, the ship of the state, the high cost of living, Republican traditions, the disadvantaged classes, messages of support?[72]

Has there ever been any more grotesque or ironic description of the rights and privileges that the *caciques* of Latin America have appropriated because of the lack of any dissenting voice? Has any Latin American writer ever stated in such denuded terms the vacuity underlying the amalgamation of rights, privileges, and taboos decreed by the Latin American oligarchy?[73] For, since there is no 'loyal dissent' of the other house, nor even the voice of the subaltern to be listened to, then the *latifundistas* can simply arrogate to themselves privileges, and rights, and things as if they were godlike. Surely it is the case that – given that the story was written in 1959 – García Márquez was attacking the grotesque arbitrariness of colonial rule in Latin America, and therefore, by implication, though not stating so as such, expressing an allegiance by one step removed to the anti-colonialist ideology of the Cuban Revolution. Indeed 'Big Mama's Funeral' might well be read as an effusive letter of self-introduction to Fidel Castro, and all that he stood for in those heady years of the 1960s, for it is a satire on the grotesque nature of the rights and privileges claimed by the conquerors of Latin America – and indeed by their successors in 'criollo' Latin America.[74] It certainly contains within it the seeds of a radical, anti-colonial reading of the history of Latin America, but this is by no means an over-obvious paradigm, and indeed may be dismissed as an over-determined interpretation by the historicist critic. Notwithstanding this, it is a potential reading and as such hovers around the text. Alternatively, it can, for example, be read as a portrayal of the lethargy of the tropics. García Márquez himself has stated that it offers 'a rather static and exclusivist vision of reality',[75] and Robin Fiddian has compared the depiction of 'the texture of tedium' in this and other of García Márquez's stories written in the mid- to late-1950s as 'reminiscent of that of Rossellini and De Sica'.[76] Certainly there are some circles – perhaps in Cuba in the early 1960s, or the left-wing intelligentsia in France or the United States, or the hierarchy in the Soviet Union – who would chuckle knowingly over the obviousness of such a political allegory, but let us for the time being read it as a short story with a number of intended meanings, political and otherwise, none of which are necessarily encoded or predetermined.

In the collection *Big Mama's Funeral* García Márquez demonstrated that he could write powerful, intensely visual short stories in which the dialogue is lapidary and the description is precise and atmospheric. The first paragraph of 'La siesta del martes' ('Tuesday Siesta'), for example, provides a number of carefully chosen details (the symmetrical and interminable banana plantations, the breeze that dies down as the train travels inland away from the coast, the offices with their electric fans, the palm trees) allowing a vivid visual picture to be created in the reader's mind. Commentary is sparse, the narration adopts the objectivity of a camera lens, thereby allowing the reader to realize only gradually the importance of the events unfolding before his eyes – the (unnamed) woman and her (unnamed) daughter whose journey we follow are arriving to pay their respects for the son who was killed as he attempted to break into the house of a woman called Rebeca, and we find this out after the midway point of the story has passed.[77] The dialogue is pithy and ironic, and has one of García Márquez's best exchanges; when the woman tells the priest that every mouthful of food tasted of the teeth her son had knocked out trying to support her, the priest remarks: 'The will of God is unfathomable' (p. 119). 'En este pueblo no hay ladrones' ('There are No Thieves in This Town') ends with a twist in that Roque reveals that he will make sure that Dámaso will pay the two hundred 'pesos' that he 'stole' along with the billiard balls (pp. 125–55 [p. 155]).

The stories are vignettes reflecting the *camera obscura* of life in Colombia's banana zone, and have more meaning when read in conjunction. Thus Baltasar's apparently Pyrrhic victory in 'La prodigiosa tarde de Baltasar' ('Balthasar's Marvellous Afternoon') when he freely gives the cage to José Montiel's son rather than waiting to be paid for it (*Cuentos*, pp. 156–64 [p. 163]) is in fact a real victory, as we understand when we read this story in the light of 'La viuda de Montiel' ('Montiel's Widow'; *Cuentos*, pp. 165–72), in which we find out that Montiel was a vicious tyrant who had never before had anyone give him orders in his own home; 'Balthasar's Marvellous Afternoon' is, thus, a story of the victory of the underdog against all the odds. By refusing to ask for payment, Baltasar deconstructs capitalism. The stories also operate like a panopticon offering glimpses of the world of Macondo which would within five years come together in the matrix of *One Hundred Years of Solitude*. In 'Un día después del sábado' ('One Day After Saturday') we find out that the thief who died in Rebeca's house was José Arcadio Buendía, the brother of the colonel (pp. 173–97 [p. 181]), whom we will meet in *One Hundred Years of Solitude*.[78] Some of the stories end on an inconclusive note, such as 'Montiel's Widow', 'One Day After Saturday' (pp. 173–97) and 'Artificial Roses' (pp. 198–204), as if they were artistic exercises in which García Márquez were honing his narrative skills in preparation for *One Hundred Years of Solitude*.

The masterpiece within the collection is 'One of These Days', written, as Robin Fiddian has noted, 'before March 1958',[79] and one of the clearest examples of the emergence of a political allegory in García Márquez's work. Barely four pages long, it uses the rather comical rivalry between a dentist, Aureliano Escovar, and the local mayor (unnamed) to draw a broader canvas; as Ernesto Volkening has pointed out, 'tooth-ache takes on metaphysical dimensions, and forces the patient to face up to the tragedy of his life as a solitary despot'.[80] The dentist forces the mayor to accept the tooth extraction without anaesthetic, and comments after the tooth has been pulled out: 'With this, lieutenant, you are paying us back for the twenty dead',[81] thereby elucidating that the local mayor has been repressing the local community, and has with impunity killed twenty of his political opponents (on whose side the 'liberal' dentist finds himself). The novelistic *coup de grâce* occurs in the hyperbolic conclusion of the short story:

> – 'Send me the bill,' he said.
> – 'To you or the town hall?'
> The mayor didn't even look at him. He closed the door and said through the metal grid:
> – 'Same difference.' (p. 26)

This hieroglyphic which traces the equals sign between impunity, corruption and state power tore the veil from the rhetoric of state discourse which had remained in power since the days of the Conquest. With these thirty-one words – in a gesture which silenced the T. S. Eliots of this world – the political allegory was born in Latin America.

4

'Even I won't be able to put up with myself'

When I met García Márquez in the Fundación del Nuevo Cine Latinoamericano in December 2007, I told him it was a great honour to meet the Cervantes of the Americas, at which point he became embarrassed, telling me not to refer to him in those terms since his friends (including Julio García Espinosa, who was there at the time), would not be able to put up with him; indeed, he added, 'ni me aguanto yo' ('even I won't be able to put up with myself'). This sense of doubleness in his being is not anything new to those who have studied García Márquez's work. We find a similar sense of disjunction in Borges' famous essay, 'Borges and I':

> Things occur to the other one, Borges. I walk around Buenos Aires and I slow down, perhaps already in a rather mechanical way, to look at the arch of a doorway and the chancel of a door, I know about Borges through the post and I see his name in a list of professors or in a biographical dictionary. . . . It would be an exaggeration to say that our relationship is one of hostility; I live and let myself live, so that Borges can construct his litera-ture, and that literature justifies my existence. . . . Gradually I am ceding everything to him . . .[1]

It is well known that Borges' work had a crucial impact on García Márquez during the latter's formative years, particularly the 1940s and '50s, and it would seem not inconceivable that a similar split between the quotidian and the writing self was one which troubled García Márquez and which came most obviously into being in the years preceding the publication of *One Hundred Years of Solitude*. Borges' dilemma was (is) an unsolvable one; his essay ends, 'I don't know which of the two is writing this page.'[2] It is the Borgesian dilemma, as I shall be arguing, that gives us a clue as to how we should interpret the role that reality and the imagination play in García Márquez's work.[3]

Let us go back to those years before *One Hundred Years of Solitude* – the book that is said by many to have earned him the Nobel Prize – was published. Now in Mexico City, García Márquez turned to script-writing, producing a number of film scripts, including *The Golden Cockerel* (1964, based on Juan Rulfo's story of that name) and *Time to Die* (1964), directed by Arturo Ripstein,[4] and in October 1964 he took part in the filming of *There are No Thieves in This Town*, based on one of his own short stories. The filmed premiered on 9 September 1965, featuring García Márquez as the ticket collector, Luis Buñuel playing the priest and Juan Rulfo one of the dominoes players.[5] Though these films have a certain dated charm, in retrospect it is clear that García Márquez was treading water, avoiding his destiny as a novelist.[6] García Márquez told William Kennedy in 1972 that the time in Mexico was suffocating: 'Nothing I did in those films was mine. It was a collaboration in which everyone's ideas were incorporated: the director's as well as the actors. I was very limited in what I could do and I was then able to appreciate that in the novel the writer has complete control.'[7] It was when he realized that his obsession with film had been counterproductive that he turned back to the novel. As he said in an interview with Miguel Fernández-Braso:

I always believed that because of its enormous visual power cinema was the perfect expressive medium. All my books before *One Hundred Years of Solitude* are deadened by this certainty. They have an excessive desire to visualize the characters and the scenes, a millimetric relationship between the time for dialogue and the time allotted for action, and even an obsession with showing the POV and the frame. While working in the film industry, however, I not only realized what could be done but also what couldn't be done; it seemed to me that the dominance of the image over other narrative elements was, of course, an advantage but it was also a limitation, and all of this was a startling discovery, because I became aware that the novel has limitless possibilities.[8]

This was a crucial turning-point in García Márquez's life, and it led to a sense of turmoil, which was evident in the interview that he gave to Luis Harss in Mexico City in 1965 (Harss and Barbara Dohmann interviewed all the important Latin American literary figures of the time between September 1964 and August 1966).[9] The transcript of the Harss interview is imaginative and perceptive, providing a glimpse of García Márquez as a writer on edge, self-absorbed, obsessed:

He has a way of startling himself with his own thoughts. Now – the night is fragrant and full of surprises – he lies back on a bed, like a psychoanalytic patient, stubbing out cigarettes. He talks fast, snatching thoughts as they cross his mind, winding and unwinding them like paper streamers, following them in one end and out the other, only to lose them before he can pin them down. A casual tone with a deep undertow suggests he is making a strategy of negligence. He has a way of eavesdropping on himself, as if he were trying to overhear bits of a conversation in the next room. What matters is what is left unsaid.[10]

What is striking about this description of García Márquez is its sense of doubleness; Luis Harss has seen that Gabo sees himself as doubled, and, rather like César Vallejo who wrote poems about himself ('César Vallejo has died', 'César Vallejo I hate you tenderly'),[11] he is sometimes startled to perceive himself as other. Harss sees Gabo as someone who is involved in self-psychoanalysis, overwhelmed by the García Márquez within him struggling to get out.

When Harss went to see García Márquez in the mid-1960s the writer's masterpiece, *One Hundred Years of Solitude*, was gestating in his soul. When asked by Plinio Apuleyo whether it was true that he had been trying to write the same novel, namely, *One Hundred Years of Solitude*, since he was eighteen years old, García Márquez replied: 'Yes, it was called *The House* because I thought the whole story would take place inside the Buendías house.'[12] In the same interview he mentions that the story just kept 'whirling' around in his head for 'another fifteen years. I couldn't find the right tone. It had to ring true for me.'[13] And then there was a trigger that inspired the whole novel. On 9 July 1965 he decided to take his family to Acapulco for a holiday, and while he was driving there from Mexico City, the novel suddenly came into being: 'One day, as Mercedes and I were driving to Acapulco with the children, it came to me in flash. I had to tell the story the way my grandmother used to tell me hers.'[14] The first sentence of the novel came into his head: 'Many years later, as he faced the firing squad, Colonel Aureliano Buendía . . .' The description García Márquez gives of the experience of the novel coming into his head is similar to Muhammad's description of the Qu'ran, as if he were simply the scribe of a story already written. There is a poignant exchange between Apuleyo and García Márquez:

Q. Is it true you turned the car round on the motorway and started writing it?
A. It's true, I never got to Acapulco. (Apuleyo, p. 74)

He turned the car round, went straight back to Mexico City and started writing the novel which would change his life.

García Márquez began writing *One Hundred Years of Solitude* in July 1965 and finished it in August 1966.[15] He gave up his film-script writing as well as his journalism. The only thing of note on the literary front during this period was that in 1966 an authorized version of *In Evil Hour* was published in Mexico. García Márquez devoted himself entirely to writing his novel in a small room in his apartment in Mexico City, a room which has since been called 'Melquíades's Room'. The novel was used as a surety against debt. As García Márquez has said: 'From the first moment, long before it was published, the book exerted a magic power on everyone who in some way came into contact with it: friends, secretaries, etc., even people like the butcher or our landlord, who were waiting for me to finish so I would pay them.'[16] The landlord, Luis Coudurier, agreed to wait to be paid nearly a year's rent until the novel was finished. He typed up sections of the novel and took it to his typist, 'Pera' (Esperanza) Araiza who produced a fair copy. In early 1966 García Márquez sold his car, a white Opel. When the money from that ran out he and Mercedes had to pawn everything: television, fridge, radio, jewellery. That Gabo was writing his own life into fiction is suggested by the sorrow he felt when he had to kill off Colonel Aureliano Buendía in chapter thirteen, as a result of which he went up to bed and wept for two hours.[17]

Finally *One Hundred Years of Solitude* was finished. In early August 1966 he and Mercedes took the novel to post it to Sud-americana publishing house in Buenos Aires. The manuscript of the novel had 490 pages and, between them, they had fifty *pesos*, which was only enough to send about half of the manuscript. They went home, pawned some more household goods, and then went back to the post office to post the second half. The editor at Sud-americana, Paco Porrúa, read it, and told Álvaro Mutis that it was 'absolutely brilliant'.[18] The initial print-run was going to be 3,000 copies, which was increased to 5,000, and then two weeks before printing, given the extra hype which accompanied the book, 8,000.

After a week the book had sold 1,800 copies and was already third in the bestsellers list, something unheard of for a 'new' writer. The subsequent success of the novel, the critics' adulation, the enormous print-runs which kept on going, took everyone by surprise including García Márquez himself. It was an international bestseller within weeks of being published,[19] the archetypal 'book of a lifetime'.[20]

One Hundred Years of Solitude, as *Living to Tell the Tale* makes clear, is based to a large degree on the vicissitudes of García Márquez's early family life; the Aracataca of Colombia becomes the Macondo of fiction.[21] Luisa Santiaga's comment to Gabo, for example, that she did not want the blood of her family roaming around in the street no doubt gave rise to the extraordinary depiction in the novel of what happened to José Arcadio's blood after his murder:

> A trickle of blood came out under the door, crossed the living-room, went out into the street, continued on in a straight line across the uneven terraces, went down steps and climbed over curbs, passed along the Street of the Turks, turned a corner to the right and another to the left, made a right angle at the Buendía house, went in under the closed door, crossed through the parlour, hugging the walls so as not to stain the rugs, went on to the other living-room, made a wide curve to avoid the dining-room table, went along the porch with the begonias, and passed without being seen under Amaranta's chair as she gave an arithmetic lesson to Aureliano José, and went through the pantry and came out in the kitchen, where Úrsula was getting ready to crack thirty-six eggs to make bread.[22]

The passage is fantastic but also highly detailed in a naturalistic sense, informing us, for example, that the terraces which the trail of blood crossed were 'uneven', that the blood hugged the walls 'so as not to stain the rugs'. We are even told how many eggs Úrsula was getting ready to break in the kitchen, all of which invests the fantastic event of self-propelled blood with a sheen of verisimilitude. García Márquez's fictional world is, indeed, a water-tight universe where everything obeys its own logic. The internal consistency of this world – which Mario Vargas Llosa was the first to recognize and analyse in his monumental study, *Historia de un deicidio* – is rooted in the dual proposition: the supernatural is depicted as if it were natural, but the natural is presented as if it were supernatural. García Márquez's fictional world, therefore, neither follows the laws of the supernatural exclusively nor the laws of the natural exclusively, but bodies forth a dynamic fusion of both.

One Hundred Years of Solitude presents the laws of the universe, and particularly the laws of science and history, not as if they were objective and self-evident facts, but instead as if they were unnatural and strange productions of man's mind.[23] The first chapter of the novel, for example, brings the arrival of the gypsies who introduce the community to natural or man-made objects such as the magnet, the telescope, the magnifying glass, and even false teeth. Márquez's presentation of the magnet is typical. The properties of the magnet, though explained rationally and coherently by physicists such as Michael Faraday (1791–1867) and John Tyndall (1820–1893), are seen animistically by Melquíades: 'Things have a life of their own . . . It's simply a matter of waking up their souls' (*One Hundred Years of Solitude*, p. 9).[24] One of the most arresting examples of García Márquez's ability to depict scientific fact as if it were unbridled fantasy occurs when José Arcadio emerges from his study having made the significant pre-Ptolemaic discovery that the world is round. The conversion of the natural into the supernatural is contrived by the skilful interpellation of Úrsula's down-to-earth scepticism:

'The earth is round, like an orange'.

Úrsula lost her patience. 'If you have to go crazy, please go crazy all by yourself!' she shouted. 'But don't try to put your gypsy ideas into the heads of the children.' (*One Hundred Years of Solitude*, p. 12)

García Márquez with the first edition of *Cien años de soledad* (One Hundred Years of Solitude), 1969.

Later on in the novel, when the commodities of technological advancement associated with the modern era, such as electricity, the cinema, the record player and the telephone, arrive in Macondo, they are greeted with gasps of amazement by the inhabitants. 'Dazzled by so many and such marvellous inventions, the people of Macondo did not know where the amazement began' (*One Hundred Years of Solitude*, p. 185).[25]

It is when this modernity – which had first appeared in the novel as an innocent, humorous gag in the form of gypsies' tricks, false teeth, a train becoming 'a kitchen dragging a village behind it' (p. 184) – shows its true colours as the harbinger of US capitalism that *One Hundred Years of Solitude* reveals itself as a political novel.

The first sign of this occurs when Mr Herbert eats a banana (p. 186), at which point the banana is studied as if it were a diamond by Mr Herbert, and then a group of engineers, agronomers, hydrologists, topographers and surveyors arrive to conduct further research (p. 187). The important point here is that the gringos do nothing to reveal their plans; Mr Herbert 'did not say anything that allowed anyone to guess his intentions' (p. 187). When Mr Brown arrives, with a team of lawyers dressed in black, once more the ignorance of the town's inhabitants is underlined: 'the suspicious inhabitants of Macondo barely began to wonder what the devil was going on when the town had already been transformed into an encampment of wooden houses with zinc roofs inhabited by foreigners who arrived on the train from halfway around the world' (p. 187). They established their own town outside Macondo, they have resources which only God would seem to possess (p. 188), and they change the town irrevocably (changing the rain, the crop cycle and even the direction of the river; p. 188); yet even then 'No one knew yet what they were after' (p. 188). Aureliano Buendía expresses their dismay pithily: 'Look at the mess we've got ourselves into . . . just because we invited a gringo to eat some bananas' (p. 189). These are the first hints that Latin America's encounter with modernity will – like the poisoned coat Herakles accepts from his wife – lead to its destruction.

Though the first gringo to discover and market the banana was Minor Keith who did so in 1871 in Costa Rica – eventually forming the United Fruit Company in 1899 – it was a story of exploitation which was common to Colombia, Costa Rica, Cuba, Nicaragua and Panama. The arrival of the banana company (p. 196) – this is, of course, the United Fruit Company, though it is never named – leads to the local functionaries being replaced by 'dictatorial foreigners' (p. 196) –and in turn to an abuse of power, epitomized by the incident in which a seven-year-old boy is killed by a policeman because he accidentally spilled his drink on him, and the boy's grandfather is beheaded (p. 196). Colonel Aureliano Buendía's reaction is to blame the gringos, whose presence has led, in his opinion, to this state of affairs, and he threatens: 'One of these days . . . I'm going to arm my boys so we can get rid of these shitty gringos!' (p. 197). As a result of this threat, his seventeen sons are shot 'by invisible criminals' (p. 197) and, though the identity of the people responsible is never clarified, the implication is that the gringos are to blame. The struggle soon becomes nakedly political. José Arcadio Segundo's trade union activities rapidly single him out as a troublemaker: 'he was pointed out as the agent of an international conspiracy against public order' (p. 242). Tension heightens, until the showdown between the army and banana workers occurs, and the three thousand dead are thrown into the sea: 'he saw the man corpses, woman corpses, child corpses who would be thrown into the sea like rejected bananas' (p. 250). García Márquez is able to build a sense of the connectiveness between the profession of the workers and the manner of their death, thrown away like 'rejected bananas'. Even the way the bodies have been piled up reminds Arcadio Segundo of banana stacking: 'those who had put them in the wagon had had time to pile them up in the same way in which they transported bunches of bananas' (translation revised by author, p. 247). Though Arcadio Segundo's recollection has the air of a hallucination about it, his statement 'There must have been three thousand of them' (p. 251) ends up having an air of believability. Thus begins the end of Macondo, and Mr Brown is revealed as an evasive person who offers to renew the contract, but only when the rain stops (p. 252), which eventually leads to the closure of the banana plantation and the 'biblical hurricane' which will destroy it completely (p. 336).

The number of dead given by García Márquez in the fifteenth chapter of *One Hundred Years of Solitude* – 3,000-plus – has been controversial since it is so much at odds with the government line. The official report of the disturbances in the Magdalena region which occurred from 13 November 1928 until 15 March 1929 was published in 1929; authored by General Carlos Cortés Vargas and entitled *Los sucesos de las bananeras*,[26] it gives the number dead in the uprising which occurred on 6 December 1928 in Ciénaga (p. 66) as nine, and at Sevilla station (pp. 103–4), as twenty-nine. It is accepted by all parties that the strike described in chapter fifteen of *One Hundred Years of Solitude* is based on the events that occurred in Ciénaga on 6 December 1928, before which there had been a month-long strike by the banana plantation workers who were working in the United Fruit Company's plantation in Ciénaga.[27] In his memoirs García Márquez emphasized that he used the number 3,000 to capture the sense of outrage that the event inspired at the time:

> I kept the number of the dead at three thousand, in order to preserve the epic proportions of the drama, and in the end real life did me justice: not long ago, on one of the anniversaries of the tragedy, the speaker of the moment in the Senate asked for a minute of silence in memory of the three thousand anonymous martyrs sacrificed by the forces of law and order.[28]

García Márquez clearly did some independent research on the event and, as his own brother Jaime recalls, he asked Jaime to go to Ciénaga to find out exactly what the General said, how much time was given to the strikers for them to disperse, and how the people responded on that fateful day in 1928. Jaime was able to provide an important detail: when the General gave the order to leave after one minute, he was greeted with the shout: 'Le regalamos el minuto que falta' (roughly translating as 'you can stick the minute left up your arse'), which he believed to have been his great discovery until Gabo brought him down a peg: Gabo told his brother years later that the phrase was already well known.[29]

Indeed, the reference to this cheeky comment is also in the official report of events given by General Carlos Cortés Vargas who stated as follows: 'In the course of the last minute, we ourselves shouted: "Withdraw, or we will shoot". "You can stick the minute left up your arse", a voice shouted from the crowd.'[30] According to the General's account the order to fire was met simultaneously by the order to 'Lay on the ground', and from that point onwards, after the first shots went off, no further shots were fired, and the workers got up and fled;[31] but subsequent research has suggested that Cortés Vargas' figures were too low.[32] It is likely that García Márquez's number of 3,000 came from the reports of the time, many of which referred to 3,000 strikers surrounding the troops,[33] but this still leaves the problem of where the figure of 3,000-plus killed came from – even taking into account García Márquez's very eloquent justification of the number in his autobiography. Is it, we ask, anything more than a false memory?

It is clear, reviewing the evidence of *El Tiempo* (*El Espectador* was not available in the Biblioteca Luis Ángel Arango for the year 1928), that the banana planation uprising was the nearest that Colombia ever got to a revolution and that, given the political implications of the strike and the fact that it was a struggle over the ownership of land, property and rural produce, it had very clear similarities with the Mexican Revolution which had occurred to the north a decade previously. It is abundantly clear from all the reports provided by the army that the insurrection was seen as a political one. Captain Alfonso Campo Serrano referred in one telegraph to: 'situation worsening by the minute. Communists have just destroyed telephone wires banana region',[34] and, in the report published that day on page four of *El Tiempo* entitled 'A Prudent Report by General Carlos Cortés Vargas', we read: 'Pamphlets circulating calling the soldiers in their ranks to communism. In the zone itself the organization of the strikers is surprising' (p. 4). A political revolution was on the brink of occurring in Colombia – although as things panned out, it became the Colombian Revolution That Never Was – which explains García Márquez's intense

Statue to the
Martyrs of the
Banana Massacre,
Main Square,
Ciénaga.

interest in this period of Colombia's history, quite apart from the
fact that it occurred on his doorstep.

If we look closely at the way in which García Márquez depicts the
Revolution of Ciénaga in his novel, it is clear, as suggested above, that
the portrayal functions on one level like a false memory. Apart from
the figure of 3,000, what else has been changed? Whereas the official
version records the expression, 'Le regalamos el minuto que falta' as
coming from the faceless crowd, as noted above, in García Márquez's
account it is José Arcadio Segundo who shouts these words out (*One
Hundred Years of Solitude*, p. 242). This means that García Márquez
is, in effect, writing his own family into the history of the insurrection, for the characters in the novel are to be understood on one level

as family members of the house in Aracataca (we may recall that *One Hundred Years of Solitude* was originally titled *La casa*, with the understanding that this was his grandparents' house in which he lived until the age of nine).[35] This is a false memory since the various members of García Márquez's family were not involved in the historic insurrection. We know this because in the official report on the insurgency, fifty-four names of those found guilty of stirring up the unrest were given, and not one of them has the surname García or Márquez or, indeed, Iguarán (the second surname of García Márquez's mother).[36] This is not surprising since García Márquez's grandfather was on friendly terms with the United Fruit Company since, as Margot recalls, the 'United Fruit Company shop of the gringos of the banana plantation was opposite our house. I don't know why but my grandfather could buy things in that shop, perhaps because he was the mayor and the treasurer of the town, and the most important liberal.'[37] So, by having José Arcadio Segundo act as the ringleader and instigator of the struggle against the United Fruit Company García Márquez was, in effect, creating a revolutionary lineage for his family that was not empiric. Notice, indeed, how the novel re-semanticizes and motivates the sheer mass of the people, giving it a name: in a sense, giving a name and face to the faceless masses. What was simply a voice in the crowd becomes a 'real' person, José Arcadio Segundo, a technique noted in García Márquez's portrayal of the *bogotazo*, as we have seen (see above pp. 33–4).

The other important point to be made about García Márquez's depiction of the failed revolution in the banana planations of Colombia is that it is acutely sensitive to the interplay between physical, martial and epistemic violence. The government, and particularly the war minister, Dr Ignacio Rengifo, was very aware of the fact that the war against the subversives had to be won with words as much as with weapons. Rengifo kept a tight control on what was known about the conflict by only releasing certain communiqués to the press, about which *El Tiempo*, clearly smelling a rat, complained. *El Tiempo* obviously took a dim view of the army's actions, questioning whether the official version was true, and even went to the extreme of publishing an incendiary and satiric cartoon of Rengifo who is presented as condoning the shooting of unarmed man by the army.[38] *El Tiempo* also called in an editorial for an official enquiry into what had really happened to cause the death of so many people,[39] and complained that the only source of information about the conflict was the communiqués permitted by the government.[40] It is also clear that the Ciénaga uprising was not the only civil disturbance to take place at the time; there were also strikes and social unrest in Sevilla Station, Santa Marta and Aracataca. Furthermore, General Cortés Vargas had been ordered to hunt down the instigators of the strike; this much is clear from the title of one of the reports published in *El Tiempo* on 11 December 1928, entitled 'El General Cortés Varga activa la persecucion'.[41] This was, indeed, Colombia's first experience of the nakedly ideological use of discourse since the new technology of the telegram allowed high numbers of potentially contradictory pieces of information to circulate, and the means of controlling the flow of information became a central plank of the ideological battle – the reporting of the War of a Thousand Days by contrast had been a far more leisurely affair. García Márquez captures this bitter struggle of words elegantly and humorously when he has the official government version described in the following terms: 'The official version, repeated a thousand times and mangled all over the country by every means of communication the government found at hand, was finally accepted; there were no dead, the satisfied workers had gone back to their families, and the banana company was suspending all activity until the rains stopped' (*One Hundred Years of Solitude*, p. 252). García Márquez's fiction, as we can see, functions as the reverse side of the official version of history controlled from Bogotá. García Márquez's political satire[42] uses the false memory as a means of destabilizing the epistemic violence of the State.

García Márquez's sense of the Borgesian dilemma –the dialectic between the writing self and the quotidian self – made him acutely sensitive to the fallibility of discourse. Just as he allowed the false memory to overcome memory, the writing self to overcome the quotidian self, so, paradoxically enough, he allowed the truth of his 'lies' to overcome the lies underlying the government's 'truth'.[43]

The political climax of the novel – the point at which the political tension between the left and the right explodes into violence – is given a highly original twist by García Márquez. The narrative informs us how José Arcadio Segundo wakes up after the troops fire on the workers in the main square of Macondo (i.e. Ciénaga), to find himself lying on top of a heap of dead people in a train trundling off to an unknown destination (p. 250). He searches in all of the carriages and estimates that the train has about two hundred carriages (p. 250); he jumps off, walks back to Macondo, goes into a woman's house where his wounds are bathed, finds that his account of the massacre is not believed, and knocks at Colonel Gavilán's house only to have the door slammed in his face; he subsequently goes home and tells his brother, Aureliano Segundo, about the massacre, but his story is once more disputed. He hides out in Melquíades' room and when the army arrives to search the house, the reader fully expects him to be apprehended. But then something extraordinary happens, forcing the reader to reinterpret what he has just read. The official asks for Melquíades' room to be opened; he first searches it with a lantern such that 'Aureliano Segundo and Santa Sofía de la Piedad saw the Arab eyes of José Arcadio Segundo at the moment when the ray of light passed over his face' (pp. 253–54). The officer notices nothing, and then turns the light on for a second time; again he is unable to see José Arcadio Segundo: 'He paused with his glance on the space where Aureliano Segundo and Santa Sofía de la Piedad were still seeing José Arcadio Segundo and the latter also realised that the soldier was looking at him without seeing him' (p. 254). It is when we read the army officer's conclusions – 'It's obvious that

no one has been in that room for at least a hundred years' (p. 254) –
that it dawns on us that José Arcadio Segundo may well be a ghost,
since he is not perceived by the military officer, and, rather in the
style of the film *The Sixth Sense*, we are encouraged to go back over
what has been described to review the possibility that José Arcadio
Segundo is already dead.

Indeed, there are details in the narrative that suggest this.
Firstly, there are José Arcadio Segundo's strange impressions of
the train in which he wakes up – that there are more than two
hundred carriages, that the dead are arranged in them like bunches
of bananas, and that, despite his searching all the carriages, the
soldiers with their machine guns never once become aware of his
presence (p. 250); and secondly, that when he goes into an unnamed
woman's house, he pronounces his own name 'in order to convince
himself that he was still alive' (translation revised, p. 247),[44] while
the woman's first impression of him is that he is an 'apparition'
since he is a figure who is 'touched with the solemnity of death'
(p. 250). The rather phantasmagorical tone that the narrative takes
on is another clue: we seem to be provided access to only part of a
story, so that all the details do not add up; why, for example, does
Colonel Gavilán's wife shut the door on José Arcadio Segundo?
As we read: '"He [Colonel Gavilán] left"; she said, frightened. "He
went back to his own country"' (p. 251), and why is she frightened
('*asustada*') simply by the sight of José Arcadio Segundo? Why is
Fernanda not allowed to know José Arcadio Segundo is in the house?
Why is his story so much at odds with everyone else's? Questions
such as these, and the characteristics of the narrative mentioned
above, can be resolved if José Arcadio Segundo is interpreted as
already dead – and as such, a ghost – who can only (with some
exceptions) be seen by members of his family. This device – very
much in the vein of magical realism – embodies that vacillation
between two opposing interpretations of one event which Todorov
identified as intrinsic to the notion of fantasy, in that José Arcadio

Segundo is alive for some people and dead for others. He is in effect the voice of the subaltern which is silenced by the state authorities.[45]

Thie massacre of the banana workers is also central to the ideological thrust of the novel since it shows how García Márquez uses the discourse of magical realism in order to make its political point. José Arcadio Segundo's version of the massacre – 3,000 people were shot and transported in a train and 'disappeared' – contrasts starkly with the official version that 'there were no dead' (p. 252), as we have seen. Thus the voice of the subaltern is also the account provided by a ghost, that is, an individual whom hegemonic discourse will not, or cannot, understand or 'hear'. In the context of the recollections of a ghost pitted against the government, the armed forces, and the media, it is clear against whom the odds are stacked. As the authorities suggest: 'You must have been dreaming' (p. 252). Yet, as García Márquez's text suggests, the voice of the subaltern is a dream which proves to be highly resilient. García Márquez's populism – his faith in the power of the people eventually to impose their will on the world around them – is the final message of *One Hundred Years of Solitude*, though it is a message which, like José Arcadio Segundo hiding in Melquíades' room, is tucked away in García Márquez's text.

One piece of historical research, Herrera Soto and Castañeda's excellent monograph, *La zona bananera del Magdalena: historia y léxico*, includes reference to a number of popular legends which had sprung up over the years following the 'massacre' of December 1928 in the Banana Zone, one of which, the fourth, may well have found its way into García Márquez's fiction. It runs as follows:

Train which went to the sea with 1,000 dead people. As soon as they had killed a thousand men, women and children they were stacked like bunches of bananas in each carriage and then thrown into the sea from the dock. The blood dripped onto the tracks, since the dead were mixed up with the injured.[46]

Herrera Soto and Castañeda, however, doubt this version of events. They argue that it could only have occurred on the railway line between Ciénaga and Santa Marta, and state that although there were some people in Santa Marta train station on the evening of 6 December 1928 waiting anxiously for news, no train is reported to have arrived, let alone a train carrying thousands of corpses. They also ask how this could have happened if no bodies were subsequently found in the bay of Santa Marta (pp. 74–5). Despite its lack of empirical veridity according to Herrera Soto and Castañeda, this is clearly the popular legend that García Márquez used for his depiction of the episode in *One Hundred Years of Solitude*. Herrera Soto and Castañeda's view would be that the description of the 'massacre' in chapter fifteen was a false memory created by the people. The important point to take from this discussion is that García Márquez did not simply pluck the account out of the air; rather he melded a number of sources, including popular stories and newspaper reports,[47] in order to creatively build a convincing false memory. Since 1967, when *One Hundred Years of Solitude* was published, this version has – paradoxically – dwarfed the other accounts. The question, however, remains: was there any truth in the popular legends about thousands of dead bodies being shipped off to the sea?[48] Are the popular legends simply societal false memories?

One individual who could not be accused of being influenced by García Márquez's version of events was Jorge Eliécer Gaitán, a young MP at the time of the 'Massacre', who spoke to the House of Representatives in September 1929 about the events in the Banana Zone. In a speech which lasted for four days (3–6 September 1929),[49] Gaitán began by reading out a letter from the priest of Aracataca, which described the cruel acts carried out by the army against women and children, even at one stage presenting the skull of a child before the House. The documents which Gaitán presented were very eloquent, and present a version of events which is diametrically opposed to General Cortés Vargas' account. One witness, Benjamin Restrepo, referred to how the army fired their machine guns in one burst and then began firing their rifles at the workers for five minutes, how the army finished off the wounded with bayonets, and how the dead were transported in trains to be disposed of in the sea.[50] This version of events, according to which the army fired their machine guns first and then shot their rifles for about five minutes, appears in another witness statement by H. Martínez M. (p. 123). There are also accounts of people being buried alive (p. 125). Perhaps the most extraordinary account in the transcript of Gaitán's speech is that of a young man called Márquez who was killed by the army at about 4.30 a.m. on 6 December 1928 in the Ciénaga train station. As Luisa Roy states:

At about 4.30 in the morning, I arrived at the railway station to wait for the train to go to Santa Marta, and near the station where they load the ice, there was a young man whose surname was Márquez, wounded, and writhing in his death agony. This young man was dressed in dark brown ['chocolate' in the original Spanish]. I could see, when 25 men started to bury him, they were also bayonetting him, each one separately until they left him lifeless. Then they turned round and when they saw me one of the soldiers hit me in the eye with the butt of his gun, knocking me to the floor. Then I ran off. (p. 128)

This testimony allows us to reconsider the role that José Arcadio Segundo plays in *One Hundred Years of Solitude* and the extent to which his story is based on this type of report. It is true that there is no mention of a García or a Márquez or a Martínez or an Iguarán in the list of those arrested (as stated above), but, as we can now see, there is a reference in one of the contemporary reports to a young man called Márquez who was bayonetted to death on 6 December 1928 in Ciénaga train station.

The question is whether this could have been a relative of García Márquez. On the face of it, this would appear to be very unlikely, but as we saw earlier there is evidence to suggest that García Márquez's grandfather spawned at least twelve illegitimate children.[51] Gerald Martin, in his family tree, gives the names of nine of these illegitimate children, with the remaining three or more listed in a box as 'Others unknown'.[52] Though a long shot there is just the possibility that one of the three-plus illegitimate offspring included in the 'Others unknown' box on is, in fact, the young man called Márquez who was killed by the army at about 4.30 a.m. on 6 December 1928 in Ciénaga train station, according to Luisa Roy's witness statement.

If this conjecture were true, it would mean that this individual dressed in dark brown, who, in effect, would have been García Márquez's illegitimate uncle, was the prototype for José Arcadio Segundo in *One Hundred Years of Solitude*, who died during the massacre, and yet also testified to it, though, as we have seen, he may also be interpreted as a ghost. García Márquez's text is ambivalent on this point: José Arcadio Segundo may, indeed, already have become a ghost by the time he returned to his family home and hid in the back room.

This allows us to offer a new interpretation of the ghosts which people García Márquez's fiction. We know from an account provided by Margot, García Márquez's sister, that Tranquilina used the discourse of superstition as a means of criticizing her husband for his extramarital affairs, and indeed for the many illegitimate children he fathered 'in the street', as the expression in Colombia has it. The conjecture that one of his illegitimate children was murdered by the army in Ciénaga raises the possibility that the ghosts which roamed freely in the house of Aracataca were also what might be called 'political ghosts'. It is known that Nicolás the grandfather was on friendly terms with the United Fruit Company and also with the commissaries where, as a result of his power, he was able to buy goods in an unhindered way. There is, therefore, a paradox – perhaps unspoken, perhaps unexpressed – that one of his natural sons had been killed by allies of the United Fruit Company (Gaitán argues very persuasively that the army, during the Banana Massacre, became the unfailing supporter of the UFC, even at the expense of the Colombian people; see *La masacre bananera*).[53] The ghosts which existed in García Márquez's childhood were the phantoms created by adultery and by the dirty politics of the UFC. They were moral as much as political ghosts, expressions of unsolved dilemmas which were rampant in the marriage of Nicolás Márquez and Tranquilina Iguarán, and constituted the emotional environment into which the young Gabito was born.

As we can see, *One Hundred Years of Solitude* is a complex and multi-layered piece of fiction which can be read on a number of levels. On a primary level the novel can be read as the exploration at an imaginative level of the tangled branches of García Márquez's own family tree, an exploration which he carried out in an empiric sense when he went on a research trip to the Guajira region in the early 1950s. Nicolás Márquez Mejía (García Márquez's grandfather) and Tranquilina Iguarán Cotes (García Márquez's grandmother) were first cousins. As Gerald Martin explains, 'his father and her mother were both children, half-brother and half-sister, of the adventurous Juanita', namely Juanita Hernández who emigrated to Colombia from Spain in the early nineteenth century.[54] García Márquez was told when he was at primary school not to go near a girl who was in his class; with hindsight he realizes this was probably because he was related to her. We find evidence within the novel of the tangled branches of García Márquez's own family as he himself discovered; thus he calculated that his grandfather had had between twelve and nineteen *hijos naturales*, mainly as a result of his travelling around Colombia during the War of a Thousand Days, and Colonel Aureliano has seventeen *hijos naturales*, who return to their father's home, and are later assassinated in mysterious circumstances. *One Hundred Years of Solitude* dramatizes the dangers inherent in incest; Arcadio nearly commits incest with his mother, Pilar Ternera – he does not know she is his mother – but is prevented from doing so when Pilar sends Santa Sofía de la Piedad to his bed; Aureliano José falls in love with his aunt, Amaranta, but they are saved from committing incest in the nick of time, and the novel in effect ends when the apocalyptic act of incest finally occurs when Aureliano has sex with his sister, Amaranta Úrsula, and the child with the pig's tail is finally born, leading to the demise of the Buendía line as well as the destruction of Macondo.

The novel is also a metaphor of the Cain and Abel struggle within Colombia's political family, in the bloody struggle between the Liberals and the Conservatives which marked the nineteenth as well as the twentieth century. This was a struggle in which, again, García Márquez's family was involved, his father being a conservative and his grandfather a liberal. These two levels are brought together in the novel in that one of the rights for which the Liberals are portrayed as fighting for was the recognition of the rights of *hijos naturales*; this surfaces on two occasions in the novel – particularly the point at which Colonel Aureliano is forced to back down on this right by the less intransigent elements within his party – and also underlies the comment, made by one of the recruits, that they are fighting for the right not only to marry one's aunt but also one's mother (p. 127). These are, of course, not rights discussed in the history books; rather they demonstrate how García Márquez was bringing together the political as well as the personal. A further dimension to the Cain and Abel struggle is provided, as we have seen, by the struggle between us capitalism (as epitomized by the United Fruit Company) and Colombian workers, projected in the Ciénaga massacre in chapter fifteen. Once more these levels are brought together in that the apocalyptic result of incest – which, as in Lévi-Strauss's account in *Les Liens de la parenté*, leads to the breakdown of human culture – is mirrored by the demise of the banana boom which swept the northern coast of Colombia in the first three decades of the twentieth century. *One Hundred Years of Solitude* thus brings together a personal exploration of the tangled roots of the author's family tree with an analysis of the struggle between workers and international capitalism, and manages to bring both plots together by using the leitmotif of the double. Incest is based on the fear of meeting the double genetically, and this leads to a number of projections of the doubleness of human identity in the novel, epitomized by the fact that Aureliano Segundo and José Arcadio Segundo are often confused – by family members, by their lovers, to such an extent that they end up in the wrong graves (p. 287). In chapter seventeen Aureliano Buendía sees his *hijos naturales* as leading to a sense of dispersion, repetition and loneliness.[55] The novel weaves these motifs into a recreation of the most important moment for García Márquez's fiction, the point at which the self sees itself die. Aureliano Buendía remarks once that he is waiting to see his own funeral going past, and Aureliano, at the end of the novel, also sees his own death when reading and deciphering Melquíades' manuscripts.

When Aureliano finally deciphers the manuscripts left by Melquíades, this leads to a 'mirada de segundo reconocimiento' ('look of second recognition'; *One Hundred Years of Solitude*, p. 296), which can be interpreted in a number of ways for, as Carlos Fuentes suggests, the novel 'presupposes two readings because it presupposes two writings'.[56] Firstly, it refers to the fact that, with the benefit of hindsight, Aureliano is able to unravel his own family history and discover, for example, that Amaranta Úrsula is his aunt rather than his half-sister (the latter would have been the case if he were an *hijo natural*, which he at first believes); thus he is committing incest rather than half-incest as it were. The look of second recognition also draws attention to the fact that the decipherment (and the reading which is its concrete embodiment) embodies Aureliano's self-recognition for, like Oedipus, he has committed the sin of incest without knowing it, and, as a result of the successful decipherment of Melquíades' manuscripts (which are to him what the oracle was to Oedipus) he achieves a second recognition which leads to his destruction (the equivalent of Oedipus' blindness).[57] The second recognition is founded crucially on the notion of the self as double, for it is in the act of Aureliano's self-recognition that the motif of the double achieves its most powerful artistic expression in García Márquez's work: it is the point at which the double becomes the self – for incest is sex with self – and leads to the collapse of humanity, history and culture.

5

'Why did he dress like a cook to receive the Nobel?'[1]

The publication of *One Hundred Years of Solitude* in 1967 led not only to enormous book sales, and translation into various languages, but also to the creation of a new global genre called magical realism. García Márquez's mixture of the magical, the real and the political was clearly a winning formula. In 1969 *One Hundred Years of Solitude* won the Chianchiano Prize in Italy and was named the Best Foreign Book in France; in 1970 it was published in English and chosen as one of twelve best books of the year by US critics. García Márquez continued to write a number of works in the magical-realist style, although a progression towards the style of *The Autumn of the Patriarch* (1975) becomes increasingly evident.[2] 'The Handsomest Drowned Man in the World' (1968), for example, is an exercise in fiction rather than a short story per se. It tells the story of a drowned man who is found in the sea by some children, and who is taken to the nearest town. He achieves almost iconic status as a result of his great beauty; an extremely 'splendid' funeral is organized on his behalf, and even the village is named after him (p. 105). Rather like a reverse image of *Leaf Storm* this short story portrays how the love of a community for an individual, even if he is not known, paradoxically can produce what is known in Latin America as a 'good death'. For this reason, no doubt, Regina Janés calls it an 'optimistic tale'.[3]

We find a similar formula in 'The Last Voyage of the Ghost Ship' (1968), which shows García Márquez plumbing the depths of Caribbean history, in its extraordinarily real description of a supernatural event, the last voyage of a ghost ship. This – the 'death' of a ghost – may be interpreted as the height of paradox (since, logic would tell, a ghost is already dead). Though phantasmal there are details which provide an empiric density to the ghost ship: 'the huge steel cask shattered the ground and one could hear the neat destruction of ninety thousand five hundred champagne glasses breaking, one after the other, from stem to stem' (p. 128). Given the recurrent reference throughout the story to the poverty of the people living on the nearby shores ('the disorder of colors of the Negro shacks on the hills', p. 124; 'the misery of the houses', p. 127), which is deliberately contrasted with the extravagance of the ocean liner, García Márquez makes it clear that his narrative style always has a political bite lurking beneath its sheen of magic. Pointing in a similar direction is 'A Very Old Man with Enormous Wings' (1968) which, like 'The Handsomest Drowned Man in the World', is an exploratory piece of fiction. It tells the story of an angel who has fallen to earth and is found 'lying face down in the mud' (p. 105) by a fisherman called Pelayo. This flesh and blood angel 'was dressed like a ragpicker. There were only a few faded hairs left on his bald skull and very few teeth in his mouth' (p. 105). Pelayo and his wife Elisenda put him in the chicken coop and then charge five cents per view. But, in a sleight of hand familiar in García Márquez's work, the magical nature of the appearance of a real angel is naturalized by the introduction of a twist in the narrative, since a new even more incredible miracle supplants interest in the angel: 'It so happened that during those days, among so many carnival attractions, there arrived in town the traveling show of the woman who had been changed into a spider for having disobeyed her parents' (p. 109). From being a miracle the angel finally ends up being a nuisance, until he one day flies away 'holding himself up in some way with the risky flapping of a senile vulture' (p. 112). The significance of this tale lies in its use as a showcase for one of García Márquez's important themes: the irony of the clash between the magical and the real.

Perhaps García Márquez's most politically outspoken short story of this period was 'Blacaman the Good, Vendor of Miracles' (1968) which, like 'A Very Old Man with Enormous Wings', explores Caribbean carnival culture, particularly the magical potions, antidotes and outlandish tricks typical of the carnivals that so fascinated Gabo as a child. The story, which can be read as a rewriting of *Lazarillo de Tormes*, the Spanish picaresque novel,[4] begins with the description of a hawker, Blacaman the Bad, trying to sell an antidote for snake venom; he is bitten by a bushmaster, survives the experience and then begins to sell his antidote to all and sundry. He takes on the services of Blacaman the Good, who is the narrator, as a fortune-teller, and they become involved in another piece of quackery (a machine called the 'electricity of suffering'; p. 117) when the story takes a rather sinister turn, and the political allegory common to a number of García Márquez's stories of this time, emerges:

We fled through Indian passes and the more lost we became, the clearer the news reached us that the marines had invaded the country under the pretext of exterminating yellow fever and were going about beheading every inveterate or eventual potter they found in their path, and not only the natives, out of precaution, but the Chinese, for distraction, the Negroes, from habit, and the Hindus, because they were snake charmers, and then they wiped out the flora and fauna and all the mineral wealth that they were able to because their specialists in our affairs had taught them that the people along the Caribbean had the ability to change their nature in order to confuse gringos. (p. 117)

This is the political twist in García Márquez's fiction. In almost the same breath in which he describes snake charmers as coming back from the dead and a man turned into a 'glob of admiral jelly' because the machine malfunctions, he describes the ruthless invasion of the Caribbean by North Americans, so that their actions (using the existence of yellow fever as a pretext to invade, beheading potters, beheading the natives, the Chinese, Negroes and Hindus, destroying the flora and fauna, draining the mineral resources from the country) catch the reader off guard and they initially seem as fantastic as the earlier events.

Then understanding dawns on the reader, and the episode is shown as a political allegory of the empiric destruction of Latin America by North America. It is apt equally that the prevalence of belief in shape-shifting among Amerindian myths and legends is here reinterpreted as a strategy used to fight back against the west, in an attempt to reverse the balance of power. Local beliefs in the supernatural are here being used as ammunition to fight against invasion by the United States. Yet the allegory is introduced with a dose of humour to lighten its political density, and make the left-wing politics more palatable. This notion is taken up later on in the story when Blacaman the Good buries Blacaman the Bad and the plaque on his grave reads: 'HERE LIES BLACAMAN THE DEAD, BADLY CALLED THE BAD, DECEIVER OF MARINES AND VICTIM OF SCIENCE' (p. 122). The irony of this story is that Blacaman the Dead stands as a symbol of Latin America's expropriation; though apparently dead and bad (i.e. executed by the West), he uses his magic to deceive the US marines, and, although a victim of science and technology, he is kept alive by Blacaman the Good, the narrator – and by extension a projection of García Márquez's own views – in his struggle against Latin America's oppressor; for, as the story concludes: 'and if by chance he has died again, I bring him back to life once more, for the beauty of the punishment is that he will keep on living in his tomb as long as I'm alive, that is, forever' (p. 122). In this sense the story of a snake-charmer is politicized to create an allegory of a political story which bites back.

Critics began writing about García Márquez's work from the 1970s onwards, leading to a flood of literary criticism which no other Hispanic author has to date rivalled. It has been estimated that about one scholarly article per week is published on García Márquez; a recent count on the academic search engine JSTOR listed no less than 2,838 separate academic articles on and reviews of his work.[5] García Márquez was proving to be that rare bird, attractive to a mass readership as well as to academia.[6] In 1971 Mario Vargas Llosa published the first book-length study of García Márquez's life and work, *García Márquez: historia de un deicidio* (*García Márquez: The History of a Decade*), an extraordinary piece of scholarship and indeed homage to García Márquez by Peru's most famous writer. *García Márquez: historia de un deicidio* provides important biographical information about the influence his parents and grandparents had on García Márquez's emotional and intellectual development. It studies his apprenticeship as a journalist and his early short stories leading up to *One Hundred Years of Solitude*. Vargas Llosa also provides some genuine insight into the Colombian writer's fondness for anecdotes:

For him everything is translated into a story, into episodes that he remembers or invents with impressive ease. Political or literary opinions, judgements about other people, things or countries, projects or ambitions: everything turns into an anecdote, and is expressed via anecdotes. His intelligence, his culture, and his sensitivity have a curiously individual and concrete seal; they flaunt their anti-intellectualism and are rabidly opposed to abstraction. When near him, life turns into a cascade of anecdotes.[7]

The admiration that seeps from the pages of Vargas Llosa's book would soon, however, turn sour. In 1968 the Cuban poet Heberto Padilla lost his job as a journalist as a result of criticizing the revolutionary writer Lisandro Otero and eulogizing the counter-revolutionary writer Guillermo Cabrera Infante; in 1971 he was imprisoned for counter-revolutionary activities. A number of

From left to right, Mario Vargas Llosa, his wife Patricia, Mercedes Barcha, José Donoso, his wife María Pilar Serrano and García Márquez, Barcelona, early 1970s.

writers – including Jean-Paul Sartre, Vargas Llosa, Juan Goytisolo, Carlos Fuentes and Octavio Paz – wrote a public letter criticizing the Cuban government for this action. Although García Márquez's name was also on the list of signatories, it had been put there by Plinio Apuleyo who had attempted to get hold of García Márquez but had failed to do so. García Márquez later said that he did not personally sign the letter,[8] which shows that, even early on, he was not prepared to tag along with fellow Boom writers such as Vargas Llosa when it came to Cuba. Indeed he has retained an unswerving loyalty to Castro over the years.

The Padilla affair led to a public rift between García Márquez and Vargas Llosa.[9] The coolness between the two men (García Márquez would never refer to Vargas Llosa, Vargas Llosa was outspoken in his rejection of left-wing politics and would not allow any part of his essay, *Gabriel García Márquez: historia de un deicidio* to be republished for many years)[10] was exacerbated by a murky fight over women, which finally flared into physical aggression. Thomas Catan takes up the story:

Various Latin American artists and intellectuals had gathered in Mexico City for a film premiere in 1976. After the film, García Márquez went to embrace his close friend, Vargas Llosa. 'Mario!' he managed to say, before receiving a 'tremendous blow' to the face from the Peruvian author.

'How dare you come and greet me after what you did to Patricia in Barcelona!' Vargas Llosa reportedly shouted, referring to his wife.

Amid the screams of some women, García Márquez sat on the floor with a profusely bleeding nose, as the Mexican writer Elena Poniatowska ran to get a steak for his eye. Two days later Mr Moya took the photos of his friend's black eye . . .

Only the two men and their wives know what really led to the fight. It is rumoured that while both families were living in Barcelona, Vargas Llosa left his wife and children for a stunning Swedish woman. According to the whispered tale, Patricia sought comfort with García Márquez and his wife, who advised her to seek a divorce. When Vargas Llosa reconciled with Patricia, she allegedly told all, leading eventually to the sucker punch. To some, however, Mr Moya's account suggests that some greater betrayal was behind Vargas Llosa's ire.[11]

The animosity is never too far beneath the surface. In 14 October 2008, for example, Vargas Llosa gave a lecture at King's College London in which he attacked the false exoticism underlying the image Europe has created of Latin America over the years, and furthermore attacked the hypocrisy of sympathizing with the Revolution as long as it is conveniently situated in a foreign country, which he argued was a similar type of exoticism based on bad faith. The battle lines had been firmly drawn in 1971 and, while there has been some cooling of animosities, the division between García Márquez and Vargas Llosa – which encompasses the personal as much as the political – shows no sign of abating. As for Mercedes,

García Márquez with his wife, Mercedes, and their sons, Gonzalo and Rodrigo, Barcelona, 1972.

she has never forgiven the Peruvian writer to this day for what she regards as an act of treachery to her husband.[12]

The success of *One Hundred Years of Solitude* led to an artistic outpouring in García Márquez's work. In 1972 he was awarded the prestigious Rómulo Gallegos Prize, and he published 'La increíble y triste historia de la cándida Eréndira y de su abuela desalmada' ('The Incredible and Sad Story of Innocent Eréndira and her Heartless Grandmother') in the same year, which could be seen as representing the zenith of his short story style. It contains its fair share of magical realism, in its dead-pan description of a fantastic event – namely, a granddaughter's consignment to sexual slavery for having accidentally burnt down the family home. This is a slavery that, furthermore, would last two hundred years if the debt the granddaughter owes for burning down the house were to be fully paid off; as such, though this event is first presented as phantasmagorical, its fantastic logarithm is allowed to produce a formula ('At this rate she'll need two hundred years to pay me back'; p. 11). Time in 'Innocent Eréndira' is portrayed as a truncated, or dislocated reality rather than an historical continuum: "'take advantage of tomorrow to wash the living-room too," she told Eréndira. "It hasn't seen the sun since the days of all the noise'" (p. 9). The novel's dialogue is punchy – "'I never saw the sea," she said. "It's like the desert but with water," said Ulises' (p. 20) – and there is also a sprinkling of absurd humour: "'Then why do they have you here as mayor?" the grandmother asked. "To make it rain," was the mayor's answer' (p. 22).

Perhaps most important, events in the novel are portrayed in such a way that they may be interpreted as a political allegory. Julio Ortega has pointed to the parodic and ironic function of this tale of a woman's woe, a tale in which the story of Cinderella is carnivalized and reversed in order to tell the story of a prostitute;[13] but the political symbolism beneath this suggests that the debt of slavery borne uncomplainingly by Eréndira may be interpreted as representative of the impossible situation of Latin America with regard to its own overwhelming debt.[14] Intriguingly – and here we can find similarities between 'Innocent Eréndira' and *One Hundred Years of Solitude*[15] – this man-made catastrophe of debt is presented not as being the result of a bad human or social decision but rather in terms of a natural disaster – that is, something that cannot be helped. Eréndira's mistake, like the 'second surge of wind' in *One Hundred Years of Solitude* (quoted above; p. 335), is also created by the wind.

Plaudits were cascading around García Márquez. In 1972 he was awarded the Books Abroad/Neusdat Prize, and the same year the English translation of *Leaf Storm and Other Stories* was published in New York. This was the beginning of one of the most significant political phases of García Márquez's life. When General Pinochet carried out his coup d'état on 11 September 1973, bombing the Casa Rosada, executing Salvador Allende, and ushering in an intensely repressive dictatorship in Chile, García Márquez experienced the event as a personal blow. He sent a telegram to Pinochet which stated the following: 'The Chilean people will never allow itself to be governed by a mob of criminals like you, who are bankrolled by North American imperialism.'[16] The following year he published an *ad hominem* attack on Pinochet – 'Chile, el Golpe y los Gringos' ('Chile, the Coup and the Gringos', 1974) – laying the blame, furthermore, for Pinochet's coup firmly at the door of the US Government, the CIA and ITT.[17] But he went even further than this by publicly stating that he would never publish another novel after *El otoño del patriarca* (*The Autumn of the Patriarch*) if Pinochet remained in power. In 1974, exploring in a more concrete vein the political problems of Latin America, he founded *Alternativa*, a left-wing magazine, in Bogotá. All of these gestures were paving the way for García Márquez's gradual ingratiation with Fidel Castro. Unlike other writers such as Vargas Llosa who had distanced themselves from Cuba, García Márquez was drawing ever closer to the Cuban regime. Thus, for example, García Márquez's first dedicated copy of *The Autumn of the Patriarch* was for Fidel Castro; he sent it to Cuba via Lisandro Otero.[18] García Márquez had met Castro on various occasions during the early years of the Revolution as a result of his work for Prensa Latina but this did not lead to any deep friendship. The friendship between the two men developed in the period between the publication of *The Autumn of the Patriarch* and his Nobel Prize award (1982).[19] César Leante has argued that *The Autumn of the Patriarch* was not released in Cuba because Fidel Castro would have seen in the portrayal of the patriarch some of his own character traits,[20] but this is a misinterpretation of the relationship between Gabo and Fidel.

The Autumn of the Patriarch (1975) is García Márquez's most political novel. A masterpiece of irony, it invented the new idiom of psychological magical realism in that it combines the depiction of an archetypal dictator's *état d'âme* with magical-realist flourishes (examples being the dictator's decision to serve up General Rodrigo de Aguilar in a cannibalistic banquet to his subalterns, pp. 104–5, and the selling of the sea to the gringos – 'but I could never have imagined that they would be capable of doing what they did to carry off the numbered locks of my old checker-board sea with gigantic suction dredges'; p. 210).[21] It was clearly a new direction for García Márquez. He had been working on the novel on and off since 1968 and, as he wrote to his friend Alfredo Iriarte on 1 April 1968: 'I work without haste, although with a great deal of difficulty . . . in an effort to take apart and dismantle the style of *One Hundred Years of Solitude*, trying to move into something truly new, so that the next novel does not profit, either involuntarily or voluntarily, from the commercial and critical success of the previous one'.[22]

The dictator leads a lonely, cut-off existence, surrounded by the cows which wander freely in the Presidential Palace, leaving their excrement wherever they roam,[23] the concubines with whom he has sporadic, frantic sex without bothering to take his clothes off, lepers and paralytics. Given that this world is viewed though his conscious-ness, we rarely as readers catch an 'objective', unmediated view of the outside world. He is visited by a string of gringo ambassadors, all with different names but making the same suggestions – that he should sell the sea to pay off his country's external debt; he is also visited by a number of military advisers such as José Ignacio Sáenz de la Barra, who provide him with (as it turns out, false) reports on what is happening in the outside world. The real world beyond the palace walls is only perceived in fragments. Having believed he was successfully seducing schoolgirls from the school opposite the palace, the dictator discovers that the school has in fact been closed down, and that the 'girls' are actually port prosti-tutes paid by the police to dress up as schoolgirls and attend to his perverted needs (pp. 188–90). He never discovers who was behind the murder of his wife, Leticia Nazareno, and their son (they were eaten by wild dogs; pp. 167–68), and on one occasion, he sees him-self on television giving a speech ('and there he was on the screen

García Márquez writing *The Autumn of the Patriarch* in the early 1970s.

thinner and trimmer, but it was me, mother, sitting in the office',
p. 198). The dictator is complicit in his own ignorance; when he
learns about the torture chambers installed by Sáenz de la Barra in
what used to be the madhouse of the Dutch adjacent to the palace,
becoming party to his underlings' lies, 'he discovered in the course

of his uncountable years that a lie is more comfortable than doubt, more useful than love, more lasting than truth' (p. 228). His paranoia knows no bounds. Thus he employs a man who looks like him, Patricio Aragonés, as his imposter, and when he is poisoned, and there is widespread rejoicing, he bides his time, enters the room as the spoils are being divided up, and has everyone executed (pp. 26–28). He has his faithful right-hand man, Rodrigo de Aguilar, served up at a cannibalistic feast, when he suspects him of betraying him (pp. 104–5).

The dictator is clearly not based on one person but is an amalgam of a number of Latin American dictators including Trujillo, the Dominican dictator who used to feed his rivals live to the sharks, as well as a number of others such as the Venezuelan dictator Pinilla. But more than a historical denunciation, *The Autumn of the Patriarch* is a searing and riveting plunge into the psychology of an archetypal dictator – a man who kills others without remorse (he even kills the soothsayer who predicts when and where he will die); a keeper of brothels; a paedophile; a rapist; a man who never knows love; whose paranoia causes him to fear sleeping for too long; a man who trusts nobody and is himself trusted by nobody; a cannibal; a man who insults moral decency and has religious men publicly humiliated, and murdered, when they go against his wishes; a man who arrogates to himself the place of God in the universe.[24]

The style of the novel is more akin to psychological realism than Realism in the canonic, nineteenth-century sense of the term. The novel begins *in medias res*, with the people's discovery of Patricio Aragonés' death, and does not provide much information about how the dictator came to power. The narrative has a basic temporal linearity, in that it begins with the death of Patricio Aragonés, describes the betrayal of Rodrigo de Aguilar, describes the dictator's relationship with his mother, then his love affair with Leticia Nazareno, his marriage and then her death, followed by the sale of the sea, the death of his adviser, Sáenz de la Barra, and then the arrival of death coming to take the dictator away. But the overall structure of the novel is closer to that of an accordion, whereby the significance of certain events is elongated through reconstruction by memory, and events are brought together through association more than historic consequentiality. This osmosis between different times is pertinent, of course, in the context of a novel that attempts to recreate the jumbled thought processes of an ailing, degenerate dictator: a strict linearity would have done no justice to the theme. This osmosis is also reflected in the effortless transitions between one person's thoughts and another's. The novel has no quotation marks, and, indeed, extends the Flaubertian formula of *style indirect libre* in a number of highly expressive ways. When Patricio Aragonés is dying, we hear about it in the customary third-person preterite voice, but a first-person present-tense voice suddenly intrudes: 'until he could no longer tell him any more because a fiery rake tore his guts apart, his heart softened again and he ended with no intent of offense but almost one of supplication I'm serious general, take advantage of the fact that I'm dying now and die with me' (p. 22). The effect is engaging, absorbing the reader's attention, allowing for flexibility and a more immediate emotional impact, for suddenly, halfway through the sentence, we hear Patricio's voice. This polyphony of voices also allows García Márquez to portray the disintegration of consciousness, presenting it as the invasion of other voices into the mind rather than the gradual extinction of one consciousness.[25] It is not the slow fading of a light that we witness; rather the novel reveals a room in the dictator's consciousness in which various lights are turned on and off sporadically, thereby breaking down the sense of its monadic hermeticism. An incisive evocation of a supremely ugly mind, the novel is nevertheless gorgeously written. As García Márquez wrote to Alfredo Iriarte in a letter dated 11 March 1970, 'there is a certain merit to treating a dirty and bloody theme in a completely lyrical style. Thus to show that even in shit there is poetry.'[26]

In 1975 García Márquez left Spain and returned to Mexico. In the spring of the following year he made a proposal to Fidel Castro that the latter could not refuse, offering his services as the writer of the epic story of the Cuban expedition to Africa. García Márquez went to Cuba to discuss his proposal, and Fidel Castro came in his jeep to pick García Márquez up at the Hotel Nacional, and they went off for a ride in the country to discuss the idea, as well other issues such as the difficulties involved in feeding a country like Cuba.[27] Castro accepted García Márquez's offer and subsequently allowed him access to the highest level of Cuba's army, in particular to Raúl Castro, head of the armed forces. In 1977 *Operación Carlota* (*Operation Carlota*), was published. In this group of essays on Cuba's role in Africa García Márquez describes in detail the military preparations made for Operation Carlota, named after a slave of that name who rose against the Spanish authorities on 5 November 1843,[28] which were designed to protect Angola against the imperialist aggression of South Africa. García Márquez argues that the war in Angola was not a military expedition so much as a 'war of the people' (*guerra popular*, p. 19), and suggests that the eventual victory in Angola was a moral boost for Cuba and the Left in the face of recent reverses such as the assassinations of Che Guevara and of Salvador Allende, and the interminable US blockade of Cuba's border.

García Márquez's visits to Cuba became more and more frequent during this period. Typically García Márquez would be staying at the Hotel Nacional with his wife, Mercedes, and Castro would turn up in his jeep and they would ride off into the country to discuss a wide range of issues: politics, literature, human rights, political asylum. Gerald Martin gives an example of one of their 'jeep' conversations:

We were in a bit of a hurry and I had six points noted down on a card that I wanted to bring up with him. Fidel laughed at my precision with each point and said: 'this yes, this no, we'll do that, we'll do the other.' When he'd answered the sixth point we were going through the tunnel to Havana and he asked me, 'And what's number seven?' There was no number seven on the card and I don't know if the devil whispered in my ear but, put like that, I thought, 'This could be the right moment.' I said, 'Point seven is here but it's really awkward!' 'OK, but tell me what it is.' Like someone throwing himself overboard in a parachute, I said, 'You know, it would give great satisfaction to a family if I could take Reinol González, liberated, to Mexico to spend Christmas with his wife and kids.' I hadn't looked behind me, but Fidel, without looking at me, looked at Mercedes and said, 'And why is Mercedes looking like that?' And I, without looking back, without seeing what expression Mercedes had on her face, answered: 'Because she's probably thinking that if I take Reinol Gonzalez and he ends up playing some dirty trick on the Revolution you're going to think I messed up.' Then Fidel answered not to me but to Mercedes: 'Look, Mercedes, Gabriel and I will do what we think is right and if after that the other guy turns out to be a louse, that's another problem!'[29]

The important point about this exchange is that it shows how intimately involved Mercedes has been in the high-level political negotiations that García Márquez and Castro have conducted over the years. García Márquez's diplomacy worked out and, in December 1977, González Reinol was released so he could spend Christmas with his family.[30]

In 1977 García Márquez and Graham Greene, the English writer who had long been a friend of Latin America,[31] were invited by President Omar Torrijos of Panama to participate in the work force established to discuss the future sovereignty of the Panama Canal. Rather mischievously, Torrijos decided to flout the visa ban that had been imposed on both García Márquez and Graham Greene as a result of their outspoken criticism of the United States, and offered to provide them with official Panamanian passports, in order to allow them to attend the signing of the treaty in Washington. They both accepted. Even President Carter laughed when he was told about the ruse later on.[32]

García Márquez has been happy over the years to let his friends make film versions of his short stories. He gave permission, for example, to Miguel Littín to produce a film version of 'Montiel's Widow' in the late 1970s. During the filming in a small Mexican village called Tlacotálcaro which Littín thought would be ideal as a setting for the mythical Macondo, he phoned García Márquez and asked him how he should explain to the actors how to make love in a hammock. The Colombian writer replied: 'Look, hang on, and I'll get there'; early one morning García Márquez and Mercedes landed at the film set in a helicopter, and gave the actors some useful tips about how best to make love in a hammock.[33]

Despite García Márquez's public declaration that he would not publish as long as Pinochet held power, he broke his literary silence in 1981 with *Crónica de una muerte anunciada* (*Chronicle of a Death Foretold*), even though Pinochet was still president, and would remain so until he was voted out by a plebiscite in 1991. It is a short though brilliantly written novel, which tipped the balance in his favour for being nominated as a candidate for the Nobel Prize. *Chronicle of a Death Foretold* had a first print-run of 1,500,000 copies; García Márquez had clearly come a long way since the early days when a private edition of *Leaf Storm* had fewer than 2,000. The success of this new novel was assured by a dramatic extraliterary event, which took place on the eve of its publication. García Márquez travelled from Mexico to Colombia to launch the novel in Bogotá and while there, he caught wind of a plot that put his life in danger, through his supposed connections with the left-wing terrorist group M-19. He took fright and made an official request to the Mexicans for political asylum. As García Márquez explained in an interview with Claudia Dreifus:

> Fortunately, I have many friends in Bogotá, and whenever anything is said in front of more than three people, one of them tells me. Three sources told me of attempts linking me to M-19. There was, apparently, a dinner at the presidential palace, where, in the presence of the president and the top military chiefs, my alleged involvement with that group was discussed. The guerrillas, meanwhile, were being held, tortured and told to sign confessions implicating me.
>
> Well, when I heard that, I was alarmed to say the least. My sources told me not to worry – the government wouldn't dare touch me, because I was too important. But it seemed to me that it might like to make an example out of me to show that it had no respect for anyone. What I did was go immediately to the Mexican embassy and ask for diplomatic protection in order to leave Colombia. It was officially stated that there was nothing against me and that I was just probably trying to get publicity for my new book.[34]

García Márquez, however, denied this. As he pointed out shortly before boarding the plane for Mexico City: 'The book has been a success ever since I wrote it.'[35] Preparations were being made for *Chronicle of a Death Foretold* to be translated into thirty-two languages. The Colombian publishers, La Oveja Negra, respected the author's request that the price of the novel be kept low which, as Benson points out,

> was no doubt responsible in part for the immediate acceptance of the book in the Spanish-speaking world. In Colombia it was sold on street corners, in drug stores, on city buses, at stop lights. Within a matter of days the country's magazines and

newspapers were interviewing the supposed real-life characters of the fictional work which the author openly admits is based on an actual occurrence of some thirty years ago.[36]

Given a scenario of this kind, it is not surprising that *Chronicle of a Death Foretold* was, and continues to be, a very successful novel. The events on which the novel was based are intrinsically dramatic. In Sucre, Colombia, on 22 January 1951 a local school-teacher, Margarita Chica,[37] married one Miguel Reyes Palencia. The wedding ceremony went ahead smoothly, but the next morning the groom returned the bride to her family declaring the marriage to be null and void since: 'La muchacha no tenía sus prendas completas' ('The girl is used goods'). Margarita Chica's deflowering was attributed to her former boyfriend, Cayetano Gentile, a twenty-two-year-old, third-year medical student at the Universidad Javeriana of Bogotá, and heir to the largest fortune in Sucre. The bride's brothers, Víctor Manuel and José Joaquín, pursued and killed Gentile because he had affronted the family's honour.[38] García Márquez knew members of the families who were involved. He counted the murder victim, Cayetano Gentile, among his friends, and, indeed, recalls attending the lavish parties that Gentile organized in Sucre the summer before his death. There was even a family connection since Gentile's mother, Julieta Chimento, was Luisa Santiaga's 'comadre' since she had been the godmother of Hernando, who was the eighth of Luisa Santiaga's children.[39]

The novel is divided into five chapters and each of them surveys the murder from a different perspective – via the consciousness of different pairs or groups of people, or refracted through the prism provided by different written documents – in order to produce a kaleidoscope effect. As in *One Hundred Years of Solitude*, none of the chapters in *Chronicle of a Death Foretold* has a title, or even a number, which leads to the impression that the chapters glide into each other, creating new intertextual resonances. It is not the case, indeed, that the various perspectives gradually fill in the blanks created by earlier chapters. There are a number of junctures in which the same event is re-visioned from a different perspective and the interpretation given of the same event is contradictory.[40] One way of understanding how these nodes of contradiction operate in the text is to analyse each chapter in terms of the spatial and temporal coordinates it provides. *Chronicle of a Death Foretold* re-visualizes – and in effect forces the reader to re-experience – Santiago's murder on five separate occasions and it is legitimate to see this as a product of the Colombian writer's artistry. Rather like Pedro Rojas in César Vallejo's poem 'Batallas III' which refers to 'Pedro y sus dos muertes', Santiago's death is recounted on five separate occasions since he, in effect, dies for different groups of people.[41] The vortex from which the conflicting accounts splay in *Chronicle of a Death Foretold* is, of course, the notion of mistaken identity),[42] and – perhaps unsurprisingly – this notion also has a parallel in García Márquez's memoirs. In his description of the murder of the charismatic liberal leader, Jorge Eliécer Gaitán, for example, he refers to a man whom he saw inciting those present at the scene to take their revenge, but no one else seems to recall having seen him.[43] This detail finds its way into *Chronicle of a Death Foretold* in that the possibility is raised that Ángela Vicario chose Santiago Nasar as a 'false assassin' in order to protect her real lover.

Each of the chapters of *Chronicle of a Death Foretold* focalizes Santiago's murder from a different point of view provided by different sets of individuals: Santiago Nasar/Plácida Linero – San Román/Angel Vicario – the Vicario twins – Carmen Amador/ Cristo Bedoya – the Investigating Judge/the town-dwellers. It uses different texts to focus on that event ranging from oral testimony (which predominates in the final chapter, but is constant through-out the novel) to written reports such as the defence lawyer's report (chapter three), the autopsy report (chapter four) and the judge's report (chapter five). Despite these differences in perspective, however, continuity between the chapters is ensured by balancing the appearance of the main characters throughout the book. Though the Vicario twins provide the focus for the reader's perception of events in chapter three they also have 'minor' parts in the other chapters. Continuity is also ensured by having the majority of the chapters viewed from within a particular household: chapter one is set within the Santiago Nasar household, chapter two in the Vicario household, chapter three is partly set within Clotilde Armenta's shop, while chapter four is viewed through the panopticon of the Riohacha prison, and chapter five set partially within 'the squalid wooden office in the town hall'.[44] In this way García Márquez is able to use the image of a gradually disappearing domestic space as an icon of the slow disintegration of social mores.

The changes which García Márquez made to the original material likewise led to a more enhanced sense of drama. First he drew in more closely the net of family ties which linked the individuals to each other. Cayetano Gentile was a family friend of García Márquez's family but he became Luisa Santiaga's godson in the novel (*Chronicle of a Death Foretold*, p. 112); the Chica brothers were turned into twins in the novel; the narrator becomes Ángela Vicario's cousin; Gentile was killed in the house of a neighbour, Etelvina Guerrero de Munive,[45] but in the novel Santiago Nasar is killed outside his own house, locked out unintentionally by his own mother. García Márquez also enhanced the dramatic impact of the events by changing certain details: the Monday of real life became the Tuesday of the novel, traditionally a day of bad luck in the Hispanic world (as *martes trece* suggests); the murder was presaged by a highly sophisticated sequence of omens, some of which are based on popular superstition, some on literary topoi and others engendered by the prolepsis built into the structure of the plot.[46] But most impressive of all García Márquez turned upside-down the chronology of the original event, allowing the murder in essence to be staged on five separate occasions, and with each chapter the suspense is intensified.

It was here that García Márquez showed the hand of the literary master; time in effect became his trump card.

In 1981 García Márquez was awarded the French Legion of Honour medal, and in the same year a French scholar, Jacques Gilard, published the first volume of a four-volume edition of the Colombian writer's journalism, *Obra períodistica: textos costeños* (*Journalism: Coastal Articles*). A screenplay, *Viva Sandino* (*Long Live Sandino*, 1982)[47] narrates the attack by the Sandinistas at the house of Dr José María Castillo Quant in Managua, their holding of the occupants as hostages, and concludes with the Sandinistas achieving a moral victory and allowing their message to be broadcast on the radio. Though politically sincere, the screenplay loses emotive intensity as a result of the distance of the narrator, and the radio becomes the vehicle of expression for the conflict rather than those involved in and suffering from the raid. In the early 1980s, before he had won the Nobel Prize, García Márquez wanted to celebrate his mother's birthday with her (which fell on 25 July); as he was exiled at the time in Colombia, Fidel Castro lent him his personal plane so he could fly clandestinely to Aracataca to spend the evening with his mother.[48]

It was in October 1982 that García Márquez was awarded the Nobel Prize for Literature, which was a shock for him as much as for the rest of the world.[49] Plinio Apuleyo remembers that he had had a conversation with García Márquez in 1981 to the effect that, if he were to receive the Nobel Prize (which they both thought highly unlikely) then he would have to wear a tuxedo, and they both agreed that this was very *pavoso*, that is, something bringing bad luck.[50] The announcement of the winner of the Nobel Prize for Literature unleashed a flurry of diplomatic activity in Bogotá (García Márquez was exiled from his home country at the time, and living in Mexico City), while, as Fernando Cruz Kronfly puts it, 'some Colombian academics felt panic in their bellies'.[51] It was highly embarrassing for the Colombian government to have the

Nobel Prize awarded to a writer who was living in exile. As if to make up for his rejection by his mother country, and coinciding with the award of the Nobel Prize, García Márquez was awarded maximum honours from Cuba (the Order Felix Varela), and from Mexico (the Aguila Ázteca).[52]

The footage of the event as it appeared on Swedish as well as Colombian TV at the time shows that García Márquez was the only person of the hundred or so on the podium and the hundreds in the audience who was not wearing a tuxedo to the event. Instead he chose to wear a white suit, the *liqui-liqui* which is normal dress in the Caribbean, and a yellow rose for luck, causing quite a stir; it was the first time a winner of the Nobel Prize received the award not dressed in a tuxedo.[53] As one of Plinio Apuleyo's friends remarked to him after the event: 'Plinio, since you are such good friends with Gabo, can you tell me something: Why did he dress as a cook to receive the Nobel prize?'[54] García Márquez was accompanied by a band of musicians who managed to breathe a bit of Caribbean life into what is normally a rather staid occasion.[55] Fidel Castro sent Gabo 1,500 bottles of rum for the celebrations after the ceremony, which led to a complaint by the Swedish Chancellery to the Cuban Embassy in Sweden as a result of the illicit distribution of alcohol.[56] García Márquez was also given a Protocol House, no. 6, in the Siboney district of Havana, after receiving the Nobel Prize, a personal gift from Fidel Castro, as well as the use of a Mercedes Benz, whenever he is in Cuba.[57] When Luisa Santiaga, his mother, was interviewed she was asked if she wanted anything more from life now that her son had won the Nobel Prize, and she said: 'How about getting the phone fixed?' (*Que me arreglen el teléfono*).[58]

García Márquez's Nobel address, 'The Solitude of Latin America', very much echoing the effrontery of his attire, attacked Europe for its complacent attitude towards Latin America. He attacked Pinochet, the President of Chile at the time, accusing him of having 'accomplished the first genocide in Latin America in our

García Márquez kissing his wife, Mercedes Barcha de García, on his arrival at the airport in Stockholm to attend the Nobel award ceremonies.

time'.[59] He went on, 'twenty million Latin American children have died before their second birthday, which is more than all those born in Europe' (p. 208), and (then referring to the *desaparecidos*) he pointed out that many women, 'arrested during pregnancy gave birth in Argentinian prisons but, still, where and who their children are is not known' (p. 209). The significance of his words is that he was referring to something happening in the present time of the listeners: 'El Salvador has created, since 1979, virtually one refugee every twenty minutes' (p. 209). He then turned to critique the ways in which Europe has used imperfect paradigms in order to understand Latin America: 'To interpret our reality through schemas which are alien to us only has the effect of making us even more unknown, even less free, even more solitary' (p. 209). García Márquez then made an impassioned plea for more comprehension:

> Perhaps venerable old Europe would be more sympathetic if
> it tried to see us in its own past; if it remembered that London

García Marquez, dressed in his *liqui-liqui*, holding his Nobel Prize for Literature medal after the award ceremony in Stockholm, Sweden, 1982.

needed three hundred years to build her first defensive wall and another three hundred before her first bishop; that Rome debated in the darkness of uncertainty for twenty centuries before an Etruscan king rooted her in history, and that even in the sixteenth century the pacifist Swiss of today, who so delight us with their mild cheeses and their cheeky clocks, made Europe bloody as soldiers of fortune. (p. 210)

It was an argument that would one day be used by Simón Bolívar in his argument with a Frenchman in García Márquez's novel *The General in his Labyrinth*. This led him to make the most important point about Europe's views of Latin America: 'Why are we granted unreservedly a recognition of our originality in literature when our attempts, in the face of enormous difficulties, to bring about social change are denied us with all sorts of mistrust?' (p. 210), clearly a nod in the direction of the Cuban Revolution. Very much like his novels, it was a speech which named without naming, using metaphor to allow a political point to emerge with greater poignancy.

A close reading of the Nobel speech shows, again, how central the notion of the double is to the Colombian writer's work. He makes perhaps his most pertinent reference to the danger of the double in the opening paragraph of his Nobel Prize speech in which he alludes to Antonio Pigafetta's description of how the first native found by Ferdinand Magallan in Patagonia was put in front of a mirror and went mad (*perdió el uso de la razón*) as a result of the fear inspired by his own image.[60] It is essentially the same terror and panic created by a vision of the double which we have seen forming the crux of early stories such as 'Tubal-Cain Forges a Star' as well as his masterpiece *One Hundred Years of Solitude*. This is expressed principally through the syntax of the plot which recreates the horror underlying the point at which the self joins physically with its double, as incest leading to the apocalypse. There are, as we have seen, many other offshoots of the same motif in the novel, such as the dream which José Arcadio Buendía has in which he leaves one room in order to go to another identical room and then another, and has to remember which room he went into first in order to be able to wake up, as well as the story of how Aureliano Segundo is mixed up with another José Arcadio Segundo, and they do not know who is buried in which grave. Beneath all of these stories – which are like tributaries streaming from the central narrative stream of the novel which identifies the double as the generator of apocalypse – is, as we have seen, the fear of the double encapsulated by the existence of a double family, illegitimate and legitimate, as created by Colonel Nicolás Márquez.

6

'A chancellor but we don't know of which country'[1]

As a result of winning the Nobel Prize in 1982, García Márquez took on the status of a rock star, a musician and a head of state, all rolled into one. What was even more extraordinary was how the novel that had earned him the Nobel Prize – *One Hundred Years of Solitude* – had hit on a formula which was then taken up by a number of writers not only in Latin America but further afield. It led to a number of 're-makes' in the Hispanic literary world, notably Isabel Allende's *The House of the Spirits* (1982), Laura Esquivel's *Like Water for Chocolate* (1989) and Luis Sepúlveda's *The Old Man who Read Love Stories* (1993).[2] But perhaps just as significant were the reformulations of the magical-realist mode of narrative which emerged in non-Hispanic countries, such as Salman Rushdie's *Midnight's Children* (1980), Nakagami Kenji's *A Thousand Years of Pleasure* (1982), William Kennedy's *Ironweed* (1983), Patrick Süskind's *Perfume* (1985), Tahar Ben Jelloun's *L'Enfant du sable* (*Sand Boy*, 1985), José Saramago's *The Stone Raft* (1986), Amitav Ghosh's *The Circle of Reason* (1986), Toni Morrison's *Beloved* (1987) and Ben Okri's *The Famished Road* (1991).

One of the reasons why magical realism appears to have attracted the attention of a wide range of writers is its ability to express 'a world fissured, distorted, and made incredible by cultural displacement'.[3] As Jean-Pierre Durix memorably puts it: 'Imperialistic powers deprived the colonized people not only of their territories and wealth but also of their imagination',[4] and, indeed, a novel such as Rushdie's *Midnight's Children* sought to remedy this by using García Márquez's formula. It was as a result of its intrinsic heterogeneity rather than its syncretism that the discourse of magical realism was able to migrate from Latin America to various cultural shores around the world. Particularly for writers in countries which had recently escaped from the clutches of colonialism, magical realism appeared to become, in Homi Bhabha's words, 'the literary language of the emergent postcolonial world'.[5]

García Márquez soon found himself fawned on by the media, invited to give lectures all round the world, and editors and publishers fell over themselves trying to get his next book. As he once told Vargas Llosa: 'I have a letter of a Spanish editor who offered me the use of his estate in Palma de Mallorca and to provide my upkeep while there for as long as I wanted in exchange for my next novel. I told him that he had probably got the wrong address, because I am not a prostitute.'[6] He started complaining about journalists who would come to see him, get drunk with him until two in the morning and then put things in their article which were said off the record.[7] So, rather than give countless interviews, he decided to use his recently won fame to help out an old friend, Plinio Apuleyo, a man who had stuck with him through thick and thin. They brought out together a collection of their conversations entitled *El olor del guayaba: conversaciones con Gabriel García Márquez* (*The Fragrance of Guava: Conversations with Gabriel García Márquez*, 1982), certainly the best source for insight into how García Márquez's mind works.[8] Indeed, Plinio proved himself to be the perfect foil for García Márquez not just because he knew him so well but because his skill at comic story-telling almost equals that of the great man himself.

After the award of the Nobel Prize the pressure on García Márquez to produce brilliant pieces of work became immense – indeed it has continued to the present day[9] – and yet he did not disappoint his readers. In 1985 he published *El amor en los tiempos del cólera* (*Love in the Time of Cholera*), the novel that many of his readers had been eagerly awaiting since it was touted as the story of the love affair of his parents. García Márquez wrote a substantial part of the text while staying in Cartagena; before returning to Mexico, and clearly unnerved by the Colombian government's statement about his political affiliation (see above, p. 17–18), he left an uncorrected copy of the manuscript with his sister Margot with the instruction that if he returned she should give it to him, but if not, then she should destroy it, in case anyone were to steal it after his death. When Gabo got to Mexico he rang his sister to confirm that he had arrived safely, and instructing her to destroy the manuscript. Margot burnt it page by page, and wondered years later how much it would be worth today.[10] The novel turned out to be an enormous success, second only in volume of print-runs to *One Hundred Years of Solitude*.

Like all of García Márquez's novels *Love in the Time of Cholera* is a patchwork of various events and episodes taken from his personal life, and given a playful twist to heighten their intensity.[11] As García Márquez pointed out in an interview published in 1988, the novel is based on his parents' love affair but the story is refracted through the prism of another story – one he read in a newspaper about two lovers who had met secretly over a period of fifty years, all the while keeping up the pretence of being happily married to their respective spouses; their story had come out when they had been murdered by a tour guide for $14.[12] The story itself is included in the novel; the news cutting is sent by Florentino Ariza to Fermina Daza 'without any comment', although it is intended as a poignant comment on their own relationship: 'the police had discovered that the elderly couple beaten to death were clandestine lovers who had taken their vacations together for forty years, but who each had a stable and happy marriage as well as very large families.'[13]

Gabriel Eligio wooed Luisa Santiaga but the latter's family were opposed to his offer of marriage and, in order to forestall any blossoming of love, sent Luisa off on a long trip to the mountains. Because Gabriel Eligio was a telegraphist he was able to keep in touch with Luisa and when she finally returned he renewed his offer; eventually the family relented and García Márquez's parents were married on 11 June 1926.[14] The love affair between Gabriel Eligio and Luisa Santiaga was clearly legendary in the family and its narration had an impact on all the children, not just Gabo; Jaime, for example, was clearly moved by the intensity with which his mother would remember the poems that his father sent her when she was banished from Aracataca to La Guajira province.[15] To this García Márquez added the story from the newspaper of a clandestine love kept secret for over fifty years, thereby allowing his novel to take a different path. Florentino Ariza falls in love with Fermina Daza, offers his hand in marriage, is refused, and Fermina is sent away to the Andes for a year, but – and here the novel diverges from the life – when she returns, she decides she no longer loves Florentino: 'Today, when I saw you, I realized that what is between us is nothing more than an illusion' (*Love in the Time of Cholera*, pp. 107–8), and she opts for a safe marriage with a local doctor, Juvenal Urbino. Florentino decides to wait for her, which means waiting for more than fifty years, until Juvenal Urbino dies.

García Márquez's decision to allow Fermina Daza two lovers rather than one – as in Luisa Santiaga's case – enables him to explore different facets of love. These range from the mundane day-to-day of official married love, characterized by stability (as Juvenal Urbino remarks, 'the most important thing in a good marriage is not happiness, but stability', p. 320), but also by childish arguments about whether or not there is soap in the bathroom (pp. 28–30), to love of the hopeless, pathetic, Romantic type with a big 'R' that Florentino aspires to. As Fermina's cousin, Hildebranda, says of him: 'He is ugly and sad . . . but he is all love' (p. 135). Such is his love for Fermina that he waits for her for more than fifty years; he plays love songs for her in the cemetery so that the wind will carry their melody to her; he buys the mirror in which he saw her reflection for two hours in order to keep an (elusive) memory of her. The difference between physical and spiritual love, love 'from the waist up' and 'from the waist down' (p. 42), is also played on.[16] Despite the very high number of his love affairs and brief sexual encounters (he has 532 of them) Florentino still manages to believe that his love for Fermina transcends the physical love he has experienced with hundreds of women, such that he can say to her: 'I've remained a virgin for you' (p. 362). But perhaps most importantly, García Márquez's use of the contrasting lovers as a narrative device allows him to present different times and perspectives occurring simultaneously; while we trace the main events of Fermina's marriage, we are made aware at crucial junctures that, all the while, Florentino is waiting in the wings. A cogent example of this occurs during the Juegos Florales event when Fermina, now a local dignitary, announces the winner of a poetry competition. Florentino has attended the event just to in order to catch a glimpse of her, and also perhaps to hear her read out his name should he win the competition, but his presence there leads to his first chance encounter with Sara Noriega, with whom he will have an affair (pp. 206–8).

The novel is shaped like a cyclical vortex: it mentions events, then traces the history that led to them; this then allows the reader to understand the events' significance, and finally to re-vision events from a different perspective. In the first chapter of the novel, for example, we see Juvenal Urbino discovering the suicide of his friend Jeremiah de Saint-Amour, visiting the body, then returning home, falling off a ladder and killing himself while attempting to capture a parrot;[17] as well as a man called Florentino declaring his eternal love to a woman, Fermina, who has just lost her husband – and it is only later on that the full significance of these events emerges. Jeremiah de Saint-Amour's love for a mulatto woman who lives in the suburbs is significant because it echoes the secret love affair Juvenal Urbino had years before with Barbara Lynch, a black woman on the outskirts of the city, and it introduces the theme of clandestine love running through the novel; it also echoes Florentino's concealed love for Fermina which gradually emerges as the novel wends its way forward.

The structure of the novel is episodic and picaresque, rather than chronological in the nineteenth-century sense; it is centrifugal and meandering, having the structure of a river with inlets and rivulets, which act like sub-plots of a story which gradually, like the River Magdalena, meanders down to the sea. Thus the narrative works in terms of eddies and undercurrents, whereby time goes backwards, and we re-vision past events. Thus, as mentioned above, we witness Florentino going to the Poetic Festival (pp. 201–6), and then we hear about Fermina's recollections of those events when they discuss them during the boat journey on the Nueva Fidelidad:

> He told her with what longing he had watched her at the Poetic Festival, on the balloon flight, on the acrobat's velocipede, with what longing he had waited all year for public festivals just so he could see her. She had often seen him as well, and she had never imagined that he was there only to see her. However, it was less than a year since she had read his letters and wondered how it was possible that he had never competed in the Poetic Festival; there was no doubt he would have won. Florentino Ariza lied to her: he wrote only for her, verses for her, and only he read them. (pp. 356–57)

All of these events – the Juegos Florales which occurs every year on the 15th of April, the journey in the air balloon, the ride on the acrobat's velocipede – have been described in detail by the narrator, and this allows the reader, in a very Proustian way, to re-experience these events as memories, and also – again in a very Proustian way – to see these memories being refashioned before our very eyes. We know that Florentino had submitted poems in a vain attempt to experience the pleasure of forcing Fermina to read out his name in public (pp. 203–4), and yet we also see the reason why he now lies to her: Florentino uses words, he uses letters, he uses poems with one sole aim: to seduce Fermina. García Márquez shows seduction to be a highly skilled activity, requiring planning, ingenuity, intelligence and determination. Even when he is on the boat with Fermina, he still needs to write letters to her, and send a white rose (p. 351–52). It is because Florentino alludes to his love poems that Fermina finally reaches out for him: 'Then it was she who reached for his hand in the darkness' (p. 357). This seduction scene also takes on more significance since it is overlaid with the reader's memory of the seduction scene which occurred immediately after the Juegos Florales many years earlier, when Florentino is seduced by the voluminous Sara Noriega (pp. 207–8). These are the under-currents and eddies in García Márquez's narrative – the significant events of a character's life, such as Florentino proposing to Fermina, Juvenal Urbino dying as a result of trying to capture a parrot, Fermina rejecting Florentino with the words, 'No, please . . . Forget it' (p. 107) – which return to haunt the flow of text.

The narrative is also haunted by a number of mysteries. Despite the apparent control of the narrator, there are events which are left unexplained and circumstances which readers must interpret for themselves. Given América Vicuña's infatuation with Florentino, the reader might surmise that it is because she has been jilted by him (p. 338) that she commits suicide. News of the incident arrives in a telegram: 'América Vicuña dead yesterday reasons unknown' (p. 358). In fact, the deciding factor prompting Vicuña's decision to take her own life is surely the love letters that she discovers: 'América Vicuña found herself alone one Saturday afternoon in the bedroom on the Street of Windows, and without looking for them, by sheer accident, she found the typed copies of the meditations of Florentino Ariza and the handwritten letters of Fermina Daza, in a wardrobe without a key' (p. 344). The narrator reports this discovery baldly, but this lack of comment does not prevent the reader from identifying this event as the main cause of América Vicuña's death. It is up to the reader to draw their own conclusions.

Occasionally the past returns in such a way as to drown the present beneath its weight. This is the case with the revelation about the true identity of Fermina Daza's father; we learn in the final and sixth chapter of the novel – as revealed by a newspaper, *La Justicia* – that his position as a muleteer was simply a front for his illegal activities as a counterfeiter, a gun smuggler and fraudster (pp. 341–42) The only indication that something had been amiss is in Lorenzo Daza's words ('We are ruined'; p. 137) before his mysterious disappearance. The second revelation made by the press, indeed the same newspaper, has more complex ramifications. It concerns the claim made by *La Justicia* that Juvenal Urbino had had an affair with Lucrecia del Real del Obispo. The narrator describes the allegation in such a way as to question its veracity:

Justicia published a front-page story, complete with photographs of the two protagonists, about the alleged secret love affair between Dr Juvenal Urbino and Lucrecia del Real del Obispo. There speculations on the details of their relationship, the frequency of their meetings and how they were arranged, and the complicity of her husband, who was given to excesses of sodomy with the blacks on his sugar plantation. The story, published in enormous black letters in an ink the color of blood, fell like a thundering cataclysm on the enfeebled local aristocracy. Not a line of it was true: Juvenal Urbino and Lucrecia del Real had been close friends in the days when they were both single, and they had continued their friendship after their marriages, but they had never been lovers. (p. 340)

Given the status of the narrator elsewhere in the novel (he knows, for example, as much about the historical evolution of cities such as Cartagena de Indias, pp. 16–17, as he does about the intimate details of the lives of the city's inhabitants) our first reaction is to take this dismissal of the story at face value as a groundless rumour. But there are a number of details added subsequently which tend to suggest that, despite the narrator's refutation, this story may have some basis in truth. The first is that another headline story by the same newspaper about Fermina's father, Lorenzo Daza – described above – is not questioned, and simply presented as the truth. Secondly, we learn that 'Lucrecia del Real did not visit Fermina Daza again, and Fermina Daza interpreted this as a confession of guilt' (p. 340). Thirdly, Fermina insults Lucrecia del Real pointedly: 'she let Lucrecia del Real know, through anyone who would repeat it to her, that she should take comfort in having had at least one real man in the crowd of people who had passed through her bed' (p. 343).

But perhaps the most important detail is the clue written in Lucrecia's name – García Márquez often uses names to say something about a character or hint at their true identity. The clues function in a number of ways. They may be ironic – as in the case of the Antillian invalid Jeremiah de Saint-Amour; or add a certain metaphorical resonance, as with Juvenal Urbino, who is as satirical about the city he lives in as the Roman poet Juvenal was about his native Rome; another function is humour. A name that Florentino mentions, that of the German emigré, Lotario Thugut, who is known for his exceptional lovemaking abilities – he makes the whores he sleeps with scream with pleasure (pp. 65–6) – refers to the character's exceptional abilities: Thugut, when pronounced according to Spanish phonetic rules, sounds like the English 'too good' (presumably what the whores say to him during lovemaking). A key to Lucrecia's real identity, then, is hidden away in her name: Lucretia is a legendary figure of classical Rome, associated with the

Roman aristocracy and also known for her rape and subsequent suicide. As such the name may be linked to a guilty aristocratic sexuality, a latent but denied sexuality, with the names 'del Real del Obispo' (suggesting connections with the king and with the bishop), hinting playfully at where the guilt might have come from. But these are only hints and innuendoes within the name itself; it should be underlined that the only act of adultery that the narrator knows Juvenal Urbino to have committed is with Barbara Lynch (as described in chapter five, pp. 256–61). Juvenal Urbino's supposed liaison with Lucrecia del Real del Obispo is a mystery not solved in the novel, revealing the narrator of *Love in the Time of Cholera* to be as unreliable as the narrator of *Chronicle of a Death Foretold*, despite the superficial impression he gives of veracity and fidelity. Curiously, given that the novel was about him, García Márquez's father died in the year *Love in the Time of Cholera* was published, 1985.[18] Like all of his brothers, Gabo was distraught at his father's funeral; the men became a bunch of 'useless crybabies'.[19]

As a result of being gifted a *casa de protocolo* by Fidel Castro, García Márquez began to make annual visits to Cuba, normally staying in his house from December to January, in order to attend the Havana Film Festival which is held in early December. He used his newly won fame to give concrete form to an ambition he had had for many years – to set up a film school in Latin America to rival European and US film schools. He worked tirelessly on this project in the period between 1983 and 1985, teaming up with two Cubans, Tomás Gutiérrez Alea, director of *Memories of Underdevelopment* (1968) and Julio García Espinosa, former head of ICAIC, the Cuban Film School, and inventor of 'imperfect cinema', as well as the iconoclastic Argentine documentarist, Fernando Birri, who had directed *Tire Dié* (*Throw us a Dime*) in 1958. García Márquez was holding long meetings at his house in Havana in the weeks before the Cuban Film Festival of 1986 and expectations were running high that the team would be able to make an official

García Márquez with Fernando Birri, Tomás Gutiérrez Alea and Julio García Espinosa at the International Film and TV School, San Antonio de los Baños, December 1986.

announcement at the inauguration of the Cuban Film Festival that year. Alfredo Bryce Echenique saw García Márquez's political guile in action as he was closing the deal: 'I saw Gabo exercise his political skills as a man who knows what he is after and what he is going to get, while he was establishing the New Latin American Cinema Foundation. This was a project that he was setting up with the attention to detail which characterizes every project he puts his mind to.'[20] Julio García Espinosa recalls that Fidel paid him a visit in November 1986 at his apartment in Nuevo Vedado and said: 'Let's go for a walk around the block and discuss what needs to be done.' So García Espinosa went for a walk with him. Fidel asked him: 'What is it you want?' and García Espinosa replied: 'A film school.' 'A film school?' Fidel said. 'That's it?' he asked, slightly bemused. 'Yes,' Garcia Espinosa said. 'That's what Gabo wants, and that's what we want.' 'OK, fine,' Fidel said.[21]

Thus was established the Fundación del Nuevo Cine Latino-americano in Havana with García Márquez as the president and the very able Alquimia Peña as the director; the Foundation was inaugurated on 4 December 1986 during the 8th Havana International Film Festival, and on 15 December 1986 the Escuela Internacional de Cine y Televisión (EICTV) was launched. The Film School had four co-founders, García Márquez, Julio García Espinosa and Tomás Gutiérrez Alea, along with Fernando Birri, who agreed to become first director of the school. All four had once studied at the Centro Sperimentale di Cinematografia in Rome, and neo-Realism had brought them together. The EICTV was able to use a disused school building on the outskirts of San Antonio de los Baños, a city thirty miles from Havana. The inaugural meal was prepared by Duquesne Smith, Castro's chef for many years, who would often cook for Gabo and Fidel in the 1980s – a Macondo-style lobster for García Márquez and a turtle consommé for Fidel, as the chef recalled.[22] García Márquez was able to finance the early days of the EICTV, which is not funded by the Cuban government, by allowing interview fees to be remitted to the school directly. In order to appear on Melvyn Bragg's *The South Bank Show*, broadcast on ITV on 29 October 1989, he charged $30,000 for a three-hour interview.[23] García Márquez also generously agreed to give a seminar each year to the EICTV students on 'How to Write a Story', and he has continued to give his seminar to the present day, barring illness.[24] The EICTV project has also led to some important link-ups such as with the Festival Internacional de Cine y TV de Cartagena in Colombia, which has now been held annually for a number of years in February/March, and for which García Márquez has acted as the official assessor in recent years.[25]

García Márquez also used his Nobel status to give political rather than literary pronouncements. The lecture he gave in Ixtapa in Mexico on 6 August 1986, 'El cataclismo de Damocles' ('Damocles' Cataclysm'), was an impassioned plea to divert the budget expended on nuclear missiles by the two superpowers to basic education, improvement of health care, and the provision of drinking water for

Statue of Gabo at the International Film and TV School, July 2008.

all; in particular he asked those present to create an 'ark of memory' which would be capable of surviving the Armageddon of nuclear war.[26] Yet García Márquez was unable to leave behind his interest in a journalistic view of the world, and in 1986 he published *La aventura de Miguel Littín, clandestino en Chile* (*Clandestine in Chile: The Adventures of Miguel Littín*). Miguel Littín had directed *The Chacal of Nahueltoro*, a searing documentary on the failures of the social system in Chile seen through the story of a psychopath, in 1968. Littín had supported Salvador Allende unreservedly during his term of office (1970–1973), and was forced to go into exile as soon as the coup occurred (11 September 1973). Since he was on Pinochet's blacklist of 5,000 who could never be allowed to return to Chile, Littín's decision to go back to Chile and film in secret was courageous (if not a little foolhardy). As with Luis Alejandro Velasco some thirty years before, García Márquez decided to keep the narrative in the first person, allow it to move along at a brisk pace, and punctuate the text with a sense of impending danger (here, though, it is not the Caribbean's sharks the narrator fears, but Pinochet's). The narrative provides a gripping description of Littín's experiences in Chile; the highlights are Littín's shock at the splendour of Santiago[27] – he was expecting it to be more rundown; his memory of when he was detained by the police and escaped just in time (pp. 36–8); the difficulties in finding people to interview (pp. 40–42); meeting his mother-in-law though she doesn't recognize him because he is incognito (pp. 61–2), the rather comical misunderstanding about the term *rasurar* (an older term meaning 'to shave' which had been replaced in the 1980s by the more neutral term *afeitar*, pp. 72–3); the sadness of visiting Neruda's house in Isla Negra (p. 87); and the escape from the three policemen who were on to them (pp. 102–4). Clearly it is the mix of journalism and literature at which García Márquez excels. Reactions to the work varied; Salman Rushdie sent a letter to Miguel Littín criticizing him for letting himself become a García-Márquezian character,[28] while Pinochet, outraged by the book, had copies of it burnt publicly in Valparaíso in 1987.[29]

In 1986 'The Story of a Shipwrecked Sailor', his tale of Luis Alejandro Velasco's survival, was published in English, in 1987 the English translation of *Clandestine in Chile* came out, and the following year *Love in the Time of Cholera* was released in the US. In 1989 García Márquez published his novel, *El general en su laberinto* (*The General in his Labyrinth*), an extraordinary evocation of the last eight months of Simón Bolívar's life, from 8 May 1830 when he left Bogotá until 17 December 1830 when he died in Santa Marta on the coast of Colombia. García Márquez derived his fascination with Simón Bolívar, Latin America's most famous man, from his grandfather who had a portrait of Bolívar above the mantelpiece in their home in Aracataca (where Gabito lived until he was nine). The basic fundamentals of the plot are historical in the sense that Simon Bolívar did leave Bogotá on 8 May 1830, he did die on 17 December, he did have an affair with Manuela Saenz, a beautiful woman from Quito who was married to an Englishman, and his *aide-de-camp* was José Palacios, as we see in the novel. His journey along the Magdalena river is meticulously followed down to the various places he stopped on the way. The novel is even correct about his shoe size, the fact that Bolívar was ambidextrous, a good dancer and a careful eater. When Alfredo Bryce Echenique stayed with García Márquez in Cuba in his *Casa de protocolo* in the summer of 1986, he noticed how attentive García Márquez was to historical details when writing *The General in his Labyrinth*:

> I have never cared a damn whether such and such an event that I narrate in my novel happens at a certain time, or a specific day, or a year, or even in what century, I was really damaged by the Carpentieresquely historicist zeal which had got into Gabo over his Bolívar. Was there or was there not a full moon on the night when Bolívar fought such and such a battle? Did Manuelita de Saenz scratch Bolívar or did she not scratch him on the eve of that battle? Listen, Peruvian, do you know if . . . ?[30]

But, despite its attention to historical detail, the novel places an extraordinary amount of novelistic flesh on these historical bones, allowing a new perception of Bolívar to emerge, a man who was not triumphant but deeply disillusioned by the course that the independence movement was taking in the late 1820s. The last eight months of his life are among the least documented of this famous man, and this provides the Colombian writer with the opportunity to expand on what is known in order to delve into what is not known (deeper questions such as what made Simón

Bolívar tick). The conversations that Bolívar has with his *aide-de-camp* and others will be familiar to any reader of García Márquez's fiction. An example is the conversation early on in the novel between Bolívar and his steward:

'Saturday, 8 May 1830, the day the English killed Joanne of Arc', announced the steward. 'It has been raining since three o' clock in the morning.'
    'Since three o'clock in the morning of the seventeenth century,' said the General, his voice still shaken by the bitter breath of insomnia.[31]

It cannot be proved that Bolívar had this conversation with his steward on 8 May 1830 nor demonstrated that he did not have this conversation. It is extremely unlikely of course that Bolívar would have used these words which are more redolent of the existentialism of the second half of the twentieth century (one thinks of Beckett, Sartre and Camus) than the mood of the second decade of the nineteenth century. Beginning with *Leaf Storm*, García Márquez had used the weather consistently as an image of the entrapment of man within the material circumstances of his world, and the same idea is present in this exchange in the sense that the political entrapment which Bolívar feels Latin America to be experiencing on 8 May 1830 has been there not simply since three in the morning but at least as far back as the seventeenth century – the century, we hardly need reminding, that Spain began asserting its power and building a colonial society in the New World in earnest.

There are other examples of the way in which García Márquez turns Bolívar's dilemma into one that a number of the characters in his earlier fiction might have recognized as similar to their own, including the colonel in *No One Writes to the Colonel* and Santiago Nasar in *Chronicle of a Death Foretold*; the best example of this occurs in those scenes in which Bolívar, as much as those around him, becomes chillingly aware of the certainty of his impending death. Thus the English diplomat remarks of Bolívar's sending-off party, 'This looks like a funeral' (*The General in his Labyrinth*, p. 39), and a woman who sees him on his way out of Bogotá says to him: 'Go with God, phantom' (p. 40). These are the indications that Bolívar is doomed in the same way as Santiago Nasar, and reveal García Márquez playing with his material, making it unmistakeably García-Márquesian, drawing history close to his chest, making history breathe.

Likewise when there is some discrepancy in the historic record García Márquez uses this as an opportunity to provide his own personal interpretation of the facts, moulding them to suit his own thesis. There was a rumour that Simón Bolívar's family had African blood somewhere in its genealogy, and while this would not have been unusual in a family living in New Granada, it is hotly debated. Some facts suggest there might be truth in the rumour, the most significant being that Bolívar's family attempted to have the family lineage vindicated in Spain resulting from his application for recognition as a member of the nobility, which was turned down (this caused a great deal of resentment in the family, it is clear).[32] However, if one looks at the various portraits of Bolívar painted at the time (this was a pre-photographic era) the vast majority show him with clearly delineated white *criollo* features; though there are a few that show him with frizzy hair, these are in the minority.[33] Still, García Márquez chooses to depict Bolívar as a creature of the Caribbean: we first see him in the novel emerging from his bath with his 'rough Caribbean curls' (p. 10). He does not feel at home in Bogotá in the Andes, remarking 'This isn't my theatre' (p. 35, translation revised). The text following this statement underlines that it is Bolívar's Caribbeanness that leads to his sense of maladjustment: 'His voice was metallic and cracked with fever, and his Caribbean accent, which so many years of travel and the tribulations of war had not softened, sounded even harsher compared to the lush diction of the Andeans' (p. 35). It is not beyond the bounds of reason to read this particular passage as well as the section that follows, in which Bolívar rather awkwardly and cagily bids Bogotá farewell, as having an autobiographical undertow; it is no secret that García Márquez, as he suggests in his autobiography, had always felt awkward in Bogotá, finding its dreariness unbearable and its snobbishness deeply offensive.[34]

There are parts of the novel in which animal symbolism is used in order to stress the underlying meaning of the narrative.[35] The mangy stray dog found by the orderly and cleaned up is an example of this:

> They had bathed him and perfumed him with baby powder, but they could not rid him of his dissolute appearance or the stench of mange. The General was taking the air in the stern when José Palacios pulled the dog over to him.
> 'What name shall we give him?' he asked.
> The General did not even have to think about it.
> 'Bolívar,' he said. (p. 91)

In the same way that the cockerel in *No One Writes to the Colonel* is symbolic of the dead son's struggle, the pueblo's hopes for a better future and perhaps even the revolution, so the dog here symbolizes the demise of Latin America's most famous man, prematurely aged, beaten down by circumstance, betrayed by his allies to die a miserable death. One other characteristic for which the novel is justly famous is its use of the poignant one-liner, the *mot juste* which, though built on paradox (or indeed because of this), epitomize the truth of the situation. When Bolívar has the long line of widows pointed out to him by José Palacios, his response reflects the irony of his own demise: 'Now we are the orphans, the wounded, the pariahs of independence' (p. 90). Bolívar has been orphaned of his own great deed.

At times García Márquez will stage-manage history in order to set up a scene of dramatic irony. This is the case in the episode in which, one evening, everyone retires except Bolívar and Iturbide, and they discuss the War of Independence. Agustín de Iturbide could not have been a member of Bolívar's entourage in 1830 since he was already dead at the time (he was executed in 1824), but he is brought in to act as a symbol of Bolívar's own demise, having himself suffered a reverse of fortune similar to Bolívar's. He fought heroically against the Spanish in Mexico, bringing the War of Independence to a successful conclusion in 1821, and crowned himself Emperor in 1822, but was then forced to abdicate in 1823, and, after a brief period of exile, was executed in 1824. Iturbide's comment, 'I'm an exile',[36] prompts Bolivar to add: 'All of us here are exiles', and this leads to his pithy summary of the tragic irony of independence: 'The damn problem is that we stopped being Spaniards and then we went here and there and everywhere in countries that changed their names and governments so much from one day to the next we don't know where the hell we come from' (pp. 163–4). The inclusion of Iturbide is all the more curious given that García Márquez decided to suppress any reference to José de San Martín, whose appearance in the novel, one would presume, would have played into García Márquez's novelistic hands. The famous Guayaquil Conference which took place between Bolívar and San Martín on 26 July 1822, and about which historians have speculated endlessly,[37] would have been ideal material for an author interested in the enigma of historical events. One can only conclude that García Márquez does not care for history's mysteries, preferring his own.

This uncertainty of origin is then translated into a deeper, more ontological insecurity. Thus an uncertainty which has an anachronistic whiff of twentieth-century existentialism about it is allowed to emerge in Bolívar's mind as he gets closer to his own death, such that he begins to doubt his own identity. When Wilson observes that not many people seem to recognize him, Bolívar explains with a laconic statement: 'I am no longer myself' (p. 43). On seeing a steam boat with the letters 'El Libertador' on the side, Bolívar remarks: 'To think I'm that man!' (p. 114), while during a discussion with Montilla in which the latter expresses his deep allegiance to Bolívar, Bolívar cuts him short with the words: 'I don't exist' (p. 127). García Márquez also uses the various commissioned portraits of Bolívar as a means of focusing on the leitmotif of the indeterminate nature of identity. He begins with a description of one of the portraits painted in oil by José María Espinosa:

> The New Granadan artist José María Espinosa had painted his portrait in Government House in Santa Fe de Bogotá not long before the September assassination attempt, and it seemed so unlike the image he had of himself that he could not resist the impulse to discuss it with General Santana, his secretary at the time, 'Do you know who the portrait looks like?' he said.
> 'Olaya, that old man from La Mesa.' (p. 160)

The conversation is fictitious but the act of sitting for the portrait was not, and even the comment is a very apt one in that it was Espinosa's style to paint the liberator in a manner which made him look like the continuation of the line of viceroys which stretched back to the beginning of Spanish rule in the Americas.[38] The novel resumes with an intriguing section on the striking variety of ethnic hues demonstrated by Bolívar in the numerous portraits made of him at the time:

> The oldest of his portraits was an anonymous miniature painted in Madrid when he was sixteen. When he was thirty-two another was painted in Haiti, and both were faithful to his age and Caribbean character. He had a strain of African blood through a paternal great-great-grandfather, who had fathered a son by

a slavewoman, and it was so evident in his features that the aristocrats in Lima called him Sambo. But as his glory increased, the painters began to idealize him, washing his blood, mythologizing him, until they established him in official memory with the Roman profile of his statues. But Espinosa's portrait resembled no one but him, wasted at the age of forty-five by the disease he did everything to hide, even from himself, until the eve of his death. (p. 160)

The portrait that García Márquez suggests resembles 'no one but him' in the above passage is the pencil drawing from life which was done in the last year of Bolívar's life, now held in the Collection Alfredo Boulton in Caracas, and in which Bolívar appears a wasted, sad figure of a man.[39] Perhaps more important to observe is the way in which García Márquez underlines Bolívar's Caribbeanness. It is true that Bolívar's skin colour is different in many of the portraits of him which were painted in the 1810s and '20s, and it is possible that the narrative voice of the novel is correct in asserting that the two lithographs made of him in Haiti were true to his Caribbean/ African heritage; but it is also true that Bolívar has never been proved to have had African descent, and also that there are more paintings that depict him as of *criollo* descent than not. But García Márquez wished to stress Bolívar's Caribbean origins, thereby drawing him closer to himself and to Fidel Castro.

There is also a little of García Márquez in the General. When Bolívar criticizes the Frenchman at dinner with the words: 'don't try to have us do well in twenty years what you have done badly in two thousand' (p. 113), and, more poignantly, 'Damn it, please let us have our Middle Ages in peace!' (p. 113), he is using the same argument that García Márquez used in his Nobel Prize speech in 1982. And there is also something of Fidel Castro in García Márquez's portrayal of Bolívar. Though his lover, Manuela Sáenz, did not undertake secretarial duties for Bolívar, her representative in the novel does: 'The General named her curator of his archives in order to keep her near him, and this made it easy for them to make love anytime, anywhere' (p. 137); this is somewhat redolent of Fidel Castro's relationship with Celia Sanchez, his secretary as well as his lover for a number of years, something García Márquez was certainly aware of. As Huber Matos remembers: 'she was a good person, very catholic, very passionate about social justice . . . When I got there it was very clear she was sleeping with Castro. She was both his secretary and his lover. He told me she was "very useful".'[40]

Rather like Balzac's *Comédie Humaine*, García Márquez's fictional world can seem like a series of interlocking canvases– such that we may find strands of larger stories whose wider significance becomes evident in later works. In *The General in his Labyrinth*, for example, we are told about a rabid dog which bit a number of people including a young white woman who had strayed into the slaves' district, and which was eventually caught, killed and strung up:

> There were still traces of the panic caused that morning by a rabid dog that had bitten several people of various ages, among them a white woman from Castiel, who had been snooping where she had no business being, and some children from the slave quarter, who had managed to stone the dog to death themselves. The body was hanging from a tree at the school door. General Montilla had it burned, not only for reasons of hygiene but also to prevent people from trying to exorcise the dog's evil spell with African magic. (p. 150)

This is precisely the story of Sierva María, a young *criolla* who was bitten by a rabid dog, and whose story we hear about in full detail in *Del amor y otros demonios* (*Of Love and Other Demons*, 1974). When *The General in his Labyrinth* was published in the US in 1990 it was not a critical success, much less a bestseller. The *New York Times* review epitomized the general view:

> Instead of exciting his imagination, the historical facts of Bolívar's life seem to have hobbled Mr. García Márquez's formidable talents, keeping this book studiously earthbound. There are frequent passages of exposition, devoted to summaries of Bolívar's ambitions and accomplishments; and for the North American reader, at least, lengthy and confusing digressions about unfamiliar battles and political campaigns.[41]

In 1992 the collection of short stories *Doce cuentos peregrinos* (*Strange Pilgrims: Twelve Stories*) was published in Madrid, and a year later an English translation appeared in the US. In this collection García Márquez brings together stories he had been working on for the previous twelve years.[42] The basic idea behind the collection are the strange things that happen to Latin Americans in Europe ('Prólogo', p. 14); García Márquez relates that this idea came to him in a dream he had in the early 1970s when he had been living in Barcelona for five years. It was a dream in which he attended his own funeral, and it was paradoxically a joyful occasion since he was able to spend some time with friends he hadn't seen in years. When they leave he tries to follow them but is informed that he is the only one who cannot leave. This dream had been going to form the basis of the third story in the original plan for the book, but it never materialized ('Prólogo', p. 15) – this is a pity since it expresses vividly one of the central themes of García Márquez´s work, the otherness of self; it is difficult to think of a situation in which the self is more other than at one's own funeral. It is suggestive, indeed, that García Márquez should use this image of otherness to express what it means to be a Latin American in Europe since this implies that a Latin American, rather uncannily, sees a dead version of his self in Europe. It is a scene which García Márquez had projected on numerous occasions in his earlier work – it is evident as far back as 'La tercera resignación' – but being in Europe allowed the contours of that dilemma to be drawn in starker colours.

The sense of the uncanny manifests itself in different ways in different stories. 'La santa' ('The Saint'), for example, tells the fantastical story of a beautiful girl who dies at the age of seven and whose body is discovered to be not only incorruptible but also weightless. This is clearly based in part on the time García Márquez spent in Rome in the 1950s studying at the Centro Sperimentale di Cinematografia; it has a cameo performance by Cesare Zavattini, who sees the girl's body but says it will not work in a film since no one would believe it.[43] All of the stories contain a level of unsolvable mystery, as is the case with 'Maria dos Prazeres' (literally, 'Maria of Pleasures'), which ends with the question of what will happen beyond the confines of the story: will it be death, sex or love? The story itself cannot give us the answer since it lies beyond the bounds of the narrative.[44] 'El rastro de tu sangre en la nieve' ('The Trail of Your Blood in the Snow', pp. 199–226), tells the story of the love between Nena Daconte and Billy Sanchez de Avila, who first meet in Marbella, fall in love, and marry. The story opens with them driving to Paris for their honeymoon. Nena cuts her wedding-ring finger and the wound refuses to heal; she braves it out during the trip, but, given the added complication that she is two months pregnant, she needs to be hospitalized as soon as they get to Paris. Billy is unable to visit her for days because of hospital rules and, when he finally does, he discovers that not only has she died but he has missed the funeral. Gerald Martin has convincingly argued that this strange, unreal tale is a veiled fictionalization of Gabo's love affair with Tachia in Paris in the 1950s, which ended in tragedy and abortion.[45] The best of the stories in this collection, 'Buen viaje, señor Presidente' ('Bon Voyage Mr President'), focuses on the strange encounter between an ambulance driver and an exiled president, both from the

Caribbean and now living in Switzerland; the former hopes to fleece the latter, but – in an odd, unexpected political twist – ends up taking pity on the president, and even paying his hospital bills. Human compassion is seen to win out over and above any political *parti pris*.

7

'The Third Pope'

In 1994 García Márquez published *Del amor y otros demonios* (*Of Love and Other Demons*; English translation 1995). It is a strong piece of fiction drawn from the rich vein of Colombia's archive of popular stories, particularly slave narratives, which underlines the strong connectiveness between fantasy, the world of the emotions, and blackness. More conventional in structure than some of his earlier works,[1] it tells the story of a young girl called Sierva María who is believed to be possessed by demons and is therefore imprisoned in the convent of Santa Clara, and examined and exorcized by her confessor, Cayetano Delaura, on the instruction of the bishop. The suspicion raised in the text is that what is understood to be the work of the devil by the Church – whose members are white, *criollo*, and racist – is simply the result of Sierva María's awareness of African religions. The magic of the African religion is centred on her necklace which she will let no one take off. When it is forcefully taken away from her, this leads to one of the party slipping and fracturing her skull. Sierva María is not only black, she is also, as her name indicates, associated with the slaves who were brought in their hordes to Colombia and specifically to Cartagena. It begins with the gloss of a modern journalist, clearly a projection of García Márquez as a young man. Sierva María is also a symbol of the magical-real in that her hair has never been cut and is twenty metres long. The novel is built around a number of oppositions, including white versus black, master versus slave, male versus female, reason versus superstition, and the real versus the magical. Sierva María, in her uncouthness (she bites, spits, fights, and never washes) is worlds apart from her confessor, Delaura, who was educated at the University of Salamanca. And yet the story tells how he gradually falls in love with her, and falls under her spell.

In a sense *Of Love and Other Demons* can be seen as a re-enactment of the drama of colonization. The novel reveals that the archive from which García Márquez draws inspiration for his magical-realist style is the African heritage of Colombia, epitomized here by Sierva María and the characteristics she represents. It is her magical nature that enables her to cause a bishop's confidant to fall desperately in love with her; she is African and speaks a number of African languages; she is superstitious – having fought tooth and nail to keep her necklace (which, when stolen, leads to the thief's demise); she is a slave, having been imprisoned by the bishop; she is fully at one with the power of the imagination (she dreams Cayetano Delaura's dream looking out on a snow-covered field in Salamanca many years before when he was training to become a priest); and she is intimately associated with vitality in that even when she dies her eyes are 'radiant' and her skin looks like that of a new-born baby. Sierva María's ability to conquer death is implied by the fact that her hair grows back on her shaven head, and 'strands of hair gushed like bubbles' (p. 160),[2] thereby suggesting that the novel ends on a note of magical realism. Indeed the hair which forms 'like bubbles' is also visually associated with the 'cluster of golden grapes, that grew back as soon as she ate them' (p. 160). The novel also weaves in a strand drawn from *Love in the Time of Cholera*, exploring the relationship between disease and love: it is not known whether Sierva María has rabies (although an objective analysis of the evidence would suggest that she does, since she is known to have been bitten by a rabid dog, and the other four individuals who were bitten by the same gray-haired dog had all subsequently died), or whether she is overwhelmed with love, or indeed protected from disease by the African

talismans which she wears. She is assumed by many to be a devil –
the warden calls her the 'beast of Beelzebub' (p. 148), she is thought
to be invisible, and the bishop has decided to have her exorcized –
but the truth of the matter is that she is deeply in love with Cayetano;
when touched by him she emits a 'sea breeze' (p. 137), and they read
Garcilaso's love poems to each other ecstatically (pp. 136–7).

García Márquez has always been a person to experiment in
different genres and he wrote a play, *Diatriba de amor contra un
hombre sentado* ('Diatribe of Love at a Man Sitting Down'), which
had been completed in November 1987, and was staged on 23
March 1994 at the National Theatre in Bogotá, Colombia, during
the Fourth Iberoamerican Theatre Festival, starring Laura García
as the lead (and indeed only) character. In a non-stop diatribe
directed at her husband, who does not answer back (the stage
directions clarify that he is a 'dummy'), on their silver wedding
anniversary,[3] Natalia laments how their love has grown cold
over the years. The monologue, in a clear departure from García
Márquez's rather wooden style of dialogue, is agile, nuanced
and passionate.

Politics were never far from García Márquez's agenda. In the
1990s he and Carlos Fuentes had an interview with President Bill
Clinton – and García Márquez had a second personal interview
with him – and one of the issues they discussed was the Cuban
blockade. García Márquez's impression was that Bill Clinton did
not have a clear anti-blockade policy and was more worried that
removing the blockade would create internal political problems
and jeopardize his success in the upcoming elections.[4]

In 1996 Garcia Marquez published *Noticia de un secuestro* (*News
of a Kidnapping*; English translation 1997) which is as much about
a story as about the way in which people tell each other stories.
It follows in the vein of the investigative New Journalism initiated
in Colombia some forty years before in his 'Story of a Shipwrecked
Sailor', and tells the dramatic tale of a number of hostages who

were held by Pablo Escobar's men in the early 1990s. Like his earlier narrative, *News of a Kidnapping* is meticulously researched and based on a series of oral interviews with a number of people, a written account by the protagonist (Maruja Pachón), as well as extensive background research of the political as much as the media backdrop. Though mainly based on the experience of one protagonist, Maruja Pachón, who was kept in a safe house in north Bogotá for 193 days (p. 301)[5] – thus the book begins with her kidnapping and ends with her release – the novel also intercalates a number of stories into this central narrative. These include the story of Pacho Santos (who was liberated at the same time as Maruja as part of Escobar's plea-bargaining to ensure that he would not be extradited to the United States if he gave himself up), Beatriz Villamizar de Guerrero (who was captured with Maruja but released early; pp. 94–5), Marina Montoya (who was murdered by her captors; p. 147), and Diana Turbay (killed during a bungled attempt by the Elite Corps to release her; pp. 164–9).

The novel manages skilfully to recreate the sense of foreboding experienced by the hostages and their relatives by keeping each of the stories separate from each other. Thus when Marina is taken away one night, supposedly to another *finca*, the truth of what will happen to her is kept from Maruja and Beatriz since their television and radio is also taken away. This withholding of information is also experienced by the reader: chapter five ends on an enigmatic note, and it is only when we turn to chapter six to read that 'At dawn the next day, Thursday 24th, Marina Montoya's body was found . . .' (p. 147), that we discover the truth. The horror of Marina's death is enhanced by the strange visions of death that she experienced before her actual death, as related by the other hostages (a man dressed in black in the laundry room looking at her; someone that only she could see; pp. 140–41). The novel also builds up the tension expertly by having the same sequence of events occur in the narrative when Beatriz is later taken away: 'the same door that opened, the same phrase that could equally mean a death sentence or freedom; the same enigma about her fate' (p. 189). At each point that a hostage is released the reader is kept in the dark about what will happen; thus we do not believe that Maruja and Pacho will be released until it happens. García Márquez avoids prolepsis and favours a style of narration in which the narrator knows as little as the reader. *News of a Kidnapping* manages to combine the narrative of the personal plight of a group of individuals with a disarmingly perceptive portrayal of behind-the-scenes negotiations in political circles, as well as the use of the media to influence public opinion and send coded messages to the hostages, always with the aim of heightening the drama of the events whether they occur in the political, personal or religious spheres.

In January 1998 Pope John Paul II visited Cuba. Fidel Castro, having moved on from the anti-religious orthodoxy of the early years of the Revolution (Castro is famous for having banned Christmas in the Revolution), had been making more conciliatory gestures of late towards Catholicism. He had had some long discussions with Frei Betto, a Brazilian theologian of the Liberation Theology persuasion, and their dialogues had been published in 1995.[6] A constant theme turning up in the book is the idea that, if Christ had lived today, he would have wanted to create a society like Cuba's. Castro had even given permission for Christmas to be celebrated in the late 1990s. Pope John Paul II's visit to Cuba on 21–5 January 1998 was thus a historic event because it was not only the first time he had been welcomed since Fidel Castro rose to power, but also because it was the first time a pope had ever visited the island nation. Castro invited García Márquez to Cuba as his personal guest during the Pope's visit, a gesture which showed the extraordinary closeness of the friendship between Castro and Gabo. So close is their relationship, indeed, that, immediately after welcoming the Pope to Cuba, Fidel Castro went to the *casa del protocolo* to pay Gabo and Mercedes a visit.[7] On 25 January the Pope held a special mass in Revolution Square in Havana, which was attended by thousands, and García Márquez sat in the front row next to Fidel Castro. While watching García Márquez sitting next to Fidel in front of John Paul II, the Spanish writer, Manuel Vázquez Montalbán, suddenly saw the Colombian writer as 'the Third Pope'.[8]

Over the years, indeed, the 'Third Pope' had been sending his manuscripts to Fidel to see if he could catch any errors. Thus he had sent him 'The Story of a Shipwrecked Sailor' and Fidel pointed out that the velocity of the boat was wrong since it would not have arrived when it did had it been going at that speed. He also pointed out an error in the description of the hunting rifle specified in *Chronicle of a Death Foretold*. Both of these errors were corrected before publication.[9] Likewise when Castro read the manuscript of *Of Love and Other Demons* he advised García Márquez to make the horse on which a man was riding a few years older, since an eleven-month-old horse was a small colt; García Márquez then changed the age of the horse to a hundred years old.[10] The Peruvian novelist Bryce Echenique has some perceptive words about their friendship:

> If there was anyone who could criticise Cuba, while being in Cuba, and to Fidel's face, it was Gabo. And, if this extraordinary writer who is also good natured (even though he can see through anything, including tar) has always been seen as the loyal suporter of Castro par excellence, the last remaining to date as I prose these pages, perhaps I believe that Gabo used to live in Cuba because it was there that they would leave him in peace, let him work in peace, make decisions in peace, cut himself off when he felt like it, and because the Caribbean has always been his favourite cup of tea, as the English say.[11]

Although García Márquez has noted his agreement with Julio Cortázar's axiom that 'There is nothing which kills a writer more rapidly than forcing him to represent his country', as Manuel

Vázquez Montalbán has argued, García Márquez, nevertheless, does represent Colombia and, to a certain degree, Cuba as well as Fidel Castro.[12] As Enrique Santos Calderón, editor-in-chief of *El Tiempo*, once said of García Márquez's fame in Colombia: 'In a country that's gone to the dogs, Gabo is a symbol of national pride.'[13]

In 1998 García Márquez decided he would try his hand at being a publisher, and on 25 November 2008, he, Mercedes, and some journalists purchased the Colombian cultural and political magazine, *Cambio*, which had reported a succession of falling circulation figures in the late 1990s. García Márquez bought it with the Nobel Prize money he had kept deposited in a Swiss bank for sixteen years; as he told Jon Lee Anderson, 'I swear it's true; I forgot about that money.'[14] A party was held in Bogotá in late January to celebrate the magazine's rebirth, attended by 2,000 invited guests. García Márquez regarded the purchase as a way of getting back to his journalistic roots. As he told journalists at the event launch: 'Journalism is the only trade I like, and I have always regarded myself as a journalist.' But things changed after he won the Nobel Prize. 'Nobody would employ me because it was too expensive. So now I pay so that I can be published.'[15] He began publishing articles in *Cambio*, and one article proved to be particularly explosive, in which he defended Bill Clinton's affair with Monica Lewinsky: 'The President only wanted to do something that ordinary men have done behind the backs of their wives since the beginning of the world, and Puritan obtuseness not only prevented him from doing it but even denied him the right to deny it. It is one thing to lie in order to deceive, and something altogether different to hide the truth in order to preserve this mythic instance of the human being that is one's private life.'[16] His reasoning infuriated feminists around the world.

Whether as a result of García Márquez's fame (some have called it the Midas touch) or as a result of the controversial nature of his articles, the magazine's fortune was transformed. In the first month newsstand sales doubled to more than 6,000, and circulation rose

Cuban President Fidel Castro with García Márquez during a dinner at the closing of the Cuban Cigars Festival, Havana, Cuba, 4 March 2000.

to 45,000. García Márquez said that *Cambio* was finding a new journalistic niche, one that avoided 'the scoop syndrome' and instead aspired to 'journalism as a literary genre'. What readers really want is for reporters 'to tell a story, to go back to the time when a reader could know what happened as if he were there himself'.[17] *Chronicle of a Death Foretold* springs to mind. García Márquez stayed until midnight at the event launch, then went back to the office to write a long article about Venezuela's recently elected president, Hugo Chávez, which he finished as the sun was rising, just ahead of deadline. 'It's been 40 years since I've done that,' he said, delight in his voice. 'It was wonderful.'[18]

And then disaster struck. In June 1999 in Bogotá García Márquez was hospitalized with fatigue. He decided to seek a second opinion,

and went to Los Angeles in September of that year, where his son
Rodrigo lives. He was diagnosed with lymphatic cancer, and when
news of his illness leaked out soon afterwards, in July 1999, a hoax
letter in rather bad taste was circulated on the internet, entitled
'Farewell Letter from Gabriel García Márquez'. It began as follows:

> Gabriel García Márquez, famous writer from Colombia, and
> Nobel Prize winner for literature, has retired from public life for
> reasons of health. He has a form of cancer, which is terminal.
> He has sent a farewell letter to his friends. 'If God, for a second,
> forgot what I have become and granted me a little bit more of life,
> I would use it to the best of my ability. I wouldn't, possibly, say
> everything that is in my mind, but I would be more thoughtful
> of all I say. I would give merit to things not for what they are
> worth, but for what they mean to express . . .'[19]

A rather maudlin letter, it concluded as follows:

> Keep your loved ones near you; tell them in their ears and to
> their faces how much you need them and love them. Love them
> and treat them well; take your time to tell them 'I am sorry';
> 'forgive me', 'please', 'thank you', and all those loving words you
> know. Nobody will know you for your secret thoughts. Ask the
> Lord for wisdom and strength to express them. Show your
> friends and loved ones how important they are to you. Send
> this letter to those you love. If you don't do it today, tomorrow
> will be like yesterday, and if you never do it, it doesn't matter
> either, the moment to do it is now. For you, With much love,
> Your Friend, Gabriel García Márquez.[20]

A number of people took the letter seriously at first, until it was
revealed that it had in fact been written by the Mexican ventriloquist
Johnny Welch, and falsely attributed to Márquez. In a subsequent

interview García Márquez commented: 'Lo que más me puede matar es la vergüenza de que alguien crea que de verdad fui yo quien escribió una cosa tan cursi' ('What really mortifies me is the shame that someone would really believe it was me who wrote such a pretentious poem').[21] García Márquez's vigorous struggle against cancer, in effect a rebuttal of this letter, continues to this day (indeed, it is extraordinary how many people still believe the letter to be authentic). García Márquez returns frequently to Los Angeles for his check-ups; he has to date had three outbreaks of the cancer.

García Márquez's support of the Cuban regime in general and Fidel Castro in particular has not faltered over the years. He wrote a warm, personal prologue for Castro's essay, 'Mañana será demasiado tarde' ('Tomorrow Will be Too Late', 2000), written in response to the collapse of the Soviet Union in 1991. It paints an intimate picture of the friendship between the two men, both of whom suffer from stage fright. As Castro once wrote to Gabo when inviting him to an official event in Cuba: 'Try to conquer for once your stage fright [*Miedo escénico*] as I have done on many occasions.'[22] García Márquez also noted that 'the "we" that he often uses to refer to his own actions is not as self-aggrandising [*mayestático*] as it at first appears; rather it is a poetic license designed to cover up his shyness' (p. 10). On 15 March 2000 García Márquez wrote an article in *Cambio* about Elián González, the young boy who had started a political tug of war between Cuba and the United States. On 22 November 1999 a Cuban, Juan Miguel González, discovered that his ex-wife, Elizabet Brotons, had kidnapped their son, Elián, and had escaped with him to Miami. Fidel Castro had turned it into a war of propaganda against the United States, and García Márquez, following Fidel's line, criticized Elián's mother as well as the extended family in Miami who were fighting tooth and nail to keep Elián in the US.[23] The article, published in English in the *New York Times* on 29 March 2000, was a small masterpiece; it told the story in the style of New Journalism, following the model used in 'Story of a Shipwrecked Sailor', allowing us to enter the world of the two parents locked in a tug of war over Elián, and keeping its political punch for the end:

> Nobody in Miami seems to care about the harm being done to Elián's mental health by the cultural uprooting to which he is being subjected. At his sixth birthday party, celebrated on 6 December in his Miami captivity, his host took a picture of him wearing a combat helmet, surrounded by weapons and wrapped in the flag of the United States, just a short while before a boy of his age in Michigan shot a classmate to death with a handgun. In other words, the real shipwreck of Elián did not take place on the high seas, but when he set foot on America soil.[24]

García Márquez's *parti pris*, predictably enough, was fiercely criticized by Vargas Llosa,[25] who wrote of the 'chilling cynicism' of Fidel Castro's campaign, which 'manipulated' the Elián case so that for months 'no one talked of the satrapy he created or the catastrophic economic condition that the Cuban people suffer, only of the boy martyr'.[26]

Despite Vargas Llosa's words, García Márquez's fame continued to grow in the new millennium. In an indication of how widespread the author's fame had become, a recipe book was published in Havana in 2000 describing how to prepare a Macondo-style lobster; its author was the chef Gilberto Smith who had often prepared meals for García Márquez when he was a special guest of Fidel Castro.[27] Julio García Espinosa, the co-founder of the Cuban Film Institute and a close personal friend of the Colombian writer, told me that whenever García Márquez comes to Havana he always likes to go to a restaurant where there is at least a three-man band playing (García Márquez is an excellent singer, particularly of *vallenatos* of which he is very fond).[28] Despite his increasing celebrity, in 2001 the 180 pages of the galley proofs of *One Hundred Years of Solitude*, containing the author's handwritten corrections, given by García Márquez to Luis Alcoriza and Janet Riesenfeld and now in a third party's hands, were auctioned at Christie's in Barcelona – but the manuscripts were not sold.[29] Christie's put the galley proofs up for auction once more, this time in London, on 20 November 2002, as Lot 106, Sales No. 642. The reserve of £300,000 was not reached, and the bid was subsequently withdrawn.

Spurred on by a sense of his own mortality, García Márquez decided to finish off a project that he had been working on for a number of years, his autobiography. *Vivir para contarla* was eventually published with great fanfare in Mexico City in October 2002, and the English translation, *Living to Tell the Tale*, was published the following year in the US. The autobiography is an extraordinary piece of work, more fiction than empiric fact, and has become one of García Márquez's most popular books. The main problem – apart from, for some readers, its literariness – is that it ends, after more than 500 well-crafted pages, in 1955 when García Márquez is about to leave for his journalistic assignment in Europe. There are those, like Ricardo Bada, who see *Living to Tell the Tale* as an exercise in self-aggrandisement since the autobiography reads more like a novel than an objective, personal account of the events of an individual's life, and there are others – such as Efraín Kristal – who see the novelistic qualities of the autobiography as a strength.[30] Indeed, it is not clear where the dividing line between fact and fiction falls in *Living to Tell the Tale*, that is, it is difficult to ascertain which events might be described as empirically valid and which are fictionalized versions.

It is clear that the autobiography is as fictional as the fiction is real, that is to say that – in García Márquez's literary system – no credible distinction is drawn between reality, fiction, history or autobiography. His autobiography in fact wilfully deconstructs the traditional notion of autobiography as an objective, empiric and chronological account in the first person of a sequence of events experienced by the writer. Thus *Living to Tell the Tale* eschews chronology: it begins with the description of a journey that García Márquez made as a young man with his mother from Baranquilla to Aracataca to help her sell the family home. It uses the people who cross his path during the journey back as a device to reconstruct the past of those individuals as it relates to his life (i.e., it uses flashback). It also deliberately stresses the connection between fiction and life by, at frequent intervals, showing how the events recounted in the novels are relived within the narrative. During the train journey, for example, he recalls the impression that the town with the name of Macondo had on him as young man, and also how he used the associations surrounding the name in his famous novel, *One Hundred Years of Solitude* (1967). Walking with his mother towards the town of Aracataca from the station reminds him of the sequence of events in the short story, 'La siesta del martes', which describes a woman arriving in town with her daughter to put flowers on the grave of her son who had been shot while attempting to break into García Márquez's aunt's house. 'I feel as I were the thief '[31] he says to himself; his auto-biographical self is beginning to live the life of the characters in his fiction. Just as significant, he refers to the fact that he is reading a Spanish translation of Faulkner's *Light in August* at the time.[32] All of these details – as well as the description of his mother and father's love affair referred to above (pp. 129–32) – contrive to give an irreducibly literary feel to the narrative of the autobiography.

The literary turn of García Márquez's autobiography reveals something more interesting than simply that the Colombian novelist is an inveterate fictionalizer. It draws attention to the fact that there is no ground zero of empiric, historical or objective fact in García Márquez's writing system. If we were to propose the common-sense view that reality is first of all worked into an objective, empiric account before achieving expression as a literary text, we would need to rec-ognize that García Márquez's writing system draws no distinction between the empiric account and the literary version. This has important implications in more general terms of how we should consider García Márquez's fiction. Thus one of the central issues governing criticism of his work has been the extent to which his fiction 'exaggerates' reality. A good example is the description of the suppression of the banana plantation workers in Ciénaga in 1928 by the United Fruit Company; how many workers were really killed on that day? Was it three, or was it (as *One Hundred Years of Solitude* suggests) more like 3,000? García Márquez discusses this issue but he does not provide a fact-hungry critic with any satisfaction: 'I kept the number of the dead at three thousand, in order to preserve the epic proportions of the drama.'[33] By emphasizing that the impact of the event meant that 3,000 was truer to the event than three, and by implying that a government official had held a minute's silence for the 3,000 workers killed meant that his version of events had won the day.[34] It is not that García Márquez is attempting to pull the wool over the reader's eyes, it is simply that his writing system excludes from view any ground-zero, objective-empirical-historical account of events. On this point his autobiography is very consistent with his fiction. The fact that his fiction is as real as his autobiography is fictional has broader implications for García Márquez's creation of magical-realist genre in fiction. His fiction collapses the difference between reality, the empiric account and the literary version, so that what is real is also literary (i.e., magical) and what is magical (i.e., literary) is also real. Given that this has been such a winning formula in García Márquez's hands, it is perhaps not surprising that he should continue to use it when writing the truth of his own life. When I met García Márquez in December 2007 in Havana at the Fundación del Nuevo Cine Latinoamericano I asked him if he was intending to publish the remaining volumes of his autobiography. He said he was, but that it was slow work.

The publication in 2004 of his novel *Memorias de mis putas tristes* (the English translation, *Memories of My Melancholy Whores*, followed a year later) came as something of a surprise to García Márquez's readers. Given that the first volume of his memoirs had come out only two years before – and had quickly become one of his most popular books – the natural next step seemed to be volume two. The novel, which was noticeably light-weight in comparison to the bulky first volume of the memoirs, told the story of an old man who decided on his ninetieth birthday to buy himself a night of passion with an adolescent virgin using the services of the local brothel's madam, Rosa Cabarcas; gradually, however, the old man falls in love with Delgadina, the young prostitute who has been provided to him by Rosa. The narrator has some things in common with his creator – like García Márquez he is a journalist[35] and his parents sound quite similar to García Márquez's grandparents ('He had been a spoilt child with a mother of many gifts who had been destroyed by TB at fifty, and with a strict father who had never been known to make an error and who was found dead in his widow's bed the day they signed the Neerlandia treaty, which put an end to the War of a Thousand Days' (p. 16). He also has features in common with other García Márquez characters: he keeps a book listing his sexual exploits ('At twenty years I began to keep a record with the name, age, place and a brief description of the circumstances and style. By the age of fifty I had been with 514 women on at least one occasion'; p. 16) – in this he is strikingly similar to Florentino in *Love in the Time of Cholera*. There are a number of themes in *Memories of My Melancholy Whores* which resonate with earlier works by García Márquez. Like *Love in the Time of Cholera*, the novel is built around the struggle between loveless sex and sexless love; it features a number of scenes set in the local brothel or that centre around the everyday life of prostitutes (as in 'Innocent Eréndira' and *Chronicle of a Death Foretold*), and it focuses obsessively on mortality and death (as do *One Hundred Years of Solitude* and *Love in the Time of Cholera*); however it marks a departure from García Márquez's marked preference for third-person objectivist narrative in that this novel – and here the intervening influence of *Living to Tell the Tale* may have been crucial – it is written in the first person. In many ways *Memories of My Melancholy Whores* might be seen as a minor spin-off from *Love in the Time of Cholera* in that its final message is that true love will finally win the day – suggested by the narrator's bout of destructive madness when he suspects that Delgadina's virginity has been taken by someone else (p. 90), as well as the late revelation that Delgadina has also fallen helplessly in love with him ('That poor creature is head over heels in love with you'; p. 109).

The novel was not to everyone's taste. Writing for the *Wall Street Journal*, Lauren Weiner argued that 'the usual García Márquez whimsy falls flat in this novel and never more so than when the charm of pederasty-plus-necrophilia is supposed to reach its piquant height', while Alberto Manguel, writing for the *Guardian*, found the novel 'flat and conventional', and Andrew Holgate was disappointed by the novel's 'unenlightening aphorisms'.[36] Offering a counter-point, however, Adam Feinstein, writing for the *TLS*, admired the novel's stylistic flourishes.[37] Rather curiously a Farsi translation of the novel was published in Iran in October 2007 with the sanitized title *Memories of My Melancholy Sweethearts*. The first print-run of 5,000 sold out within three weeks, at which point it was banned by Iran's Ministry of Culture on the grounds that it promoted in-decency.[38] Clearly not as successful as some of his early novels, the main problem was not so much the theme as the use of the first-person narrative which does not ring as true as the third-person perspective of García Márquez's earlier novels.

In the summer of 2006 the mayor of Aracataca, Pedro Javier Sánchez Rueda, began a campaign to whip up support for a motion to rename the town Aracataca-Macondo, but fewer than the required 7,400 voters (out of the 53,000 registered voters of the town) showed up for the referendum. Soon after the polls closed late in the afternoon on 25 June 2006, the mayor reported that more than 90 per cent of the votes cast were in favour of the proposal but 'the turnout was not high enough for the vote to count'.[39] On 6 March 2007 Aracataca celebrated García Márquez's eightieth birthday with a military parade, a special Mass and eighty fireworks set off at 5 a.m.[40] Sánchez Rueda said in an interview: 'We're still waiting for the maestro to appear.'[41] The culture minister of Colombia, Elvira Cuervo de Jaramillo subsequently announced that the government would spend US $500,000 to reconstruct the house where Gabo lived with his grandparents for the first eight years of his life. 'The importance of this home to the work of García Márquez is that the original title of *One Hundred Years of Solitude* was going to be *La Casa*', said Jaramillo.[42] Because of prior commitments, however, García Márquez was unable to attend the celebrations that day, but he did visit Aracataca three months later, on 31 May 2007:

On Wednesday, a vintage train – dubbed the Yellow Train of Macondo – rumbled past shantytowns on the coast and through what the author called the 'hermetic realm of the banana region' before coming to a halt in Aracataca. Thousands of people had lined the route, screaming 'Gabo, Gabo, Gabo' and holding up giant posters featuring the irreverent author's smiling face framed by enormous glasses. They threw confetti, set off fireworks and let loose yellow balloons. Brass bands played and pint-sized schoolgirls performed, dressed as butterflies. 'Look at all these people and then say that it was me who invented Macondo', remarked García Márquez, his eyes tearing up.[43]

When he finally got to Aracataca, García Márquez was at first triumphant. 'Like a politician on the campaign train, he signed autographs, posed for photographs and clasped hands with his admirers, who had waited outside for his arrival undeterred by the blazing sun and dripping humidity.'[44] But when he arrived outside

García Márquez waving from the train on visit to Aracataca, 31 May 2007.

the house in Aracataca, he was not able to get out, first because there were so many people there, and secondly, because it was too difficult for him emotionally. 'He simply stood up, and then he burst into tears. Because he had spent the best ten years of his life here.'[45]

The reconstruction of the house, based on the original plans, began soon after the government's official announcement. Aída, García Márquez's sister, oversaw the reconstruction. The various rooms – the room where Gabito slept, the room where his grandfather used to entertain his friends (and where no women were allowed), the silversmith workshop where Colonel Nicolás would do his metalwork, the kitchen, the dining room, the room for guests – were completed in the spring of 2009, and the plan is that original furniture of the period will now be placed in the rooms ready for the official inauguration. Rubiela Reyes, the official guide of the Aracataca house, doubts, though, that García Márquez will be able to visit and walk around the house because of the very strong emotions it evokes in him; his sister Margarita (Margot), the only sibling who lived with Gabo in the house, cried when she visited the house recently, so much so that she felt unwell.[46]

García Márquez still gives a workshop to the *curso regular* students of the EICTV in December when the Cuban International Film Festival is taking place. The workshop is called 'Cómo se cuenta un cuento' ('How to Tell a Story') and it more or less follows the same format each year. Students come up with ideas for their own stories, and García Márquez offers them advice on how best to make them work – whether as a novel, a short story or a film script. It does not matter which since the essence of the conversation revolves around the way a narrative is told. There is a film on YouTube which gives a flavour of the type of advice that García Márquez provides to participants; the film clip is based on the scriptwriting workshop held in December 2006.[47] On that occasion in the EICTV Dolores Calviño, Julio García Espinosa's wife, remarked to García Márquez that it was strange that he now seemed so interested in having film versions of his novels made, since he had always been so dead against it in the past. García Márquez told her that he had been disappointed with some of the film versions produced in Latin America in the past, and that he was therefore more interested in European versions. However, this change of heart did not apply to *One Hundred Years of Solitude*, which will never be filmed during his lifetime – this is stipulated in his will.[48]

In March 2007 several events were held in Cartagena, organized by the Spanish Academy of the Language, to celebrate the fortieth anniversary of the publication of *One Hundred Years of Solitude*, as well as García Márquez's eightieth birthday (6 March 2007). Films of his work were shown at the annual Cartagena Film Festival (2–9 March 2007), including *La viuda de Montiel* (*Montiel's Widow*; 1979; dir. Miguel Littín), *María de mi corazón* (*Maria My Dearest*, 1979; dir. Jaime Hermosillo), *Fábula de la bella palomera* (*The Fable of the Beautiful Pigeon-Fancier*, 1988; dir. Ruy Guerra), *Tiempo de morir*

(*Time to Die*, 1966; dir. Arturo Ripstein), *El coronel no tiene quien le escriba* (*No One Writes to the Colonel*, 1999; dir. Arturo Ripstein), *Cartas del parque* (*Letters from the Park*, 1988; dir. Tomás Gutiérrez Alea), and *Edipo Alcalde* (*Oedipus Mayor*, 1996; dir. Jorge Alí Triana). Though a number of the film directors – including Fernando Birri, Miguel Littín and Jorge Alí Triana – turned up for the ceremony, García Márquez did not put in a guest appearance.

In mid-March 2007 the sixty-third annual meeting of the Inter-American Press Association was held in Cartagena, and, no doubt because of the two guests of honour – Bill Gates, the inventor of Microsoft and the richest man in the world, and the former president of the United States, Bill Clinton – García Márquez this time decided to attend. But he was mobbed when he appeared at a luncheon held on 19 March:

> The publicity-shy Nobel laureate arrived just as the richest man in the world, Bill Gates, was leaving the meeting. But the author clearly wished he had the security detail afforded the Microsoft chairman to fend off overzealous admirers. . . . People treated him like a museum piece as he dined with journalist friends in a big tent at the event. Dozens jostled with police officers standing guard to have their pictures taken with him and to have books autographed.[49]

He could have done with his former minder, Don Chepe, a tough, no-nonsense ex-member of FARC who used to be his bodyguard as well as driver in the 1990s.[50] Despite García Márquez's well-known aversion to interviews, one young interviewer tried his luck anyway:

> 'How about a few words for Caracol radio?' he said, thrusting a microphone in front of the 80-year-old writer. 'If I give you an interview I have to give an interview to everyone,' the writer

García Márquez with Bill Clinton in Cartagena, March 2007.

responded. Noting the reporter's crushed expression, García Márquez then softened. 'I love you, young man', he said. After lunch, the mustachioed writer shuffled slowly to a friend's waiting sport utility vehicle, looking exhausted. He threw up his hands before getting into the vehicle. 'I can't take any more of this. I'm going to Mexico. I'm going to Mexico.'[51]

García Márquez,
Havana, December
2008.

On 26 March 2007 a ceremony was held in the Cartagena Convention Centre specifically to mark the publication of the commemorative edition of *One Hundred Years of Solitude*. In addition to the author himself, the event was attended by three Colombian ex-presidents – Andrés Pastrana, César Gaviria and Ernesto Samper – as well as the current president, Álvaro Uribe Vélez,[52] along with the former president of Uruguay, Julio María Sanguinetti; President Martín Torrijos of Panama; Bill Clinton; Carlos Fuentes, Mexico's most famous writer; Tomás Eloy Martínez, Argentina's most famous

García Márquez signing book at the Fundación del Nuevo Cine Latinoamericano, Cuba, December 2007.

writer; the King and Queen of Spain, Don Juan Carlos and Doña Sofía; and last but not least, García Márquez's wife Mercedes.[53] As Frank Bajak reported: 'Hailed by a crowd of 1,200 with a standing ovation and thunderous applause as he entered the auditorium of Cartagena's Convention Center, the white-suited, mustachioed writer, who turned 80 this month, clasped his hands above his head like a prizefighter.'[54] A number of speeches were given, including by the king and also by García de la Concha who presented the commemorative edition of the novel to García Márquez, but none was more eagerly awaited than García Márquez's. As Gerald Martin recalls: 'Mercedes looked on anxiously and sombrely and prayed that this man who had got through so many challenges would get through this one too.'[55] As Frank Bajak reported:

In a 13-minute speech, he recounted how his wife Mercedes had to hock her jewels to pay the rent and put food on the table for their two boys during the 18 months it took him to finish the novel, which was published in 1967. . . . 'I only know that from the time I was 17 until this morning I've done nothing more than wake up early every day, sit in front of a set of keys to fill a blank page or a blank screen with the sole mission of writing a story never before told that will make life happy for a reader who doesn't exist . . . To think that a million people would read something written in the solitariness of my room with 28 letters of the alphabet and two fingers as my sole arsenal seems insane.'[56]

The presentation of the deluxe edition of *One Hundred Years of Solitude* was an occasion for much gushing praise: '"I believe he's the most important writer of fiction in any language since William Faulkner died," said Mr Clinton, who recalled reading *One Hundred Years of Solitude* when he was in law school and not being able to put it down – even during classes. Fellow writers Carlos Fuentes and Tomás Eloy Martínez praised García Márquez for breathing new life into a language now spoken by nearly 500 million people'.[57]

In the summer of 2007 García Márquez went to Cuba to stay in the *casa de protocolo* which has a large pool in the back garden.[58] Thinking he would take a dip García Márquez was surprised to find an enormous alligator lying at the bottom of the pool. One of his neighbours, the painter Kcho (Alexis Leyra), kept the alligator as a pet (as well as a number of other animals such as hens, chickens and peacocks) and, while García Márquez was away, it had slipped into his swimming pool to cool off.[59] A magical-real moment.

In December 2007 the workshop on 'How to Write a Story' García Márquez routinely gives to the final-year students of the Escuela Internacional de Cine y Televisión was held in the Fundación del Nuevo Cine Latinoamericano, at the invitation of the director, Alquimia Peña, rather than in its normal venue at the EICTV. It was a more rushed occasion than usual; García Márquez had originally phoned his close friends to say that he would not be coming because he was suffering from flu, but then, seemingly miraculously, he was able to fly to Havana and was rushed straight to the Fundación del Nuevo Cine Latinoamericano where the third-year students of the EICTV were waiting for their seminar with the maestro. Each of the students was presented personally to García

Márquez, as is the custom, before they took their seats. Just before the workshop García Márquez spoke about how annoyed he was over the panning of the film of his book, *Love in the Time of Cholera*, in the international and particularly the Colombian press. García Márquez had not been intimately involved in the film, but in December 2006 he had met with one of the art team assistants, a young man called Juan Pablo Bustamante Restrepo, and was very impressed with the rough cut of the film Bustamante brought from Colombia to Cuba to show him on that occasion. As Bustamante recalls, no expense was spared in the filming: 'Cartagena became a giant film set.'[60] Although *Love in the Time of Cholera* (2007; dir. Mike Newell) was badly received (the *Guardian* review called it a 'horrifically boring festival of middlebrow good taste'),[61] its redeeming feature was the atmospheric portrayal of the city of Cartagena. García Márquez's hopes had been built up. He has no English and it is likely that he was simply impressed with the visual aspect of the film, and therefore assumed (wrongly) that it was going to be a success.

In December 2008 Plinio Apuleyo Mendoza announced that García Márquez was writing a new novel. It was to be a love story. As Apuleyo suggested: 'He has four versions of it. He told me that he was now trying to get the best from each of them.'[62] The hope that García Márquez was about to bring out a new novel was dashed in April 2009, however, when his publisher, Carmen Balcells, confirmed that she was not expecting a new novel. She told the Chilean newspaper *La Tercera*, 'I don't think that García Márquez will write anything else.' His biographer, Gerald Martin, concurred: 'I also believe that Gabo won't write any more books, but I don't think this is too regrettable, because as a writer it was his destiny to have the immense satisfaction of having a totally coherent literary career many years before the end of his natural life.'[63] García Márquez has a number of unpublished manuscripts in his possession – some are drafts of a novel – and it was not long before he issued a rebuttal of these remarks. As Elizabeth Nash reported, he 'set pages fluttering in publishing circles by furiously denying reports that he'll never write again'.[64] García Márquez went on to say: 'Not only is that not true, but what is true is that I do nothing else but write. . . . I'm a writer, not a publisher. But only I know when the cakes I'm baking in the oven are ready to eat.'[65] García Márquez told me in December 2007 that he was working on the second volume of his autobiography, and it is likely that this will be the book most eagerly awaited by his readers all around the world. His 1996 novel, *News of a Kidnapping*, is in the process of being adapted for the screen; Pablo Pedro Ibarra will be directing, Eduardo Costantini will be producing, and the Mexican actress, Salma Hayek, is likely to star in the movie.[66]

References

1 'He won't be playing chess any more'

1 'He won't be playing chess any more' (the comment Gabo made when he found out that Don Emilio, a friend of his grandfather's, had committed suicide); see Gabriel García Márquez, *Living to Tell the Tale*, trans. Edith Grossman (London, 2003), p. 93. Occasionally I refer to the original Spanish version of the autobiography.

2 *Living to Tell the Tale*, p. 60.

3 As Gabo's brother Luis Enrique has pointed out, Gabo was born on 6 March 1927, not 1928, as many still believe. This mistake arose in 1955 when Gabo had to leave Colombia after his publication of *Relato de un náufrago* in *El Espectador* resulted in problems with Rojas Pinilla's government. The papers he presented on leaving listed his date of birth as 1928 – a date that has only been rectified recently: see 'Ni yo soy diablo ni Gabito es santo', in Silvia Galvis, *Los García Márquez*, 4th edn (Medellín, 2007), pp. 115–39. Luis Enrique has said that Gabo changed his birth date to make it coincide with the year of the banana massacre; see Dasso Saldívar, *García Márquez: el viaje a la semilla: la biografía* (Madrid, 1997), p. 68.

4 *Vivir para contarla*, p. 75; illus. 4.

5 Saldívar, *García Márquez*, p. 86.

6 Luisa Santiaga died in 2002; García Márquez refers to his mother's death in *Vivir para contarla* (Barcelona, 2002), p. 58.

7 Gerald Martin, *Gabriel García Márquez: A Life* (London, 2008), p. 31.

8 Saldívar, *García Márquez*, p. 111.

9 Father Angarita's letter was read out in parliament in January 1929 by a Liberal politician who was barely known at the time, Jorge Eliécer

Gaitán, the man destined to transform Colombia before he was
cruelly cut down in his prime in April 1948; see Eliécer Gaitán,
La Masacre en las bananeras: documentos testimonios (Bogotá, n.d.).

10 Apuleyo Mendoza, *The Fragrance of Guava* (London, 1983), p. 17.

11 Rubiela Reyes, interview with the author, Aracataca, 26 February
2009.

12 Ibid.

13 Colonel Nicolás encouraged Gabito to draw and believed he would
become a painter; *Living to Tell the Tale*, pp. 82–3. The drawing of the
rabbit is held in the Casa Natal in Aracataca.

14 Saldívar, *García Márquez*, p. 110.

15 Rubiela Reyes, interview with the author, Aracataca, 26 February 2009.

16 J. G. Cobo Borda, 'En el corazón de Macondo: Aracataca', in *Gabriel
García Márquez: los cuentos de mi abuelo el coronel* (Cali, 1988), pp. 1–3
(p. 3).

17 Gerald Martin, *García Márquez: A Life* (London, 2008), p. 35.

18 Rubiela Reyes, interview with the author, Aracataca, 26 February 2009.

19 Galvis, *Los García Márquez*, p. 65.

20 Martin, *Gabriel García Márquez*, p. 37.

21 Rubiela Reyes, interview with the author, Aracataca, Colombia,
26 February 2009.

22 The number nineteen was given by García Márquez to Dasso
Saldívar; see *García Márquez: el viaje a la semilla*, p. 103, and Gerald
Martin speculates that Nicolás 'spawned many, maybe dozens more
illegitimate children'; Martin, *Gabriel García Márquez*, p. 5.

23 Jaime has calculated that his grandfather, Colonel Nicolás, had twelve
illegitimate children; see Galvis, *Los García Márquez*, p. 41. Since nine
have been positively identified this would leave three which have not,
though there may have been more (see previous footnote). The García
Márquez legitimate family was also shot through with illegitimacy:
García Márquez's father and his grandmother were illegitimate, and
his father sired four illegitimate children.

24 Saldívar, *García Márquez*, p. 103.

25 See Guiomar Dueñas Vargas, *Los hijos del pecado: legitimidad y vida
familiar en la Santafe de Bogotá colonial* (Bogotá, 1997), p. 17.

26 Maria Emma Mannarelli, *Pecados públicos: la ilegitimidad en Lima,
Siglo XVII* (Lima, 1994), p. 23.

27 Dueñas Vargas, *Los hijos del pecado*, pp. 44–5.

28 Thus Juan Ortega, founder and mayor of Bogotá, left 6,000 pesos for his *hijo natural*; Dueñas Vargas, *Los hijos del pecado*, p. 56.

29 Dalín de Jesús Miranda Salcedo, *Legitimad e ilegitimidad familar: el problema del control social en Barranquilla 1880–1930* (Barranquilla, 2000), p. 97.

30 Miranda Salcedo, *Legitimad e ilegitimidad familar*, p. 108.

31 Saldívar, *García Márquez*, p. 30.

32 Miranda Salcedo, *Legitimad e ilegitimidad familar*, p. 116; my translation.

33 The names of nine of the illegitimate children are known. According to Saldívar they are: José María Valdeblánquez Márquez, Carlos Alberto Valdeblánquez Márquez, Sara Noriega Márquez, María Gregoria Ruiz Márquez, Esteban Carrillo Márquez, Elvira Carrillo Márquez, Nicolás Gómez Márquez, Remedios Núñez Márquez, Petronila Arias Márquez (see appendix, 'Los Márquez Iguarán). Martin, *García Márquez*, pp. 572–3, provides these nine names but in all but one case, Petronila, the surname Márquez has been removed.

34 *Living to Tell the Tale*, p. 89.

35 Rubiela Reyes, interview with the author, Aracataca, 26 February 2009.

36 Ibid.

37 Saldívar, *García Márquez*, pp. 26–7.

38 Ibid., p. 32.

39 Ibid., pp. 41–5.

40 Ibid., p. 49.

41 Ibid., p. 44.

42 Ibid., p. 26.

43 Ibid., p. 27. Saldívar states that after Colonel Márquez had served his prison sentence for the murder of Medardo Pacheco Romero (a year in the prison of Santa Marta) he and his family moved to Ciénaga in 1909, and he also states that 'the main reason for this was that Isabelita Ruiz lived there, the lover that the colonel had known in Panama in 1885 and with whom he had María Gregoria Ruiz the following year' (p. 45). It was only at the end of August 1910 that the colonel moved with his family (his wife and his three children, Juan de Dios, Margarita and Luisa Santiaga) to Aracataca, given the recent expansion of the United Fruit Company in Aracataca (p. 45). One

might even speculate that, as a parting gift, Colonel Nicolás Márquez left Isabelita Ruiz with a child, a child who would be murdered by government troops on 6 December 1928, eighteen years later.

44 *Living to Tell the Tale*, p. 79.
45 Saldívar, *García Márquez*, p. 105.
46 Martin, *García Márquez*, p. 48.
47 Margot, 'Mi vida ha sido una lucha contra la pobreza de todos', Galvis, *Los García Márquez*, pp. 59–88 (p. 63).
48 Martin, *García Márquez*, p. 47.
49 According to Margot; see Galvis, *Los García Márquez*, p. 64.
50 From a lecture given at London Metropolitan University on 8 December 2008. Saldívar states something similar in his book about these 'muertos de verdad'; see *García Márquez*, p. 98.
51 Martin, *García Márquez*, p. 50.
52 *Living to Tell the Tale*, p. 92.
53 Ibid., p. 92.
54 *Vivir para contarla*, pp. 118–19.
55 *Living to Tell the Tale*, p. 138.
56 Rubiela Reyes, interview with the author, Aracataca, 26 February 2009.
57 *Living to Tell the Tale*, p. 139.
58 Ibid., pp. 88–9.
59 Galvis, *Los García Márquez*, pp. 67–8.
60 Rubiela Reyes, interview with the author, Aracataca, 26 February 2009.
61 Ibid; see also *Living to Tell the Tale*, p. 97.
62 *Living to Tell the Tale*, p. 154.
63 Plinio Apuleyo Mendoza, *The Fragrance of Guava: Conversations with Gabriel García Márquez* (London, 1983), p. 21.
64 *Living to Tell the Tale*, esp. pp. 3–5.
65 Apuleyo, *The Fragrance of Guava*, p. 20. García Márquez is known in Colombia as a *mamagallista* (see Jon Lee Anderson, 'El poder de Gabo', *Semana*, 4–11 October 1999, pp. 46–66), and Silvia Galvis has argued that Luisa Santiaga is the source of the gene of *mamagallismo* which characterizes the García Márquez family. 'Mamagallismo' roughly translates as 'pulling someone's leg' based on the verb *mamarle el gallo a alguien* (Galvis, *Los García Márquez*, p. 17 and p. 13); see also Margret

S. de Oliveira Castro, *La lengua ladina de García Márquez* (Bogotá, 2007), pp. 167–8.

66 Saldívar, *García Márquez*, pp. 133–4; my translation.

67 Margot, 'Mi vida ha sido una lucha contra la pobreza de todos', in Galvis, *Los García Márquez*, pp. 54–88 (p. 70).

68 Aída, 'Jamás me convencieron de que bailar fuera pecado', in Galvis, *Los García Márquez*, pp. 89–114 (p. 93).

69 Apuleyo, *The Fragrance of Guava*, p. 21.

70 García Márquez discusses the 'transgressions' of both his grandfather and father, but dismisses them as not interesting in the slightest (*Living to Tell the Tale*, p. 51), which does not appear to be borne out by his fiction.

71 52.4 per cent were legitimate while 46.9 per cent were *hijos naturales*; Mirando Salcedo, *Legitimad e ilegitimidad familiar*, p. 99.

72 *Living to Tell the Tale*, p. 49.

73 Rubiela Reyes, interview with the author, Aracataca, 26 February 2009.

74 Martin, *García Márquez*, p. 70.

75 Galvis, *Los García Márquez*, p. 55.

76 Quoted in Martin, *García Márquez*, p. 70.

77 *Living to Tell the Tale*, pp. 51–2.

78 Luis Enrique, 'No yo soy diablo ni Gabito es santo', in Galvis, *Los García Márquez*, 4th edn (Medellín, 2007), pp. 115–39.

79 *Living to Tell the Tale*, pp. 161–2.

80 *Living to Tell the Tale*, p. 168.

81 Ibid.

82 Ibid., pp. 184–87. Gómez Tamar also lent him a copy of Dostoevsky's novel, *The Double*, and the notion of the double was destined to become one of García Márquez's favoured literary tropes (see discussion in chapter Four of this text).

83 Ibid., p. 70.

84 Ibid., p. 216.

85 Ibid.

86 According to Luis, in Galvis, *Los García Márquez*, p. 137; see also *Living to Tell the Tale*, p. 217.

87 *Living to Tell the Tale*, p. 218.

88 Jon Lee Anderson, 'El poder de Gabo', p. 48.

89 Apuleyo, *The Fragrance of Guava*, p. 22.
90 Martin, *García Márquez*, p. 84.

2 '10 per cent inspiration, 90 per cent perspiration'

1   '10 per cent inspiration and 90 per cent perspiration'; this is the secret
    to García Márquez's work, as he told J. G. Cobo Borda; see 'Vueltas en
    redondo en torno a Gabriel García Márquez', in *Para llegar a García
    Márquez* (Bogotá, 1997), pp. 45–100 (p. 63).
2   A plaque near the corner of the two roads commemorates the spot
    where the deed occurred.
3   The road is now called carrera 8; Dasso Salvídar, *García Márquez: el
    viaje a la semilla: la biografía* (Madrid, 1997), p. 176.
4   The classical study of violence in Colombia is Germán Guzmán
    Campos's two-volume study, *La violencia en Colombia: estudio de un
    proceso social* (Bogotá, 1977), 8th edn, which, though adopting a
    moralist perspective, opened up the debate in a sociological sense.
5   Quoted in Gerald Martin, *Gabriel García Márquez: A Life* (London,
    2008), p. 106.
6   Gabriel García Márquez, *Living to Tell the Tale*, trans. Edith Grossman
    (London, 2003), p. 281.
7   García Márquez refers to false memories in his memoirs; see *Living
    to Tell the Tale*, p. 52, p. 63. They appear as real as the purportedly true
    memories.
8   Martin, for example, states: 'García Márquez ran out immediately to
    the site of the murder but Gaitán's dying body had already been
    rushed to the hospital'; *Gabriel García Márquez*, p. 106.
9   *Living to Tell the Tale*, p. 282.
10 Ibid., p. 283.
11 'Cómo se llevó a cabo el crimen más horrendo cometido en el país',
    El Tiempo, xxxviii/13147 (12 April 1948), p. 1.
12 Jaime Quijano Caballero, 'Cómo nació el motín en Bogotá: una
    reconstrucción de los hechos del 9 de abril, por un testigo presencial',
    El Tiempo, xxxviii/13149 (16 April 1948), p. 11.
13 Saldívar, *García Márquez*, p. 195.
14 Stephen Hart, *A Companion to Latin American Literature* (London,

2007), pp. 277–78.

15 For an excellent study of García Márquez's journalism and its foundational role in his fiction, see Pedro Sorela, *El otro García Márquez: los años difíciles* (Madrid, 1988).

16 Jorge García Usta, *Como aprendió a escribir García Márquez* (Medellín, 1995), p. 24.

17 Ibid., pp. 16-B, C (illus. nos), p. 22.

18 As he wrote in an editorial in *El Universal* on 2 August 1949: 'The laws of the language are in force for those who wish to write, even during a Conservative regime. And, as our Constitution informs us, ignorance of the law is no excuse' (García Usta, *Como aprendió a escribir García Márquez*, p. 21). He was famous for using a red pen to correct every single sentence written by the journalists who worked for him, including García Márquez (García Usta, p. 68). García Márquez began to write with the pseudonym of Septimus from 24 June 1949 onwards (García Usta, p. 91). García Usta has identified one of the techniques García Márquez developed during his early journalism: a real – though extraordinary – 'event is treated humorously so that the arbitrary nature of the event reveals something about the social backdrop to the event' (García Usta, p. 135).

19 See illus. 32 of his 'Punto y aparte' in *El Universal* of 22 May 1948, beginning 'No sé qué tiene el acordeón de comunicativo . . . ' (García Usta, *Como aprendió a escribir García Márquez*, p. 144-c).

20 *Gabriel García Márquez: textos costeños: obra periodística*, vol. 1, ed. Jacques Gilard (Madrid, 1981), p. 59, p. 63, pp. 72–3. See also Gilard's 'Pistes temporelles de García Márquez', *Silex*, 11 (1979), pp. 37–44.

21 Gilard, ed., *Textos costeños*, 1, pp. 77–8. For a discussion of the articles published in *El Universal*, see Conrado Zuluaga Osorio, *Puerta abierta a Gabriel García Márquez: aproximación a la obra del Nobel colombiano* (Barcelona, 2001), pp. 31–5.

22 Interview in a documentary, *Buscando a Gabo*; Señal Colombia/ Universidad del Magdalena, broadcast in Cartagena on 6 March 2009.

23 Jacques Gilard found and transcribed thirty-eight texts published in *El Universal* under the section 'Punto y Aparte', and Gustavo Arango, more recently, has discovered five additional articles – see *Un ramo de nomeolvides: García Márquez en El Universal* (Cartagena, 1995), p. 138n. These are 'Sobre el libro de Payan Archer', *El Universal* (8 December

1948), p. 4; 'Viernes', *El Universal* (24 June 1949), p. 4 (with pseudonym of Septimus); 'Contribución a los censos', *El Universal* (2 October 1949); 'La vorágine en el cine', *El Universal* (23 October 1949), p. 4; 'Dos nuevos abogados', *El Universal* (9 November 1949), p. 4. These articles may be consulted in Arango's book as follows: pp. 156–8; 161–2; 158–9; 159–60; 137–8. It is not clear why these texts have not been transcribed in chronological order.

24 For further discussion of how García Márquez's work intermingles with that of his contemporaries in Cartagena such as Héctor Rojas Herazo, see Arango, *Un ramo de nomeolvides*. For further analysis of how his work relates to his journalism and to film, see Juan Cristóbal, *García Márquez y los medios de comunicación* (Lima, 1999).

25 'Un infanticidio en el Barrio de La Esperanza'; see Arango, *Un ramo de nomeolvides*, p. 251.

26 It is likely that García Márquez wrote the story which ran in *El Universal* on 27 October 1949 about a pilgrimage of the Virgin of Fatima in Cartagena, and perhaps used it in order to draw up some of the details in *Of Love and Other Demons* (Report in *El Universal*, 27 October 1949, p. 2; see Arango, *Un ramo de nomeolvides*, p. 2.) Conrado Zuluaga has suggested that García Márquez's work as a ournalist shows that he did not always write so well; during the 1948–52 period he was often overwhelmed by 'metaphor, synecdoche, metonym and hyberbole'; see *García Márquez: el vicio incurable de contar* (Bogotá, 2006), p. 35.

27 Saldívar, *García Márquez*, p. 223; see illus. 26.

28 'Yo no tengo ojo pa'muerto', in Silvia Galvis, *Los García Márquez*, 4th edn (Medellín, 2007), pp. 141–70 (p. 157). It is likely that the name of *La Jirafa* was inspired not only by Mercedes' long neck but also by the definition of a giraffe given by Ramón Gómez de la Serna as 'a horse elongated by curiosity' (quoted in García Usta, *Como aprendió*, p. 154), given that the *Jirafas* show a deep curiosity about human actions and culture. García Usta has emphasized the similarity between Gómez de la Serna's 'greguerías' and the type of wit found in García Márquez's early journalism; one example he gives is particularly illuminating. In García Márquez's 'Defensa de los ataúdes' ('In Defence of Coffins') published in *El Universal* on 9 March 1950 we find the line: 'Death might simply be a change in civil status' (García Usta, p. 167).

29 For an excellent discussion of the Barranquilla literary group, see Saldívar, *García Márquez*, pp. 226–38.

30 Rubiela Reyes, interview with the author, Aracataca, Colombia, 26 February 2009.

31 Jorge García Usta has questioned the emphasis placed on the Barranquilla literary group in reference to García Márquez's development as a writer, and indeed has blamed Jacques Gilard for the unfair treatment that Cartagena's literary scene has received as a result; see Jorge García Usta, *García Márquez en Cartagena: sus inicios literarios* (Bogotá, 2007), pp. 13–17. García Usta's book is an attempt to set the record straight; he points out that García Márquez was already reading and discussing writers such as Faulkner and Virginia Woolf with his literary-minded colleagues at the newspaper he worked for in Cartagena (pp. 73–81), and that he was influenced by Gómez de la Serna while in Cartagena (pp. 125–49). Indeed Ibarra Merlano remembers that García Márquez was reading Faulkner and Virginia Woolf in the late 1940s, and breaking down their technique in order to learn the secrets of their craft: 'He [García Márquez] already knew Faulkner and Virginia Woolf. He went around with their books which he had annotated and underlined since he was subjecting them to a minute process of breaking them down [*desmonte*]. You would see him studying the point of view, the monologue, all the greatness and minutiae of pure novelistic technique' (quoted in García Usta, p. 217).

32 Jon Lee Anderson, 'El poder de Gabo', *Semana*, 909 (4–11 October 1999), 46–66 (p. 52).

33 The address as listed in the 2008–2009 Cartagena *Yellow Pages* is San Diego Cra. 7, 38–205 Calle del Curato (p. 213). Apart from the house in Cartagena, and a spacious duplex apartment in Bogotá, García Márquez has his main residence in Mexico City and a 'casa del protocolo' in Havana, Cuba.

34 Gilard, *Gabriel García Márquez: textos costeños*, p. 140.

35 Ibid., p. 156.

36 *Vivir para contarla*, p. 145.

37 Luis Enrique, interviewed in a documentary, *Buscando a Gabo*, Señal Colombia, broadcast in Cartagena, 6 March 2009.

38 See Martin, *Gabriel García Márquez*, p. 150.

39 García Usta, *Como aprendió*, pp. 59–60.

40 Ibid., pp. 60–61.

41 Quoted in García Usta, *Como apendió a escribir García Márquez*, p. 208-A.

42 See Osvaldo Rodríguez Jiménez, 'Ortodoxia y heterodoxia en el campo literario nacional: el caso de García Márquez', MA thesis, University of Cartagena, 1998, 45 pp. T. C863 R696 (p. 22). This led García Márquez to make his famous comment that 'literary provincialism in Colombia begins at 2,500 metres above sea level' (Gilard, ed., *Textos costeños*, p. 293).

43 Eligio García Márquez, *Tras las claves de Melquíades: historia de 'Cien años de soledad'* (Bogotá, 2001), pp. 234–35.

44 Ibid., pp. 256–8.

45 'Comerás papel'; quoted in Galvis, *Los García Márquez*, p. 45.

46 Saldívar, *García Márquez*, pp. 286–7.

47 Ibid., pp. 287–8.

48 Ibid., pp. 288–9.

49 *El doble*, trans. Alfonso Nadal (Madrid, 1930).

50 As Michael Bell suggests, 'although the "double" is a well-worn device of modern fiction, Márquez has already given it his own metaphysical inflection'; see *Gabriel García Márquez: Solitude and Solidarity* (London, 1993), p. 17.

51 *El doble*, pp. 290–1.

52 For further discussion see Stephen Hart, 'García Márquez's Short Fiction', in *A Companion to Gabriel García Márquez* (Cambridge, forthcoming).

53 *Vivir para contarla*, p. 297.

54 García Usta, *Cómo leer a Gabriel García Márquez* (Madrid, 1991), p. 14.

55 All references are to 'The Third Resignation', in *Innocent Eréndira and other stories*, trans. Gregory Rabassa (London, 1981), pp. 68–75.

56 All references are to 'Eva is Inside her Cat', in *Innocent Eréndira and other stories*, pp. 83–91.

57 For a discussion of Kafka's influence on García Márquez's fiction, see Hannelore Hahn, *The Influence of Franz Kafka on Three Novels by Gabriel García Márquez* (New York, 1993).

58 *El Espectador*, Año 60, No. 11,895, p. 5.

59 Grau, by then an already established painter (he had held his first exhibition at the National Library in Bogotá the previous year, 1946), would study for two years in Italy (1954–5) and he met García

Márquez when he arrived as *El Espectador*'s foreign correspondent in Sienna, Italy in December 1955. See Enrique Grau, *El pequeño viaje del Baron Von Humboldt* (Bogotá, 1984), p. 111.

60 Mario Vargas Llosa, 'A Morbid Prehistory (The Early Stories)', *Books Abroad*, XLVII/3 (1973), pp. 451–60 (p. 454). Likewise Raymond Leslie Williams suggests that the story 'does not actually reach any coherent conclusion'; *A Companion to Gabriel García Márquez* (Woodbridge, 2010), p. 3.

61 'Tubal-Cain forja una estrella', p. 5. All translations of this short story are my own.

62 It is likely, since García Márquez´s father was still alive in 1948 when the story was written, that the father in the story is a projection of the grandfather, Nicolás Márquez, who embodied the role of father when Gabo lived in his grandparents' house in Aracataca.

63 'La otra costilla de la muerte', in *Gabriel García Márquez: Cuentos 1947–1992* (Bogotá, 1999), pp. 23–32 (p. 24). All translations are my own.

64 Vargas Llosa describes this story as 'a surrealistic dream in which anguish and black humour are fused'; Vargos Llosa, 'A Morbid Prehistory', p. 455.

65 All references are to 'The Other Side of Death', in *Innocent Eréndira and other stories*, pp. 76–82.

66 All references are to 'Dialogue with the Mirror', in *Innocent Eréndira and other stories*, pp. 92–7.

67 All references are to 'Eyes of a Blue Dog', in *Innocent Eréndira and other stories*, pp. 102–7.

68 All references are to 'The Woman Who Came at Six o'clock', in *Innocent Eréndira and other stories*, pp. 108–17.

69 All references are to 'Someone Has Been Disarranging These Roses', in *Innocent Eréndira and other stories*, pp. 118–21.

3 'Same difference'

1 'Same difference' – words used by the mayor which conclude the short story, 'One of These Days'.

2 Martha Canfield, 'Gabriel García Márquez', in *Colecciones Clásicos Colombianos* (Bogotá, 1991), p. 1.

3   García Márquez joined an excellent team. In 1954–5 the 'Día a día' (Day by Day) was written by Guillermo Cano, Gonzalo González (GOG) and Eduardo Zalamea Borda ('Ulises'). See Jacques Gilard, 'Prólogo', in *Gabriel García Márquez: Obra periodística III: Entre cachacos* (Bogotá, 1983), p. 6.

4   Gilard, *Gabriel García Márquez*, pp. 5–72 (p. 5).

5   Dasso Saldívar, *García Márquez: el viaje a la semilla: la biografía* (Madrid, 1997), p. 218.

6   Gilard, *Gabriel García Márquez*, p. 8n.

7   Saldívar, *García Márquez*, pp. 307–8.

8   Gilard, *Gabriel García Márquez*, p. 37.

9   Ibid., pp. 27–31.

10 Gilard, 'Milagro en Milan', in *Gabriel García Márquez*, pp. 142–4 (p. 142).

11 Gilard, *Gabriel García Márquez*, pp. 21–2.

12 'La Marquesita de la Sierpe', in *Crónicas y reportajes* (Bogotá, 1976), pp. 11–18 (pp. 11–12).

13 'El muerto alegre', *Crónicas y reportajes*, pp. 43–50.

14 Jacques Gilard, *Gabriel García Márquez*, p. 53.

15 Juan Cruz, 'Tomás Eloy Martínez: El anonimato digital potencia el periodismo amarillo', *El País*, no. 11560 (8 February 2009), pp. 8–9 (p. 9).

16 Gabriel García Márquez, *Living to Tell the Tale*, trans. Edith Grossman (London, 2003), p. 472.

17 Ibid., p. 473. The articles were published as follows: 'La verdad sobre mi aventura I', *El Espectador*, 67, no. 14261 (5 April 1955), p. 1, p. 3; 'La verdad . . . II', *El Espectador*, 67, no. 14262 (6 April 1955), p. 1, p. 16; 'La verdad . . . III', *El Espectador*, 67, no. 14265 (9 April 1955), p. 1, p. 10; 'La verdad . . . IV', *El Espectador*, 67, no. 14267 (11 April 1955), p. 1, p. 13; 'La verdad . . . V', *El Espectador*, 67, no. 14256 (error in sequence but *sic*) (12 April 1955), p. 1, p. 13; 'La verdad . . . VI', *El Espectador*, 67, no. 14266 (13 April 1955), p.1, p. 17; 'La verdad . . . VII', *El Espectador*, 67, no. 14267 (14 April 1955), p. 1, p. 9; 'La verdad . . . VIII', *El Espectador*, 67, no. 14268 (15 April 1955), p. 1, p. 16; 'La verdad . . . IX', *El Espectador*, 67, no. 14269 (16 April 1955), p. 1, p. 14; 'La verdad . . . X', *El Espectador*, 67, no. 14271 (18 April 1955), p. 1, p. 17; 'La verdad . . . XI', *El Espectador*, 67, no. 14272 (19 April 1955), p. 1, p. 11; 'La verdad . . . XII', *El Espectador*, 67, no. 14273 (20 April 1955), p. 1, p. 15; 'La verdad . . . XIII', *El Espectador*, 67,

no. 14274 (21 April 1955), p. 1, p. 17; 'La verdad . . . xiv', *El Espectador*, 67, no. 14275 (22 April 1955), p. 1, p. 17. The complete edition was announced in *El Espectador* on 23 April 1955, 67, no. 14276, p. 1, which would be available on 28 April 1955, such had been the demand for copies of the story.

18 *Living to Tell the Tale*, p. 475.

19 García Márquez, 'La historia de esta historia', in *Relato de un náufrago que estuvo diez días a la deriva en una balsa sin comer ni beber, que fue proclamado héroe de la patria, besado por las reinas de la belleza y hecho rico por la publicidad, y luego aborrecido por el gobierno y olvidado para siempre* (Barcelona, 1970), 3rd edn, pp. 7–10 (p. 9).

20 *Relato de un náufrago* (Barcelona, 1970), pp. 38–9; my translation. In the preface to the 1970 edition of the story, García Márquez stated that he wished the royalties to go to Velasco (p. 10), and this continued for fourteen years, until – as a result of some legal advice – Velasco decided to sue García Márquez. The court decided in García Márquez's favour and he decided to pay the royalites to an educational foundation (*Living to Tell the Tale*, pp. 478–9).

21 Gerald Martin, *Gabriel García Márquez: A Life* (London, 2008), pp. 183–4.

22 Saldívar, *García Márquez*, p. 335.

23 Ibid., p. 337.

24 Raymond Williams, *Novela y poder en Colombia, 1844–1987*, trans. Alvaro Pineda Botero (Bogotá, 1991), p. 143.

25 For further discussion see Pedro Lastra, 'La tragedia como fundamento estructural de *La hojarasca*', in *Gabriel García Márquez*, ed. Peter G. Earle (Madrid, 1981), pp. 40–49.

26 Martin, *Gabriel García Márquez*, p. 145.

27 This character is no doubt based on the house servant of the same name who lived in the grandparents' house in Aracataca: 'I never knew Meme, the Goajiro slave whom the family brought from Barrancas and who, one stormy night, ran away with Alirio, her adolescent brother, but I always heard that they were the ones who most peppered the language of the house with their native language' (*Living to Tell the Tale*, p. 77). Meme lived in the servants' abode, the only original structure of the house in Aracataca to survive to the present day.

28 *Leaf Storm*, trans. Gregory Rabassa (London, 1979), p. 24.

29 Ángel Rama, *García Márquez, edificación de un arte nacional y popular* (Montevideo, 1987), p. 35. In his important early study Rama also draws attention to the interplay of the three monologues in *Leaf Storm* (pp. 36–42), the theme of decomposition (pp. 45–46), the importance of journalism and film to Gabo's work (pp. 47–55), the tradition of the *Novela de la Violencia* in Colombia (pp. 56–59) and how García Márquez rewrites the genre by focusing on the moments of peace between explosions of violence (p. 60), concluding with an analysis of time and structure in *One Hundred Years of Solitude* (pp. 68–105).

30 J. G. Cobo Borda, 'Vueltas en redondo en torno a Gabriel García Márquez', in *Para llegar a García Márquez* (Bogotá, 1997), p. 85.

31 García Márquez has spoken of his admiration for Hemingway's theory of the iceberg in literature. Only an eighth of an iceberg is visible and seven-eighths of its volume is hidden beneath the surface of the ocean: 'As a result of this I realized that each sentence, each episode, each risk that one runs when writing, has seven-eighths below holding it up. The first thing I do is write the visible part, and afterwards I investigate the seven-eighths which are below the surface, in case there is any contradiction' (Eligio García Márquez, *Tras las claves de Melquíades: historia de 'Cien años de soledad'* (Bogotá, 2001), p. 466).

32 For a good discussion of the journey from *Leaf Storm* to *One Hundred Years of Solitude*, see Robert Louis Sims, *The Evolution of Myth in Gabriel García Márquez: From 'La hojarasca' to 'Cien años de soledad'* (Miami, 1981).

33 Martin, *Gabriel García Márquez*, p. 195.

34 Plinio Apuleyo made this point in his lecture given on 8 December 2008 at London Metropolitan University.

35 Saldívar, *García Márquez*, pp. 349–50.

36 Martin, *Gabriel García Márquez*, p. 199. García Márquez later asked Mercedes to destroy these letters – there were 650 sheets – once they were married and living in Caracas; she agreed, accepting the symbolic sum of 100 *bolívares*, and the letters were burnt (p. 243).

37 'El año más famoso del mundo', in *Cuando era feliz e indocumentado* (Caracas, 1973), pp. 11–28 (p. 11).

38 'Condenados a 20 años, pero son inocentes', *Cuando era feliz e indocumentado*, pp. 119–31 (p. 121).

39 Saldívar, *García Márquez*, p. 353.

40 García Márquez, *De viaje por los países socialistas* (Bogotá, 1978), p. 136.

41 Lecture given on 8 December 2008 at London Metropolitan University. See also Ilan Stavans, *Gabriel García Márquez: The Early Years* (New York, 2010), p. 9.

42 Saldívar, *García Márquez*, p. 362.

43 Ibid.

44 Ibid., pp. 367–68.

45 Ibid., pp. 375–76.

46 Martin, *Gabriel García Márquez*, p. 236.

47 Ibid, p. 239.

48 Quoted in ibid., p. 239.

49 Saldívar, *García Márquez*, pp. 372–3.

50 'El poder de Gabo', *Semana*, no. 909, 4–11 October 1999, pp. 46–66 (p. 48).

51 Angel Esteban and Stephanie Panichelli, *Gabo y Fidel: el paisaje de una amistad* (Bogotá, 2004), p. 38.

52 Quoted in Minta, *Gabriel García Márquez: Writer of Colombia* (London, 1987), pp. 59–60.

53 As Stephen Minta suggests: 'García Márquez's enthusiasm for the Cuban Revolution has remained undiminished to the present day, and, if he has had some private reservations about the direction which the revolution has taken, he has never doubted that its achievements have been of far greater significance than its limitations' (p. 59). Over the years García Márquez has been able to use his personal influence with Castro to obtain political asylum for a number of Cuban writers and personae non gratae, such as Armando Valladares, Severo Sarduy's parents, Eliseo Diego's son, Eliseo Alberto, and Norberto Fuentes (Esteban and Panichelli, *Gabo y Fidel*, pp. 246–7).

54 Martin, *Gabriel García Márquez*, p. 264.

55 Eligio García Márquez, *Tras las claves de Melquíades*, p. 437.

56 Ibid.

57 Ibid., p. 438.

58 Ibid.

59 Martin, *Gabriel García Márquez*, p. 271.

60 Ibid, pp. 278–89.

61 For a discussion of the overlap between *In Evil Hour* and *No One Writes to the Colonel*, see George R. McMurray, *Gabriel García Márquez*

(New York, 1977), pp. 21–46.

62 *La mala hora* (Barcelona, 1974), p. 21.

63 All references are to *El coronel no tiene quien le escriba* (Barcelona, 1979). All translations are mine.

64 Rubén Pelayo, *Gabriel García Márquez: A Critical Companion* (Westport, CT, 2001), p. 54.

65 Martin, *Gabriel García Márquez*, pp. 206–7.

66 See the first line of Eliot's *The Waste Land*; *T. S. Eliot: Selected Poems* (London, 1975), p. 51.

67 See Plinio Apuleyo Mendoza, *The Fragrance of Guava: Conversations with Gabriel García Márquez* (London, 1983), p. 26. See also Ben Box, *García Márquez: 'El coronel no tiene quien le escriba'* (London, 2000), 3rd ed., p. 9. For a detailed study of the ways in which the cinematic techniques of Italian neo-Realism were incorporated in *No One Writes to the Colonel*, see the MA thesis, Elmer Morillo Valdelamar, 'García Márquez y el lenguaje fílmico: visión y escritura cinematográfica en *El coronel no tiene quien le escriba*', University of Cartagena, 2000, T. C863 M857, 57 pp. This study identifies a number of techniques, including the use of the backdrop of war (pp. 26–7); description of objects (p. 28); the use of anonymity (as in De Sica's *Umberto D.*) (p. 29); moralism (pp. 30–33); abrupt beginning to scenes (pp. 34–5); the gradual delivery of information ('dosficacion de la información') (pp. 35–8); laconic dialogue (pp. 38–41); frequent visual references, such as the description of the arrival of the post boat on Fridays (pp. 42–7); and the use of cinematic ocularization and auricularization, that is, points at which the reader is encouraged to 'see' a sequence of actions, or 'hear' a noise (such as the bell indicating the curfew) (pp. 47–51).

68 Martin, *Gabriel García Márquez*, p. 211.

69 Ibid., p. 213.

70 'Un novelista de la violencia americana', in *9 asedios a García Márquez* (Santiago de Chile, 1969), pp. 106–25 (p. 113).

71 Saldívar, *García Márquez*, p. 356.

72 'Los funerals de la Mamá Grande', in *Los funerales de la Mamá Grande* (Buenos Aires, 1977), p. 137. All translations are mine.

73 Philip Swanson argues that 'Los funerales de la Mamá Grande' satirizes 'la influencia de las oligarquías rurales en América Latina'; *Cómo leer a Gabriel García Márquez* (Madrid, 1991), p. 26.

74 See Edgar Paiewonsky-Conde, 'La escritura como acto revolucionario: *Los funerales de la Mamá Grande*', in *En el punto de mira: Gabriel García Márquez*, ed. Ana María Hernández de López (Madrid, 1985), pp. 33–53.

75 Quoted in Philip Swanson, *Cómo leer a Gabriel García Márquez*, p. 22.

76 Robin Fiddian, *Cine-Lit v*, 1 (2004), 7–13 (p. 9). Special number, *Essays on Hispanic Film and Fiction*, eds George Cabello-Castellet, Jaume Martí-Olivella and Guy H. Wood (Corvallis, OR, 2004).

77 'La siesta del martes', *Cuentos 1947–1992*, pp. 113–20 (p. 118).

78 In an earlier version of this event the thief's name was Carlos Centeno; see 'La siesta del martes', *Cuentos*, p. 118).

79 Robin Fiddian, *García Márquez: Los funerales de la Mamá Grande* (London, 2006), Critical Guides to Spanish Texts, no. 70, p. 51.

80 'A propósito de *La mala hora*', in *9 asedios a García Márquez* (Santiago de Chile, 1969), pp. 164–73 (p. 168). My translation.

81 'Un día de éstos', in *Los funerales de la Mamá Grande* (Buenos Aires, 1977), pp. 21–26 (p. 25).

4 'Even I won't be able to put up with myself.'

1 'Borges y yo', in *Jorge Luis Borges: obras completas 1923–1972* (Buenos Aires, 1974), p. 808, my translation.

2 Ibid., p. 808.

3 For a discussion of Borges in García Márquez, see Emir Rodríguez Monegal, '*One Hundred Years of Solitude*: The Last Three Pages', *Books Abroad*, XLVII/3 (1973), pp. 485–9; and Juan-Manuel García Ramos, *Cien años de soledad* (Madrid, 1989), pp. 17–18.

4 Gerald Martin, *Gabriel García Márquez: A Life* (London, 2008), p. 289.

5 Ibid., pp. 290–91.

6 García Márquez's relationship with film has been a constant if ambiguous one. When asked whether the cinema can teach the writer useful techniques, he responded: 'Well, I don't really know. In my case, the cinema has been both help and hindrance. What it did help me with was how to think in images. But at the same time, I now see an exaggerated zeal for visualizing characters and scenes, and even an obsession with camera angles and frames, in all my books prior to *One Hundred Years of Solitude*' (Apuleyo Mendoza, *The Fragrance of Guava:*

Conversations with Gabriel García Márquez (London, 1983), p. 33). He once mentioned to Dolores Calviño that he has been disappointed over the years by the film versions made of his novels and short stories.

7 Quoted in Eligio García Márquez, *Tras las claves de Melquíades: historia de 'Cien años de soledad'* (Bogotá, 2001), p. 578.

8 Miguel Fernández-Braso, *Gabriel García Márquez: una conversación infinita* (Madrid, 1969), pp. 36–7; my translation.

9 'Prologue, with Musical Chairs', in *Into the Mainstream: Conversations with Latin American Writers* (New York, 1967), pp. 1–36 (p. 35).

10 Luis Harss, 'Gabriel García Márquez, or the Lost Chord', in *Into the Mainstream: Conversations with Latin American Writers*, pp. 310–41 (p. 317).

11 See 'Black Stone on a White Stone', and 'In short, I have only my death to express my life . . .', in *César Vallejo: Complete Late Poems 1923–1938*, ed. and trans. by Valentino Gianuzzi and Michael Smith (Exeter, 2005), p. 104, and p. 265.

12 Plinio Apuleyo Mendoza, *The Fragrance of Guava*, p. 73.

13 Ibid., p. 74.

14 Ibid.

15 Martin, *Gabriel García Márquez*, p. 296.

16 Eligio García Márquez, *Tras las claves de Melquíades*, p. 617.

17 Apuleyo Mendoza, *The Fragrance of Guava*, pp. 33–4.

18 Martin, *Gabriel García Márquez*, p. 313.

19 Fausto Avendano, 'El factor del best-seller en *Cien anos de soledad*', in *Explicación de 'Cien anos de soledad'*, ed. Francisco E. Porrata (San José, 1976), pp. 65–77.

20 T. C. Boyle, 'Book of a Lifetime: *One Hundred Years of Solitude*', *Independent* (20 March 2009), p. 33.

21 Macondo was the name of one of the largest ranches of the United Fruit Company, 336 hectares, which was situated on the edge of the Sevilla river (Dasso Saldívar, *García Márquez: el viaje a la semilla: la biografía* (Madrid, 1997), p. 115). While this was its empiric root, it went beyond its empirical roots. As García Márquez once said: 'Macondo is not a place, it is a state of mind which allows you to see what you want to see and see it as you want to see it' (interview, Rubiela Reyes, 26 February 2009, Aracataca). For a dictionary-cum-encyclopaedia of places, names and characters in *One Hundred Years*

of Solitude, see Cristóbal Acosta Torres, *Macondo al desnudo: intimidades reales y ficticias en 'Cien años de soledad'* (Bucamaranga, 2005).

22 *One Hundred Years of Solitude*, trans. Gregory Rabassa (London, 1978), pp. 113–14.

23 For an excellent discussion of the portrayal of the scientific consciousness in the novel, see Roberto González Echevarría, '*Cien años de soledad*: The Novel as Myth and Archive', in *Gabriel García Márquez's 'One Hundred Years of Solitude'*, ed. Harold Bloom (Philadelphia, 2003), pp. 15–36.

24 For a discussion of the connections between science and alchemy in the novel, see Chester S. Halka, *Melquíades, Alchemy and Narrative Theory: The Quest for Gold in 'Cien años de soledad'* (Lathrup Village, MI, 1981).

25 For further discussion see Stephen Hart, 'Magical Realism in Gabriel García Márquez's *Cien años de soledad*', *Inti*, 16–17 (1982–3), 37–52.

26 *Historia de los acontecimientos que se desarrollaron en la zona bananera del Departamento del Magdalena – 13 de noviembre de 1928 al 15 de marzo de 1929* (Bogotá, 1929), 175pp. The copy in the Biblioteca Luis Ángel Arango (331.892986C67s) has a signed dedication by the General himself on the frontispiece.

27 Because Thomas Bradshaw, the manager of the United Fruit Company, refused to talk to the USTM (Unión Sindical de Trabajadores del Magdalena), the union representing the workers at the Ciénaga Banana Plantation, which had made nine demands – including collective insurance, indemnification for work-related accidents, hygienic houses, a 50 per cent increase for lower-paid workers, the closing down of the company's commissaries (*comisariatos*), the replacement of credit slips by money, the replacement of bi-weekly by weekly payments, the elimination of contractors, and the establishment of hospitals; see Marcelo Bucheli, 'The United Fruit Company in Colombia: Labour, Local Elite, and Multinational Enterprise, 1900–1970', PhD, Stanford University, 2002, p. 105), a strike was called for 11 November 1928 (p. 110). The stalemate caused by the strike meant that the UFC was unable to export any fruit out of Colombia during this period, and led to the showdown in the main square of Ciénaga on 6 December 1928.

28 Gabriel García Márquez, *Living to Tell the Tale*, trans. Edith Grossman

(London, 2003), p. 63.

29 Silvia Galvis, *Los García Márquez*, 4th edn (Medellín, 2007), p. 38.

30 Carlos Cortés Vargas, *Los sucesos de las bananeras (Historia de los acontecimientos que se desarrollaron en la zona bananera de Departamento del Magdalena – 13 de noviembre de 1928 al 15 de marzo de 1929)* (Bogotá, 1929), p. 65.

31 Ibid., pp. 65–6.

32 Cortés Vargas admitted to killing thirteen (as listed above, his report states that eight were found dead in the square, and five more found dead in the near vicinity of the square, bringing the total to thirteen), while historians gave different estimates 'from 60, to 100, 400, 800, 1,000, 1,500 and 2,000' (Bucheli, 'The United Fruit Company in Colombia', pp. 113–14). The figure of 2,000 was given by Judith White, *La United Fruit en Colombia: historia de una ignomina* (Bogotá, 1978), p. 100.

Roberto Herrera Soto and Rafael Romero Castañeda, *La zona bananera del Magdalena: historia y léxico* (Bogotá, 1979), recognize that the number of dead in the Banana Zone as a result of the conflict ranges from forty-seven in total, as given by Cortés Vargas (this is the figure for the whole region and not just for Ciénaga), to more than 2,000 as given by Marco Córdoba. In the work *Elementos de sindicalismo* (Bogotá, 1977), 3rd edn, he states that 'more than 2,000 workers were killed by official bullets on 6 December 1928' (p. 18), although no evidence is adduced to substantiate this statement, and it may well be a reaction to García Márquez's text rather than a piece of information culled from independent sources. For their part, Herrera Soto and Castañeda propose a number of between 60 and 75 (p. 79).

33 One report entitled 'A Prudent Report by General Carlos Cortés Vargas' published in *El Tiempo* on 9 December 1928, read as follows: 'Upon returning with the troops there [Ciénaga], an enormous crowd, of about 3,000 people of both sexes, surrounded the trains, shouting "Long Live the Army!" and "All we are asking for is an increase in our daily wages!" A peaceful but firm attitude prevented and prevents the movement of the trains' (p. 4). It is possible that a published account such as this one, or indeed an oral report reaching the same conclusion of people involved, found its way to García Márquez when he was drawing up his fictional version of the event in Ciénaga.

34 *El Tiempo*, xvii/6181 (9 December 1928), p. 4.

35 For a study of the characters in the novel, see Anonymous, *'Cien años de soledad': análisis y estudio sobre la obra, el autor y su épica* (Madrid, 2003).

36 See Cortés Vargas, *Los sucesos de las bananeras*, pp. 140–42.

37 Silvia Galvis, *Los García Márquez*, p. 60.

38 *El Tiempo*, xvii/6186 (14 December 1928), p. 1.

39 'Ni reacción ni impunidad', *El Tiempo* (14 December 1928), p. 3.

40 'Los partes de guerra', *El Tiempo*, xvii/6180 (8 December 1928), p. 3.

41 *El Tiempo*, xvii/6183 (11 December 1928), p. 2.

42 Carmen Arnau, *El mundo mítico de Gabriel García Márquez* (Barcelona, 1971), pp. 75–78.

43 In March 2009 I visited the site of the old, now disused river port of Ciénaga where merchandise used to be loaded during the banana boom and met a fifty-year-old inhabitant of Ciénaga who laughed when I said that the official report of those killed in the Main Square of Ciénaga on 6 December 1928 was nine. He said it must have been more than 3,000; his grandfather who was an eye-witness had told him that the square was ankle-deep in blood after the massacre. He would not allow me to take his name, or record an interview with him. I also visited the main square of Ciénaga where the statue to the Martyrs has been erected. All that is left of the Ciénaga railway station which originally backed onto the main square (which has now been turned into a road packed on both sides with market stalls) is the outer shell of the Ciénaga station itself, which is now used as a hardware shop. The shop assistant pointed to the train rails which had been used to buttress up the shop roof; I asked for permission to take a photograph of the roof but the manager refused. The rails of the track out of Ciénaga were torn up soon after the massacre took place. The hesitance of everyone I spoke to about the massacre suggested that the events of 6 December 1928 are still a very sensitive issue even eighty years later.

44 The original Spanish says 'para convencerse de que estaba vivo', *Cien años de soledad* (Barcelona, 1980), p. 247, translated incorrectly as 'in order to convince her' in the English edition (*One Hundred Years of Solitude*, p. 250).

45 For further discussion, see Stephen Hart, 'Magical Realism in the

Americas: Politicised Ghosts in *One Hundred Years of Solitude, The House of the Spirits*, and *Beloved*', *Journal of Iberian and Latin American Studies*, IX/2 (2003), 115–23.

46 Herrera Soto and Castañeda, *La zona bananera del Magdalena*, p. 74; my translation.

47 For an excellent discussion of the conflict between the oral and the written modes in the novel, see James Higgins, '*Cien años de soledad*', in *Gabriel García Márquez's 'One Hundred Years of Solitude': A Casebook*, ed. Gene H. Bell-Villada (Oxford, 2002), pp. 33–51.

48 Carmenza Kline underlines the importance of the child who witnessed the events in her analysis; see *Fiction and Reality in the Works of Gabriel García Márquez*, trans. Daniel Linder (Salamanca, 2002), pp. 104–6.

49 See Judith White, *La United Fruit en Colombia*, pp. 106–8.

50 Jorge Eliécer Gaitán, *La Masacre en las bananeras: documentos testimonios* (Bogotá, n.d.), pp. 117–18.

51 This is the estimate provided by Jaime García Márquez; see chapter One, note 18.

52 Martin also makes the following statement: 'None of Nicolás Márquez's "natural children" inherited his name: they all carried their mother's surname' (*Gabriel García Márquez*, n. 5, p. 576). This is not borne out, however, by the table on page 573 which shows that the youngest offspring has the name Petronila Arias Márquez, which raises the possibility that, though it was more common (especially for the older children) to take the mother's surname, adopting the father's surname also occurred (though, perhaps, less frequently).

53 The unknown Márquez might have been born between about 1900 and 1910, possibly in Ciénaga, where the murder occurred; after all Colonel Nicolás is known to have fathered illegitimate children with a woman, Isabel Ruiz, who lived in that city (Martin, *Gabriel García Márquez*, p. 19).

54 Martin, *Gabriel García Márquez*, p. 5.

55 For further discussion of repetition and the mirror motif in the novel, see María Eulalia Montaner, *Guía para la lectura de 'Cien años de soledad'* (Madrid, 1981), pp. 199–211.

56 Carlos Fuentes, *Gabriel García Márquez and the Invention of America* (Liverpool, 1987), p. 9.

57 For a discussion of the role of Oedipal myth see Josefina Ludmer, '*Cien*

años de soledad': una interpretación (Buenos Aires, 1972), pp. 22–30.
For an insightful Freudian analysis of Melquíades' hieroglyphs, see
Emerita Fuenmayor, 'Histoire d'un paradoxe', *Silex*, 11 (1979), 94–99.

5 'Why did he dress like a cook to receive the Nobel?'

1 'Why did he dress like a cook to receive the Nobel Prize?' – a comment
   made to Plinio Apuleyo Mendoza by one of his friends about García
   Márquez. From a lecture by Apuleyo Mendoza at London
   Metropolitan University, 8 December 2008.
2 Michael Palencia-Roth, *Gabriel García Márquez: la línea, el círculo y las
   metamorfosis del mito* (Madrid, 1983), p. 137.
3 Regina James, *Gabriel García Márquez: Revolution in Wonderland*
   (Columbia, SC, 1981), p. 78.
4 Jacques Joset, *Gabriel García Márquez: coétano de la eternidad*
   (Amsterdam, 1984), pp. 25–29.
5 As consulted on 15 January 2008.
6 Examples of academic works published early on on magical realism
   are Emir Rodríguez Monegal, 'Realismo mágico versus literatura
   fantástica: un diálogo de sordos', in *Otros mundos, otros fuegos: fantasía
   y realismo mágico en Iberoamérica: memoria del XVI Congreso Internacional de Literatura Iberoamericana*, ed. Donald A. Yates (East
   Lansing, MI, 1975), pp. 25–37; Juan Barroso, *'Realismo mágico' y 'lo
   real maravilloso' en* El reino de este mundo *y* El siglo de las luces
   (Miami, 1977); Irlemar Chiampi, *El realismo maravilloso: forma e
   ideología en la novela hispanoamericana* (Caracas, 1983). For further
   information see Stephen M. Hart and Kenneth Reeds, 'Guide to
   Further Reading', in *A Companion to Magical Realism*, eds Stephen
   M. Hart and Wen-chin Ouyang (London, 2005), pp. 281–4.
7 Mario Vargas Llosa, *García Márquez: historia de un deicidio* (Barcelona,
   1971), p. 81. The publication of Vargas Llosa's *Historia de un deicidio*
   led to a colourful exchange between him and Ángel Rama, now
   published as Ángel Rama, Mario Vargas Llosa, *García Márquez y la
   problemática de la novela* (Buenos Aires, 1973). Rama criticized Vargas
   Llosa for his out of date Romantic aesthetics (p.8), and Vargas Llosa
   responded by criticizing the latter's anachronistic 'neo-Lukácsian

convictions' (p. 22). In his first reply Rama attacks the individualism underpinning Vargas Llosa's position, arguing instead that the writer is part of a social group (pp. 28–9), to which Vargas Llosa replied that a writer could form part of a society and also be an individualist as well as a dissident within that society (pp. 50–52). Rama's second and final reply underscored the importance in his view of the classist understanding of the social function of literature (p. 60).

8 Angel Esteban and Stephanie Panichelli, *Gabo y Fidel: el paisaje de una amistad* (Bogotá, 2004), pp. 48–55.

9 Vargas Llosa began calling García Márquez 'Castro´s courtesane' (*el cortesano de Castro*, see Esteban and Panichelli, *Gabo y Fidel*, p. 66).

10 Vargas Llosa did, however, finally relent and, in 2007, he allowed part of his essay to be reprinted in the commemorative edition of *One Hundred Years of Solitude* published by the Spanish Language Academy.

11 Thomas Catán, 'The truth behind two giants of literature, one black eye and 30 years of silence', *The Times* (13 March 2007), p. 33. See Rodrigo Moya, 'La terrífica historia de un ojo morado', *La Jornada* (6 March 2007). The article contains a photograph of García Marquez with a black eye. García Márquez and Mercedes went to see Rodrigo Moya and asked for the photograph to be taken as evidence. Mercedes was incandescent about the event, and called Vargas Llosa a 'stupid jealous man' (*un celoso estúpido*) repeatedly while the photographs were being taken.

12 Gerald Martin, *Gabriel García Márquez: A Life* (London, 2008), p. 390.

13 'García Márquez posmoderno: el relativismo de la verdad', *Ínsula*, 723 (March 2007), 12–15 (p. 12). Special number entitled 'Ciento cuarenta años de soledad y ochenta de vida'.

14 See Arnold M. Penuel, 'The Theme of Colonialism in *La increíble y triste historia de la cándida Eréndira y de su abuela desalmada*', in his *Intertextuality in García Márquez* (York, SC, 1994), pp. 88–106.

15 Elena Clementelli points to solitude as a theme linking the two novels, *García Márquez* (Florence, 1975), p. 126.

16 Esteban and Panichelli, *Gabo y Fidel*, pp. 98–99.

17 *Chile, el Golpe y los Gringos* (Bogotá, 1974), pp. 11–34.

18 Gerald Martin, *Gabriel García Márquez*, p. 389.

19 Esteban and Panichelli, *Gabo y Fidel*, p. 95.

20 Quoted in ibid., p. 117.

21 *The Autumn of the Patriarch*, trans. Gregory Rabassa (London, 1977. All references are to this edition.

22 See www.christies.com/LotFinder/lot_details.aspx?from=search results&intObjectID=1524776&sid=ee49b30a-a86b-47eb-8bcf-of8cfff705ea (accessed 29 December 2009).

23 Martha L. Canfield analyses the 'excremental motif' in the novel; *El 'patriarca' de García Márquez: arquetipo literario del dictador his-panoamericano* (Florence, 1984), pp. 39–45.

24 For an excellent discussion of the satiric qualities of *The Autumn of the Patriarch*, see Isabel Rodríguez-Vergara, *El mundo satírico de Gabriel García Márquez* (Madrid, 1991), pp. 21–75.

25 As Jo Labanyi suggests, the novel has 'a bewildering profusion of intermediary narrators, all of them unreliable'; '*El otoño del patriarca*', in *Gabriel García Márquez*, ed. Harold Bloom (Philadelphia, PA, 2007), pp. 145–58 (p. 152). For a discussion of how the various voices play off against each other, see Kalman Barsy, *La estructura dialéctica de 'El otoño del patriarca'* (Río Piedras, 1989).

26 See www.christies.com/LotFinder/lot_details.aspx?from=search results&intObjectID=1524776&sid=ee49b30a-a86b-47eb-8bcf-of8cfff705ea (accessed 29 December 2009).

27 Martin, *Gabriel García Márquez*, p. 391.

28 *Operación Carlota* (Lima: Prensa Latina, 1977), p. 15.

29 Martin, *Gabriel García Márquez*, pp. 393–94.

30 Ibid., p. 396.

31 Mohan Ramahan, 'Graham Greene's Latin America', in *García Márquez and Latin America*, ed. Alok Bhalla (London, 1987), pp. 116–28.

32 Esteban and Panichelli, *Gabo y Fidel*, pp. 174–75.

33 Restrepo Sánchez, *Gabriel García Márquez y el cine*, pp. 74–75. Miguel Littín has argued that the expression of the unconscious which is central to García Márquez's literary works does not transfer well to the silver screen (Restrepo Sánchez, p. 77). Littín has suggested furthermore that there are two Gabos, one the literary writer who is 'difficult to classify', and the other who is the cineaste who loves neo-Realist cinema (Restrepo Sánchez, p. 76).

34 Claudia Dreyfus, 'Playboy Interview: Gabriel García Márquez', *Playboy*, 30.2 (February 1983), 65–77, 172–78 (p. 73).

35 Quoted in John Benson, '*Cronica de una muerte anunciada*', *Latin American Literary Review*, 11 (1982), 63–67 (p. 64).

36 Ibid., p. 64.

37 Gabriel García Márquez, *Living to Tell the Tale*, trans. Edith Grossman (London, 2003), pp. 382–83.

38 Julio Roca and Camilo Calderón, 'García Márquez lo vio morir', *Al Día*, no. 1 (28 April 1981), 52–60, 108–9. Julio Roca, 'Sí, la devolví la noche de bodas', *Al Día*, no. 3 (12 May 1981), 24–27.

39 *Living to Tell the Tale*, p. 383.

40 See Donald Shaw's excellent article, '*Chronicle of a Death Foretold*: Narrative Function and Interpretation', in Bradley A. Shaw and Nora Vera-Godwin (eds), *Critical Perspectives on Gabriel García Márquez* (Lincoln, NE, 1986), pp. 91–104.

41 In his poem 'Batallas III' from *España, aparta de mí este cáliz*, Vallejo gives a sense of the magnitude of the death of the republican militiaman by referring to how Pedro Rojas dies not only as a 'man', but also a 'father' to his children, as a 'husband' to his wife, and as a 'railway worker' to his friends at work, thereby suggesting that his death has various ramifications in the community rather than simply being the death of 'one' person; see *César Vallejo: Selected Poems*, ed. Stephen Hart (London, 2000), pp. 84–86.

42 Amelia S. Simpson, *Detective Fiction from Latin America* (Toronto, 1990), pp. 167–75.

43 *Living to Tell the Tale*, p. 283.

44 *Chronicle of a Death Foretold*, trans. Gregory Rabassa (London, 1983), p. 99.

45 Eligio García Márquez, *La tercera muerte de Santago Nasar* (Mexico City, 1989), pp. 40–41.

46 Josefa Salmon, 'El poder de la anunciación en *Cien años de soledad* y *Crónica de una muerte anunciada*', *Discurso Literario: Revista de Temas Hispánicos*, 1 (1983), 67–77.

47 The screenplay was subsequently retitled *El asalto: El operativo que el FSLN se lanzó al mundo. Un relato cinematográfico* (Managua, 1982).

48 Esteban and Panichelli, *Gabo y Fidel*, pp. 167–68.

49 As Arthur Lundkvist, the member on the 18-person panel that made up the Nobel Prize Committee acting as the Spanish and Latin America literature expert, pointed out in an interview, García Márquez

was awarded the Nobel Prize mainly as a result of *One Hundred Years of Solitude*, although this novel had been published fifteen years earlier; see Eligio García Márquez, 'Entrevista a Arthur Lundkvist', in *La soledad de América Latina*, pp. 49–58 (p. 56).

50 In a lecture given at London Metropolitan University on 8 December 2008. See definition of *pavoso* in Margret S. de Oliveira Castro, *La lengua ladina de García Márquez* (Bogotá, 2007), p. 279.

51 'La soledad del Nobel', in *La soledad de América Latina*, pp. 31–48 (p. 35).

52 See Esteban and Panichelli, *Gabo y Fidel*, p. 196.

53 Ibid., p. 199

54 In a lecture given by Plinio Apuleyo Mendoza at London Metropolitan University on 8 December 2008.

55 The footage of the event can be seen on YouTube at http://uk.youtube.com/watch?v=GFIYyesVAE8&feature=related.

56 Esteban and Panichelli, *Gabo y Fidel*, p. 199.

57 Ibid., p. 209.

58 Silvia Galvis, *Los García Márquez*, 4th ed. (Medellín, 2007), p. 18.

59 'The Solitude of Latin America: Nobel address 1982', trans. Richard Cardwell, in *Gabriel García Márquez: New Readings*, ed. Bernard McGuirk and Richard Cardwell (Cambridge, 1987), pp. 207–11 (p. 208).

60 Gabriel García Márquez, 'La soledad de América Latina (Conferencia Nobel 1982)', in *La soledad de América Latina: brindis por la poesía* (Cali, 1983), pp. 3–12 (p. 3).

6 'A chancellor but we don't know of which country'

1 'He's a chancellor but we don't know of which country.' This is what Fidel Castro once said of García Márquez; see Silvia Galvis, *Los García Márquez*, 4th edn (Medellín, 2007), p. 53.

2 Isabel Allende, *La casa de los espíritus* (Barcelona, 1982); *The House of the Spirits*, trans. Magda Bodin (New York, 1985). Laura Esquivel, *Como agua para chocolate* (Mexico City, 1989); *Like Water for Chocolate*, trans. Carol Christensen and Thomas Christensen (New York, 1993). There has been an important film version of the book directed by Alfonso Arau; see Stephen Hart, *Companion to Latin American Film*

(London, 2004), pp. 171–78. Luis Sepúlveda, *Un viejo que leía novelas de amor* (Barcelona, 1993); *The Old Man who Read Love Stories*, trans. Peter Bush (London, 2002). For a discussion of the magical-real elements in Isabel Allende's novel, see Stephen Hart, '*The House of the Spirits* by Isabel Allende', in *The Cambridge Companion to the Latin American Novel*, ed. Efraín Kristal (Cambridge, 2005), 270–82.

3 Elleke Boehmer, *Colonial and Post Colonial Literature: Migrant Metaphors* (Oxford, 2005), p. 235.

4 Jean-Pierre Durix, *Mimesis, Genres and Post-Colonial Discourse: Deconstructing Magic Realism* (London, 1998), p. 187.

5 Homi Bhabha, 'Introduction', *Nation and Narration* (London, 1995), pp. 1–7 (pp. 6–7).

6 Mario Vargas Llosa, *García Márquez: historia de un deicidio* (Barcelona, 1971), p. 84.

7 Ibid., p. 83.

8 Translated into English as Plinio Apuleyo Mendoza, *The Fragrance of Guava: Conversations with Gabriel García Márquez* (London: Verso, 1983).

9 García Márquez is keenly aware of the need to maintain his reputation as the only living Nobel Prize writer of Latin America, and thus he seeks to retain a tight control over the ways his ideas are reported in the press (hence his reluctance to give interviews); he is also well aware that any work he publishes will be judged according to the high standards set by his earlier work. There have been times when he has felt 'oppressed' by his fame as a result; interview with Dolores Calviño, Havana, 5 December 2007.

10 Galvis, *Los García Márquez*, p. 67.

11 García Márquez's brother, Jaime, has argued that, rather than the family members getting ideas from Gabo, the reverse occurs: 'it's [Gabo] who draws sustenance from the phrases and the atmosphere in our family; that is the most important source [of his work]', Galvis, *Los García Márquez*, p. 32.

12 Marlise Simons, 'The Best Years of His Life: An Interview with Gabriel García Márquez', *New York Times Book Review* (10 April 1988), pp. 22–24.

13 *Love in the Time of Cholera*, trans. Edith Grossman (London, 1991), pp. 339–40.

14 Gabriel García Márquez, *Living to Tell the Tale*, trans. Edith Grossman

206

(London, 2003), p. 59.

15 'Yo soy racionalmente ateo, pero católico en el corazón', in Galvis,
    Los García Márquez, pp. 21–58.

16 See Thomas Fahy, *Gabriel García Márquez's 'Love in the Time of
    Cholera'* (London, 2003), pp. 42–48.

17 For a discussion of the role of the parrot in the novel, see Jean Franco,
    'Dr Urbino's Parrot', in *Gabriel García Márquez's 'Love in the Time of
    Cholera'*, ed. Harold Bloom (Philadelphia, PA, 2005), pp. 99–112.

18 Galvis, *Los García Márquez*, p. 44.

19 'Llorones inservibles', as Jaime recalls; see Galvis, *Los García Márquez*,
    p. 56.

20 *Permiso para vivir (Antimemerias)* (Barcelona, 1998), p. 450.

21 Conversation with Julio García Espinosa in Nuevo Vedado, Havana,
    15 July 2009.

22 For the reference to Fidel Castro's favourite meal see Manuel Vázquez
    Montalbán, *Y Dios entró en La Habana* (Madrid, 1998), p. 254. For
    he recipe of 'Langosta a lo Macondo', see *Rey langosta: creaciones del
    maestro Gilberto Smith* (Havana, 2000), pp. 18–19.

23 Holly Aylett set up the interview, filmed the footage in Colombia,
    and directed the documentary on García Márquez; presentation
    given at UCL at the Festival of the Moving Image, Bloomsbury
    Theatre, 30 October 2007.

24 See García Márquez, *Cómo se cuenta un cuento: taller de guión de Gabriel
    García Márquez* (San Antonio de los Baños, 1996). I am grateful to
    Vladimir Smith for lending me a copy of this book. There is also a
    CD-ROM based on the seminar, García Márquez, *Cómo se cuenta un
    cuento*, read by Luis Gabriel González N. (Bogotá, 2004).

25 See, for example, *44 Festival Internacional de Cine y TV de Cartagena
    2004. 27 de Febrero al 5 de marzo* (Cartagena, 2004).

26 *El cataclismo de Damocles* (Bogotá, 1986), p. 13.

27 *La aventura de Miguel Littín clandestino en Chile: un reportaje de Gabriel
    García Márquez* (Buenos Aires, 1986), p. 28.

28 Restrepo Sánchez, *Gabriel García Márquez y el cine* (Barranquilla, 2001),
    p. 79.

29 Angel Esteban and Stephanie Panichelli, *Gabo y Fidel: el paisaje de una
    amistad* (Bogotá, 2004), p. 101.

30 Alfredo Bryce Echenique, *Permiso para vivir (Antimemorias)*

(Barcelona, 1998), p. 428; my translation.

31 Based on *The General in his Labyrinth*, trans. Edith Grossman (New York, 2004), p. 10, though revised. The original Spanish runs as follows: "'Sábado ocho de mayo del año de treinta, día en que los ingleses flecharon a Juana de Arco," anunció el mayordomo. "Está lloviendo desde las tres de la madrugada." "Desde las tres de la madrugada del siglo diecisiete", dijo el general con la voz todavía perturbada por el aliento acre del insomnio.' *El general en su laberinto*, 5th edn (Barcelona, 1998), p. 10. The English edition provides the translation of the first sentence as follows: 'Saturday, May 8, 1830, the Day of the Blessed Virgin, Mediatrix of all Grace' (p. 10). This is incorrect since it does not refer to the way the English mistreated Joan of Arc and, thereby, misses one of the crucial motifs of the novel, that is, Bolívar's obsession with Europe, including England. Hence the rather odd comment made by Bolívar to the English diplomat: 'I hope there is not much fog this autumn in Hyde Park' (*The General in his Labyrinth*, p. 34, revised).

32 Stephen M. Hart, 'Blood, Ink and Proteus: Simón Bolívar as Proteus', *Bulletin of Spanish Studies*, LXXXII/3–4 (2005), 335–52 (p. 346).

33 Compare José Gil de Castro's *Portrait of Simón Bolívar in Lima* (1825) with Dubois's *Here is Your Liberator* (nineteenth century, precise date unknown); see *Art in Latin America: The Modern Era, 1820–1980*, ed. Dawn Ades (London, 1989), p. 20, p. 17. See also the discussion in Stephen M. Hart, 'Blood, Ink and Proteus', pp. 341–47.

34 *Living to Tell the Tale*, pp. 183–4.

35 Pablo Carrascosa Miguel points to the role of zoomorphism in the novel; *'El general en su laberinto': G. García Márquez* (Barcelona, 1989), p. 72.

36 *The General in his Labyrinth*, p. 163; in the original Spanish, 'soy un desterrado', *El general en su laberinto*, p. 190.

37 As Thomas E. Skidmore and Peter H. Smith point out: 'Exactly what happened there has never been established'; *Modern Latin America* (Oxford, 1992), p. 34.

38 See José María Espinosa, *Bolívar: Portrait of the Liberator*, in *Art in Latin America* (London, 1984), p. 18.

39 Ibid., p. 21.

40 Christine Toomey, 'The life and loves of inFidelity Castro', *Sunday Times Magazine* (28 December 2008), pp. 13–17 (p. 15).

41 Michiko Kakuti, 'Books of the Times; The Human Behind the Heroic Pose', *New York Times* (11 September 1990), The Arts.

42 'Prólogo: porqué doce, porqué cuentos y porqué peregrinos', in *Doce cuentos peregrinos* (Bogotá, 1992), pp. 13–14 (p. 13).

43 'La santa', *Doce cuentos peregrinos*, pp. 57–73 (p. 69).

44 Olga Sigüenza Ponce has argued that the main themes of the whole collection are death, solitude, the lack of communication and love; see 'Elementos estilísticos en *Doce cuentos peregrinos*', in Jesús Humberto Florencia Zaldívar, Luis Quintana Tejera, and Olga Sigüenza Ponce, *Tres perspectivas de análisis en el marco de la obra de Gabriel García Márquez* (Mexico City, 2002), pp. 101–65 (p. 162).

45 Gerald Martin, *Gabriel García Márquez: A Life* (London, 2008), pp. 213–14.

7 'The Third Pope'

1 Dagmar Ploetz, *Gabriel García Márquez* (Madrid, 2004), pp. 158–61.

2 *Of Love and Other Demons*, trans. Edith Grossman (London, 1996). All references are to this edition.

3 *Diatriba de amor contra un hombre sentado* (Bogotá, 1994), p. 10.

4 Manuel Vázquez Montalbán, *Y Dios entró en La Habana* (Madrid, 1998), pp. 51–52.

5 All references are to *Noticias de un secuestro* (Barcelona, 2007). All translations are my own.

6 Frei Betto, *Fidel Castro y la religión: conversaciones con Frei Betto* (Mexico City, 1986).

7 Vázquez Montalbán, *Y Dios entró en La Habana*, p. 560.

8 Ibid., p. 567.

9 Angel Esteban and Stephanie Panichelli, *Gabo y Fidel: el paisaje de una amistad* (Bogotá, 2004), p. 217.

10 Ibid., p. 219.

11 Bryce Echenique, *Permiso para vivir*, p. 440; my translation. 'Cuba is the only place where I am as I am', as Gabo once told a journalist; see Bernard Marqués, 'García Márquez, pasado y presente de una obra', *Alternativa*, 93 (9–16 August 1978), pp. 6–7 (p. 7).

12 Vázquez Montalbán, *Y Dios entró en La Habana*, p. 560.

13 Jon Lee Anderson, 'El poder de Gabo', *Semana*, no. 909 (4–11 October 1999), 46–66 (p. 49).

14 Ibid., p. 49.

15 Larry Rohter, 'Bogotá Journals: García Márquez Embraces Old Love (That's News!), *New York Times* (27 January 1999).

16 Quoted in ibid.

17 Quoted in ibid.

18 Quoted in ibid.

19 See http://dewereldstaatstil.web-log.nl/mijn_weblog/2008/12/farewell-letter.html (accessed 1 February 2009).

20 Ibid.

21 Raúl Trejo Delarbe, 'Ciberperiodismo, nuevo periodismo, viejos dilemas', www.portalcomunicacion.com/both/aab/ent/trejo/pc_trejo_ciberperiodismo.pdf (accessed 28 January 2009).

22 'Prólogo', in *Mañana será demasiado tarde* (Tafalla, 2000), pp. 7–20 (p. 11).

23 Esteban and Panichelli, *Gabo y Fidel*, p. 295.

24 See www.cuba-junky.com/cuba/article-elian.html (accessed 20 March 2009).

25 Esteban and Panichelli, *Gabo y Fidel*, pp. 306–9.

26 *Miami Herald*, 29 June 2000; consulted at www.cubanet.org/CNews/y00/jun00/29e11.htm (accessed 20 March 2009).

27 The recipe is as follows: '2 lobsters, peppered salt according to taste, 4–5 garlic cloves, juice from 4 lemons, 240 ml (1 tablespoon) of vegetable oil, 1 twig of coriander, 1 medium-sized white onion, 2 green peppers, $^1/_4$ teaspoon of paprika, 240g (1 cup) of soft boiled rice, 100g (3.5 oz) of butter, 60 ml ($^1/_4$ cup) of rum, 60 ml ($^1/_4$ cup) of white wine, a few drops of Tabasco sauce, Worcester sauce (*salsa inglesa*) according to taste, 200g (7 oz) of grated Parmesan cheese (optional). Clean the lobsters thoroughly and cut them longways into two halves. Marinate the lobsters with peppered salt, crushed garlic, lemon juice and a little vegetable oil, to avoid the acid pickling the mixture. Prepare a garnish with oil with the garlic, coriander, onion, peppers, which should all be finely cut and seasoned with a little paprika. Half of this garnish should be mixed with the soft rice. Cut the flesh of the lobster into small pieces and sauté the pieces in equal measures of butter and oil to seal. Flambé with rum and extinguish the

flames with the white wine. Add the rest of the garnish to the lobster and mix it up thoroughly. Add paprika, a few drops of Tabasco sauce and Worcester sauce, according to taste. The head of the lobster is covered with the rice and the tail is stuffed with the sauteed mixture. If desired, Parmesan grated cheese can be sprinkled on top and cooked au gratin. Serve piping hot'; see *Rey langosta: creaciones del Maestro Gilberto Smith* (Havana, 2000), p. 17). I visited Maestro Gilberto Smith in July 2006 and he prepared a wonderful Macondo-style lobster. Gilberto Smith was for many years Fidel Castro's personal chef and mentioned how relaxed Castro always was in Gabo's company.

28 Interview with Julio García Espinosa, 3 December 2007, Havana, Cuba.

29 Conrado Zuluaga, *García Márquez: el vicio incurable de contar* (Bogotá, 2006), p. 125.

30 Ricardo Bada, 'La ficción de la ficción', *Cuadernos Hispanoamericanos*, 633 (March 2003), 122–26; Efraín Kristal, 'Lessons from the Golden Age in Gabriel García Márquez's *Living to Tell the Tale*', in *A Companion to Magical Realism*, ed. Stephen Hart and Wen-chin Ouyang, pp. 88–97.

31 Gabriel García Márquez, *Living to Tell the Tale*, trans. Edith Grossman (London, 2003), p. 23.

32 Ibid., p. 16.

33 Ibid., p. 63.

34 See the discussion of the interplay between reality and fiction as mediated by the creative false memory in chapter four of this book.

35 'La nota dominical que he escrito sin desmayos durante más de medio siglo'; *Memorias de mis putas tristes* (Barcelona, 2004), p. 12. All translations are mine.

36 Lauren Weiner, 'In Love With a Child Prostitute', *Wall Street Journal* (29 October 2005), Books Section; Alberto Manguel, 'A sad affair', *Guardian* (12 November 2005), Books; Andrew Holgate, 'Love's redemptive Powers', *The Times* (23 October 2005), Books section.

37 Adam Feinstein, 'Sleeping Seamstress', *TLS*, no. 5306 (10 December 2004), p. 23.

38 BBC News, 16 November 2007; http://news.bbc.co.uk/2/hi/americas/7098233.stm (date accessed 30 December 2009).

39 'Birthplace of "Magic Realism" Wonders What's in a Name', *New York Times* (26 June 2006), Americas section.

40 Simon Romero, 'The Town's Biggest Event Since the Banana Fever Ended', *New York Times* (7 March 2007), World News section.

41 Ibid.

42 Joshua Goodman, 'On 80th birthday, Colombia vows to rebuild García Márquez's home', *Herald Tribune* (6 March 2007), Americas section.

43 Juan Forero, 'For García Márquez, a Magical Homecoming', *Washington Post* (2 June 2007), A01.

44 'Colombian writer García Márquez feted in homecoming', see www.reuters.com/article/idusN3146707120070531.

45 Rubiela Reyes, interview with the author, Aracataca, 26 February 2009.

46 Rubiela Reyes, interview with the author, Aracataca, 26 February 2009.

47 See http://uk.youtube.com/watch?v=yv7T7XQBE.

48 Interview with Dolores Calviño, Havana, 3 December 2007.

49 Anonymous, 'Famed Colombian writer García Márquez mobbed at press gathering', see www.cbc.ca/arts/books/story/2007/03/20/marquez-columbia-mob.html (accessed 28 January 2009).

50 Jon Lee Anderson, 'El poder de Gabo', *Semana* (4–11 October 1999), 46–66 (p. 46). Translated from the original article, 'The Power of Gabriel García Márquez', *New York Times* (27 September 1999); see www.themodernword.com/gabo/gabo_power.html. His driver when he is in Colombia nowadays is Rafael.

51 Anonymous, 'Famed Colombian writer García Márquez mobbed at press gathering'.

52 Gerald Martin, *Gabriel García Márquez: A Life* (London, 2008), p. 564.

53 Frank Bajak, 'Colombia honors García Márquez', see www.cartagenainfo.net/english/garcia-marquez.html (accessed 28 January 2009).

54 Bajak, 'Colombia Honors García Márquez'.

55 Martin, *Gabriel García Márquez*, pp. 565–66.

56 Bajak, 'Colombia Honors García Márquez'.

57 Frank Bajak, '80 Years of García Márquez: tributes mark writer's birthday', *Guardian* (28 March 2007), International Section, p. 26. For information about the deluxe commemorative edition of *Cien años de soledad* on its fortieth anniversary, see Juan Cruz, 'Días de alboroto

caribeño', *El País* (27 March 2007), 45–46.

58 Although the Protocol House was a gift from Fidel Castro, García
Márquez took the precaution of finding out who its former owner
was in the pre-Revolutionary days, and has purchased it from that
individual who now lives in the United States.

59 Email from Dolores Calviño, 10 February 2009.

60 Juan Pablo Bustamante, '*El amor en los tiempos del cólera* se filmó en
Macondo', *Cine Cubano*, 165 (July–September 2007), 69–75 (p. 73).

61 Peter Bradshaw, 'Love in the Time of Cholera', *Guardian* (21 March
2008), Features section, p. 8.

62 Giles Tremlett, 'Magical and real: García Márquez is writing new
novel, says friend', *Guardian* (10 December 2008), International
Section, p. 23; see www.guardian.co.uk/books/2008/dec/10/
gabriel-garcia-marquez-new-novel (accessed 15 January 2009).

63 Paul Hamilos, 'Gabriel García Márquez, literary giant, lays down
his pen', *Guardian* (2 April 2009), International section, p. 20; see
www.guardian.co.uk/books/2009/apr/02/columbia-gabriel-garcia-
marquez-books (accessed 9 April 2009).

64 Elizabeth Nash, 'Furious Garcia Marquez denies he will never write
again', *Independent* (8 April 2009); see www.independent.co.uk/
news/world/europe/furious-garcia-marquez-denies-he-will-never-
write-again-1665373.html (accessed 9 April 2009).

65 Ibid. García Márquez's daily routine in the 1990s was described by Jon
Lee Anderson: Gabo normally gets up at five o'clock in the morning,
reads a book until seven o'clock, gets dressed, reads the newspapers,
answers his email until ten o'clock, and then – *come what may* – he
writes from ten o'clock until 2.30 p.m.; 'El poder de Gabo', *Semana*,
no. 909 (4–11 October 1999), 46–66 (p. 48).

66 See http://globedia.com/pronto-comenzara-rodaje-noticia-pelicula.

Select Bibliography

Works by Gabriel García Márquez

García Márquez, Gabriel, *Vivir para contarla* (Barcelona, 2002), *Living to Tell the Tale*, trans. Edith Grossman (London, 2003)
——, *Innocent Eréndira and other stories*, trans. Gregory Rabassa (London, 1981)
——, *Gabriel García Márquez: cuentos 1947–1992* (Bogotá, 1999)
——, *Crónicas y reportajes* (Bogotá, 1976)
——, *Relato de un náufrago que estuvo diez días a la deriva en una balsa sin comer ni beber, que fue proclamado héroe de la patria, besado por las reinas de la belleza y hecho rico por la publicidad, y luego aborrecido por el gobierno y olvidado para siempre* (Barcelona, 1970), 3rd edition
——, *Leaf Storm*, trans. Gregory Rabassa (London, 1979)
——, *Cuando era feliz e indocumentado* (Caracas, 1973)
——, *De viaje por los países socialistas* (Bogotá, 1978)
——, *La mala hora* (Barcelona, 1974).
——, *Los funerales de la Mamá Grande* (Buenos Aires, 1977)
——, *One Hundred Years of Solitude*, trans. Gregory Rabassa (London, 1978)
——, *La soledad de América Latina: brindis por la poesía* (Cali, 1983)
——, *Operación Carlota* (Lima, 1977)
——, *Memorias de mis putas tristes* (Barcelona, 2004)
——, *Noticias de un secuestro* (Barcelona, 2007)
——, *Of Love and Other Demons*, trans. Edith Grossman (London, 1996)
——, *Diatriba de amor contra un hombre sentado* (Bogotá, 1994)
——, *Doce cuentos peregrinos* (Bogotá, 1992)
——, *The General in his Labyrinth*, trans. Edith Grossman (New York, 2004)
——, *El general en su laberinto*, 5th edition (Barcelona, 1998)

——, *El cataclismo de Damocles* (Bogotá, 1986)

——, *La aventura de Miguel Littín clandestino en Chile: un reportaje de Gabriel García Márquez* (Buenos Aires, 1986)

——, *Cómo se cuenta un cuento: taller de guión de Gabriel García Márquez* (San Antonio de los Baños, 1996)

——, *Love in the Time of Cholera*, trans. Edith Grossman (London, 1991)

——, *El asalto: El operativo que el FSLN se lanzó al mundo. Un relato cinematográfico* (Managua, 1982)

——, *Chile, el Golpe y los Gringos* (Bogotá, 1974)

——, *The Autumn of the Patriarch*, trans. Gregory Rabassa (London, 1977)

——, *Chronicle of a Death Foretold*, trans. Gregory Rabassa (London, 1983)

——, *Cien años de soledad* (Barcelona, 1980)

Journalism

Gilard, Jacques, ed., *Gabriel García Márquez: textos costeños: obra periodística vol. I* (Madrid, 1981)

—— ed., *Gabriel García Márquez: Obra periodística III: Entre cachacos* (Bogotá, 1983)

Interviews

Anderson, Jon Lee, 'El poder de Gabo', *Semana*, no. 909 (4–11 October 1999), 46–66

Apuleyo Mendoza, Plinio, *The Fragrance of Guava: Conversations with Gabriel García Márquez* (London, 1983)

Dreyfus, Claudia, 'Playboy Interview: Gabriel García Márquez', *Playboy*, xxx/2 (February 1983), 65–77, 172–78

Harss, Luis, *Into the Mainstream: Conversations with Latin American Writers* (New York, 1967)

Simons, Marlise, 'The Best Years of His Life: An Interview with Gabriel García Márquez', *New York Times Book Review* (10 April 1988), 22–24

Reviews

Bada, Ricardo, 'La ficción de la ficción', *Cuadernos Hispanoamericanos*, 633 (March 2003), pp. 122–6

Boyle, T. C., 'Book of a Lifetime: *One Hundred Years of Solitude*', *Independent* (20 March 2009), p. 33

Bradshaw, Peter, 'Love in the Time of Cholera', *Guardian* (21 March 2008), Features section, p. 8

Feinstein, Adam, 'Sleeping Seamstress', *TLS*, no. 5306 (10 December 2004), p. 23

Holgate, Andrew, 'Love's redemptive Powers', *The Times* (23 October 2005), Books section

Kakuti, Michiko, 'Books of the Times; The Human Behind the Heroic Pose', *New York Times* (11 September 1990), The Arts

Manguel, Alberto, 'A sad affair', *Guardian* (12 November 2005), Books.

Weiner, Lauren, 'In Love With a Child Prostitute', *Wall Street Journal* (29 October 2005), Books Section

Biographies

Esteban, Ángel, and Stephanie Panichelli, *Gabo y Fidel: el paisaje de una amistad* (Bogotá, 2004)

Galvis, Silvia, *Los García Márquez*, 4th edition (Medellín, 2007)

García Usta, Jorge, *Como aprendió a escribir García Márquez* (Medellín, 1995)

——, *García Márquez en Cartagena: sus inicios literarios* (Bogotá, 2007)

Martin, Gerald, *Gabriel García Márquez: A Life* (London, 2008)

Pelayo, Rubén, *Gabriel García Márquez: A Biography* (Santa Barbara, CA, 2008)

Saldívar, Dasso, *García Márquez: el viaje a la semilla: la biografía* (Madrid, 1997)

Starans, Ilan, *Gabriel García Márquez: The Early Years* (New York, 2010)

Vázquez Montalbán, Manuel, *Y Dios entró en La Habana* (Madrid, 1998)

Secondary Criticism

Acosta Torres, Cristóbal, *Macondo al desnudo: intimidades reales y ficticias en 'Cien años de soledad'* (Bucamaranga, 2005)

Anonymous, *'Cien años de soledad': análisis y estudio sobre la obra, el autor y su épica* (Madrid, 2003)

Arango, Gustavo, *Un ramo de nomeolvides: García Márquez en El Universal* (Cartagena, 1995).

Arnau, Carmen, *El mundo mítico de Gabriel García Márquez* (Barcelona, 1971)

Barroso, Juan, *'Realismo mágico' y 'lo real maravilloso' en 'El reino de este mundo' y 'El siglo de las luces'* (Miami, 1977)

Barsy, Kalman, *La estructura dialéctica de 'El otoño del patriarca'* (Río Piedras, 1989)

Bell, Michael, *Gabriel García Márquez: Solitude and Solidarity* (London, 1993)

Bell-Villada, Gene H. ed., *Gabriel García Márquez's 'One Hundred Years of Solitude': A Casebook* (Oxford, 2002)

Benedetti, Mario, et al., *9 asedios a García Márquez* (Santiago de Chile, 1969)

Benjamin, Walter, *Illuminations*, ed. Hannah Arendt, trans. Harry Zohn (London, 1992)

Benson, John, *'Cronica de una muerte anunciada'*, *Latin American Literary Review*, 11 (1982), pp. 63–7

Betto, Frei, *Fidel Castro y la religión: conversaciones con Frei Betto* (Mexico City, 1986)

Bhalla, Alok, ed., *García Márquez and Latin America* (London, 1987)

Bloom, Harold, ed., *Gabriel García Márquez's 'One Hundred Years of Solitude'* (Philadelphia, PA, 2003)

——, ed., *Gabriel García Márquez's 'Love in the Time of Cholera'* (Philadelphia, PA, 2005)

Box, Ben, *García Márquez: 'El coronel no tiene quien le escriba'* (London, 2000), 3rd edition

Bryce Echenique, Alfredo, *Permiso para vivir (Antimemorias)* (Barcelona, 1998)

Bucheli, Marcelo, 'The United Fruit Company in Colombia: Labour, Local Elite, and Multinational Enterprise, 1900–1970', PhD, Stanford University, 2002

Bustamante, Juan Pablo, *'El amor en los tiempos del cólera* se filmó en Macondo', *Cine Cubano*, 165 (July–September 2007), pp. 69–75

Canfield, Martha L., *El 'patriarca' de García Márquez: arquetipo literario del dictador hispanoamericano* (Florence, 1984)

Carrascosa Miguel, Pablo *'El general en su laberinto': G. García Márquez* (Barcelona, 1989)

Cartín de Guier, Estrella, *Una interpretación de 'Cien años de soledad'* (San José, 1981)

Catan, Thomas, 'The truth behind two giants of literature, one black eye and 30 years of silence', *The Times* (13 March 2007), p. 33

Chiampi, Irlemar, *El realismo maravilloso: forma e ideología en la novella hispanoamericana* (Caracas, 1983)

Clementelli, Elena, *García Márquez* (Florence, 1975)

Cobo Borda, J. G., *Gabriel García Márquez: los cuentos de mi abuelo el coronel* (Cali, 1988)

——, *Para llegar a García Márquez* (Bogotá, 1997)

Córdoba A, Marco A., *Elementos de sindicalismo* (Bogotá, 1977), 3rd edition

Cortés Vargas, Carlos, *Los sucesos de las bananeras (Historia de los acontecimientos que se desarrollaron en la zona bananera de Departamento del Magdalena – 13 de noviembre de 1928 al 15 de marzo de 1929* (Bogotá, 1929)

Cristóbal, Juan, *García Márquez y los medios de comunicación* (Lima, 1999)

Dueñas Vargas, Guiomar, *Los hijos del pecado: legitimidad y vida familiar en la Santafe de Bogotá colonial* (Bogotá, 1997)

Durix, Jean-Pierre, *Mimesis, Genres and Post-Colonial Discourse: Deconstructing Magic* Realism (London, 1998)

Earle, Peter G. ed., *Gabriel García Márquez* (Madrid, 1981)

Eliécer Gaitán, Jorge, *La Masacre en las bananeras: documentos testimonios* (Bogotá, n.d.)

Fahy, Thomas, *Gabriel García Márquez's 'Love in the Time of Cholera'* (London, 2003)

Fernández-Braso, Miguel, *Gabriel García Márquez: una conversación infinita* (Madrid, 1969)

Fiddian, Robin, *García Márquez: Los funerales de la Mamá Grande* (London, 2006), Critical Guides to Spanish Texts, no. 70

Forero, Juan, 'For García Márquez, a Magical Homecoming', *Washington Post* (2 June 2007), A01

Fuentes, Carlos, *Gabriel García Márquez and the Invention of America* (Liverpool, 1987)

García Márquez, Eligio, *La tercera muerte de Santiago Nasar* (Mexico City, 1989)

——, *Tras las claves de Melquíades: historia de 'Cien años de soledad'* (Bogotá, 2001)

García Ramos, Juan-Manuel, *Cien años de soledad* (Madrid, 1989)

Giacoman, Helmy, F. (ed.), *Homenaje a G. García Márquez* (New York, 1972)

Goodman, Joshua, 'On 80th birthday, Colombia vows to rebuild García Márquez's home', *Herald Tribune* (6 March 2007), Americas section

Hahn, Hannelore, *The Influence of Franz Kafka on Three Novels by Gabriel García Márquez* (New York, 1993)

Halka, Chester S., *Melquíades, Alchemy and Narrative Theory: The Quest for Gold in 'Cien años de soledad'* (Lathrup Village, MI, 1981)

Hamilos, Paul, 'Gabriel García Márquez, literary giant, lays down his pen', *Guardian* (2 April 2009), International section, p. 20

Hart, Stephen, 'Magical Realism in Gabriel García Márquez's *Cien años de soledad*', *Inti*, 16–17 (1982–1983), pp. 37–52

——, 'Magical Realism in the Americas: Politicised Ghosts in *One Hundred Years of Solitude*, *The House of the Spirits*, and *Beloved*', in *Journal of Iberian and Latin American Studies*, 9.2 (2003), pp. 115–23

——, *Companion to Latin American Film* (London, 2004)

——, and Kenneth Reeds, 'Guide to Further Reading', in *A Companion to Magical Realism*, ed. Stephen M. Hart and Wen-chin Ouyang (London, 2005), pp. 281–4

——, 'Blood, Ink and Proteus: Simón Bolívar as Proteus', in *Bulletin of Spanish Studies*, LXXXII/3–4 (2005), pp. 335–52

——, *A Companion to Latin American Literature* (London, 2007)

Hernández de López, Ana María ed., *En el punto de mira: Gabriel García Márquez* (Madrid, 1985)

Herrera Soto, Roberto and Rafael Romero Castañeda, *La zona bananera del Magdalena: historia y léxico* (Bogotá, 1979)

Joset, Jacques, *Gabriel García Márquez: coétano de la eternidad* (Amsterdam, 1984)

Kline, Carmenza, *Fiction and Reality in the Works of Gabriel García Márquez*, trans. Daniel Linder (Salamanca, 2002)

Kristal, Efraín, 'Lessons from the Golden Age in Gabriel García Márquez's *Living to Tell the Tale*', in *A Companion to Magical Realism*, ed. Stephen Hart and Wen-chin Ouyang (London, 2005), pp. 88–97

Labanyi, Jo, '*El otoño del patriarca*', in *Gabriel García Márquez*, ed. Harold Bloom (Philadelphia, PA, 2007), pp. 145–58

Mannarelli, Maria Emma, *Pecados públicos: la ilegitimidad en Lima, Siglo XVII* (Lima, 1994)

Marqués, Bernard, 'García Márquez , pasado y presente de una obra', *Alternativa*, 93, (9–16 August 1978), pp. 6–7

May, Stacy, and Galo Plaza, *La United Fruit Company en América Latina* (Mexico, 1959)

McGuirk, Bernard, and Richard Cardwell eds, *Gabriel García Márquez: New Readings* (Cambridge, 1987)

McMurray, George R., *Gabriel García Márquez* (New York, 1977)

Miranda Salcedo, Dalin de Jesús, *Legitimad e ilegitimidad familar: el problema del control social en Barranquilla* 1880–1930 (Barranquilla, 2000), p. 97

Montaner, María Eulalia *Guía para la lectura de 'Cien años de soledad'* (Madrid, 1981)

Morillo Valdelamar, Elmer, 'García Márquez y el lenguaje fílmico: visión y escritura cinematográfica en *El coronel no tiene quien le escriba*', University of Cartagena, 2000, T. C863 M857, 57pp

Moya, Rodrigo, 'La terrífica historia de un ojo morado', *La Jornada* (6 March 2007)

Müller-Bergh, Klaus, '*Relato de un náufrago*: Gabriel García Márquez's Tale of Shipwreck and Survival at Sea', *Books Abroad*, 47.3 (1973), pp. 460–66

Nash, Elisabeth, 'Furious Garcia Marquez denies he will never write again', *Independent* (8 April 2009)

Oliveira Castro, Margret S. de, *La lengua ladina de García Márquez* (Bogotá, 2007)

Palencia-Roth, Michael, *Gabriel García Márquez: la línea, el círculo y las metamorfosis del mito* (Madrid, 1983)

Pelayo, Rubén, *Gabriel García Márquez: A Critical Companion* (Westport, CT, 2001)

Penuel, Arnold M., *Intertextuality in García Márquez* (York, SC, 1994)

Ploetz, Dagmar, *Gabriel García Márquez* (Madrid, 2004)

Porrata, Francisco E., ed., *Explicación de 'Cien anos de soledad'* (San José, 1976)

Rama, Angel, *García Márquez, edificación de un arte nacional y popular* (Montevideo, 1987)

——, and Mario Vargas Llosa, *García Márquez y la problemática de la novela* (Buenos Aires, 1973)

Roca, Julio, 'Sí, la devolví la noche de bodas', *Al Día*, no. 3 (12 May 1981), pp. 24–7

———, and Camilo Calderón, 'García Márquez lo vio morir', *Al Día*, no. 1 (28 April 1981), pp. 52–60, 108–9

Rodríguez Jiménez, Osvaldo, 'Ortodoxia y heterodoxia en el campo literario nacional: el caso de García Márquez', MA thesis, University of Cartagena, 1998, 45pp. T. C863 R696.

Rodríguez Monegal, Emir, '*One Hundred Years of Solitude*: The Last Three Pages', *Books Abroad*, 47.3 (1973), 485–89

———, 'Realismo mágico versus literatura fantástica: un diálogo de sordos', in *Otros mundos, otros fuegos: fantasía y realismo mágico en Iberoamérica: memoria del XVI Congreso Internacional de Literatura Iberoamericana*, ed. Donald A. Yates (East Lansing, MI, 1975), pp. 25–37

Rodríguez-Vergara, Isabel, *El mundo satírico de Gabriel García Márquez* (Madrid, 1991)

Rohter, Larry, 'Bogotá Journals: García Márquez Embraces Old Love (That's News!), *New York Times* (27 January 1999)

Romero, Simon, 'The Town's Biggest Event Since the Banana Fever Ended', *New York Times* (7 March 2007), World News section

Salmon, Josefa, 'El poder de la anunciación en *Cien años de soledad* y *Crónica de una muerte anunciada*', *Discurso Literario: Revista de Temas Hispánicos*, 1 (1983), pp. 67–77

Shaw, Donald, '*Chronicle of a Death Foretold*: Narrative Function and Interpretation', in Bradley A. Shaw and Nora Vera-Godwin (eds), *Critical Perspectives on Gabriel García Márquez* (Lincoln, 1986), pp. 91–104

Simpson, Amelia S., *Detective Fiction from Latin America* (Toronto, 1990)

Sims, Robert Louis, *The Evolution of Myth in Gabriel García Márquez: From 'La hojarasca' to 'Cien años de soledad'* (Miami, 1981)

———, *The First García Márquez: A Study of His Journalistic Writing From 1948 to 1955* (Lanham, MA, 1992)

Skidmore, Thomas E. and Peter H. Smith, *Modern Latin America* (Oxford, 1992)

Sorela, Pedro, *El otro García Márquez: los años difíciles* (Madrid, 1988)

Swanson, Philip, *Cómo leer a Gabriel García Márquez* (Madrid, 1991)

Toomey, Christine, 'The life and loves of inFidelity Castro', *Sunday Times Magazine* (28 December 2008), pp. 13–17

Tremlett, Giles, 'Magical and real: García Márquez is writing new novel, says friend', *Guardian* (10 December 2008), International Section, p. 23

Vargas Llosa, Mario, *García Márquez: historia de un deicidio* (Barcelona,

1971)

——, 'A Morbid Prehistory (The Early Stories)', *Books Abroad*, XLVII/3 (1973), pp. 451–60

White, Judith, *La United Fruit en Colombia: historia de una ignomina* (Bogotá, 1978)

Williams, Raymond Leslie, *A Companion to Gabriel García Márquez* (Woodbridge, 2010)

Zaldívar, Jesús Humberto Florencia, Luis Quintana Tejera, and Olga Sigüenza Ponce, *Tres perspectivas de análisis en el marco de la obra de Gabriel García Márquez* (Mexico City, 2002)

Zuluaga Osorio, Conrado, *Puerta abierta a Gabriel García Márquez: aproximación a la obra del Nobel colombiano* (Barcelona, 2001)

——, *García Márquez: el vicio incurable de contar* (Bogotá, 2006)

Acknowledgements

My thanks to Jason Wilson with whom over the years I have enjoyed many discussions about recent developments in Latin American literature, to Julio García Espinosa, Fernando Birri and Russell Porter for their insights about Gabo, to Dolores Calviño and Alquimia Peña who set up my meeting with García Márquez at the Fundación del Nuevo Cine Latinoamericano in Havana in December 2007, to the librarians at the Biblioteca Luis Ángel Arango in Bogotá who skilfully guided me to the right archives, and to Rubiela Reyes whose magisterial tour of the house, the church and the tele-graph office in Aracataca on 26 February 2009 was a revelation. I record my gratitude to the British Academy for funding a research trip to Colombia in February–March 2009 which allowed this book to take its present form, and to the UCL Dean's Research Fund for covering the reproduction costs of the images. Lastly, many thanks to Vivian Constantinopoulos at Reaktion Books, for her forbearance.

Photo Acknowledgements

The author and publishers wish to express their thanks to the following sources of illustrative material and/or permission to reproduce it:

Courtesy of the Biblioteca Luis Angel Arango, Bogotá: pp. 43, 45; Corbis: pp. 129 (Bettmann), 174 (Fredy Builes/Reuters), 178 (Cesar Carrion/EPA); Courtesy of Julio Garcia Espinosa: pp. 141, 143, 181; Courtesy of Fundación del Nuevo Cine LatinoAmericano: pp. 38, 86, 108; Getty Images: p. 163; Courtesy of Stephen Hart: pp. 10, 90, 180; Courtesy of The Casa Natal García Márquez, Aracataca: pp. 6, 8, 9, 23, 37, 67; Rex Features: pp. 69 (CSU Archives/Everett Collection), 114 (Everett Collection); Topfoto: pp. 112, 127.